THE FORDS

OF

DEARBORN

Henry Ford in 1904

THE FORDS
OF
DEARBORN

SECOND EDITION

Ford R. Bryan

Ford Books, Dearborn, Michigan, 2004

08   07   06   05   04   1   2   3   4   5

ISBN 0–9727843-1-4

Designed by Mary Primeau

The Publication of this book was made possible by the
Ford R. Bryan Publication Fund

*Front end paper: This dry-stone cottage near Crohane, Ireland, is thought to have
been the Ford family home.*

Back end paper: A mid-summer afternoon river view of Fair Lane, about 1927.

This book is dedicated to my grandmother
Emma Althea Ford,
who more than one hundred years ago enjoyed as I do
the pastime of writing and publishing.
Although her style was poetry while mine is prose,
there cannot but exist a kindred spirit.

Contents

Foreword to First Edition
The Fords of Dearborn

I first encountered the work of Ford R. Bryan while I was one of the researchers gathering material from the treasure trove that is the Ford Archives in the Edison Institute at Dearborn. Every so often I would come across a learned article that seemed particularly fresh and original, based on truly new research. The writing stood out from the common academic rut by virtue of the firsthand knowledge that the author clearly possessed. These articles were all bylined Ford R. Bryan.

Then I got to know him. I discovered that Ford R. Bryan was one of the researchers working in the Ford Archives, and that he was to be found there almost every day, combing through documents and diaries in search of fresh discoveries. I came to learn that Ford R. Bryan had a modesty and generosity to match his historical passion. He gave me advice and shared his findings with all the enthusiasm of a true explorer.

I heartily commend his work. You will discover more that is truly new about the Fords inside this book than in many a volume twice the size. These are the bricks of history — crafted, patient, meticulous, accurate, and strong.

— Robert Lacey
June 30, 1987

About the Author

Ford Richardson Bryan
1912 – 2004
Teacher, Engineer, Researcher, Genealogist, Author, and Friend.

Ford Richardson Bryan was fortunate to have had more than one career in his lifetime.

He was educated by both Eastern Michigan University and the University of Michigan to teach science in the secondary schools of Michigan. World War II interrupted his teaching career when he went to work for the Ford Motor Company as a spectrochemical analyst, and later worked in the Ford Scientific Laboratory. Ford R. Bryan authored many articles about the Ford family and company for *The Dearborn Historian*. These articles later became the basis for the seven books he authored: *The Fords of Dearborn* (two editions), *Beyond the Model T: The Other Ventures of Henry Ford* (two editions), *Henry's Lieutenants, Henry's Attic: Some Fascinating Gifts to Henry Ford and His Museum, Clara: Mrs. Henry Ford, Friends, Families & Forays: Scenes from the Life and Times of Henry Ford, Rouge: Pictured in Its Prime, Covering the Years 1917-1940.*

Ford Bryan when working at the Rouge with a Master of Science degree and a badge #685.

The author in his 1923 Model-T Roadster purchased in 1927 for $50.
(Photo courtesy the author and his $3 Brownie No. 2A camera)

Preface

This book consists of a series of illustrated articles pertaining to various branches of the Ford families of Dearborn. Several of these articles were first published in the *Dearborn Historian*, a quarterly sponsored by the Dearborn Historical Commission. In a large part, the material is derived from the vast Ford Archives housed in the Benson Ford Research Center of The Henry Ford (formerly known as Henry Ford Museum and Greenfield Village). Unless otherwise noted, the photographs are reproduced with permission of the Benson Ford Archives.

Since the articles were published individually over a period of 26 years, this accounts for the substantial variation in format and considerable redundancy. Based on records from a great variety of sources, there are more than a few contradictory statements. Inconsistencies in spelling of names, for example: Forde vs. Ford, Ahern vs. O'Hern, and Starwell vs. Starvell vs. Stawel, are conspicuous.

Although directed largely to the Dearborn community, we feel that these short accounts may be of some general interest because of the immense popularity of the Henry Ford associated with automobiles. The stories presented depict Ford family history from the early nineteenth century to the mid-twentieth century during which interval the Dearborn Fords were moderately influential as well as reasonably prolific. Descendants of the Dearborn Fords are now scattered far and wide, very few carrying the Ford name and very few carrying the burden of wealth.

Acknowledgements

The writer is especially grateful to Winfeld H. Arneson, Chief Curator of the Dearborn Historical Museum and Editor of *The Dearborn Historian,* for his wholehearted acceptance of this material, story by story. His enthusiastic support has provided the incentive to proceed with the work. The entire Dearborn Historical Museum staff has been supportive in every respect.

The staff of the Archives and Library of The Henry Ford–Benson Ford Research Center have not only permitted but have singularly encouraged me to utilize the great wealth of material housed in their seemingly endless collections. Among the many accommodative people have been Steven Hamp, Judith Endelman, Terry Hoover, and Cynthia Read Miller. James Orr scanned the photographs for this book.

To produce the book, Alice Nigoghosian has been publication consultant, Mary Primeau has been book designer and compositor, and Wendy Warren Keebler created the index.

❧❧ 1 ❧❧
SAMUEL FORD

First of the Fords to Come to Dearborn,
Ford Ancestry in England and Ireland,
Leaving for America

Many words have been printed about Dearborn's best-known native, the late Henry Ford. However, readers may be interested in learning about other Fords before him who migrated to America from Europe. One such person was Samuel Forde who was the first of the Fords to settle in Dearborn. The following material is taken largely from notes collected by Raymond H. Laird for Henry Ford during the period 1924–1940. These are now on file in the Archives of the Benson Ford Research Center.

de la FORDE, de FORDE, FOORD, FORDE, FORD*

It is quite well known that the Dearborn Fords came to the United States from Ireland. What is more interesting is where they may have been before that, inasmuch as records show they had been in Ireland for some 250 years. There is remarkable evidence that they were in England during the time of Queen Elizabeth I. Beyond that, their derivation is more questionable.

A George Ford of Fordmore,[1] who died in 1702, was said to be the last male heir of an ancient family which had settled in Fordmore as early as the reign of Edward I (A.D. 1272–1307). There is said to be a document called the Bruton Cartulary[1] in which is the record of a grant made by Walter de Ford to Robert de Ford of certain lands in Bruton and Shipwick (two villages in

---

*In the old tithe book of Kilmeen Parish, Samuel Ford is on the same page written Samuel Forde. In the course of time one branch of the family spelled its name with an *e* at the end, while another omitted it.

Samuel Forde

A Ford crest, representative of several on file at the Ford Archives, Henry Ford Museum & Greenfield Village. None is thought to relate specifically to the Dearborn Fords, however.
(188-74817)

Somersetshire) in the early years of the thirteenth century. It is especially notable that the witness to that grant was a William de Starvella, because the Forde and Starvella names are associated for three centuries in England, and again in Ireland. The French spelling of the names would indicate that perhaps both the Starvella and Forde families came from Normandy following William the Conqueror.

Many prominent Fords inhabited England in the 1600–1700s,[2] and there is a village known as Fordstown (in Meath County) in the neighborhood of which many of the name Ford were settled. It would seem that these Fords came from Lancashire. It is also said that there were four distinct old families of Fords in Devonshire, each bearing a different coat-of-arms.[2] Another reference[4] indicates that in all of England there were about 20 different crests belonging to the various branches of the Ford family. Still another source[5] presents a single coat-of-arms said to represent the similarities of all. However, a letter from Frank Campsall to Edsel B. Ford, dated November 3, 1939,[6] reads, "Through the Ford family Genealogy, we have been endeavoring to connect the ancestors of Mr. Henry Ford with one of these crests, but so far have not been successful." (The crest appearing on the 1950 model Ford cars is a stylist's rendition based on features common to several. The three lions were taken from the crest of a Charles Ford, and there is believed to be no connection with the Dearborn Ford family.)

There were Fords, possibly or possibly not, related to the Dearborn Fords, who were very distinguished. There was Sir Henry Ford, M.P. for Exeter in 1669; and Rev. Thomas Ford, physician to Queen Charlotte and close friend of George III. There was Sir Richard Ford, noted art and literary figure, and a Henry Ford,[3] "an ingenious mechanical gentleman who raised the Thames water into the highest streets of the city (London) 93 feet high in 8 pipes, and built a great water engine near Somerset house; and suggested many other useful places which did not meet with equal encouragement." He died in 1670.

Another interesting but questionable genealogical lead deals with the 7,000-acre Stopham Estate in Sussex County, England.[7] Fords were reported to be the Saxon owners of this estate in A.D. 1066. After the battle of Hastings, William the Conqueror turned over all the land in and around Sussex, the Stopham Estate going to Sir Brian de Stopham, one of his soldiers. The Fords remained on the estate, intermarried with the new neighbors, and therefore are of both Saxon and Norman blood. The Stopham Estate was never in the hands of the Church or the King, the only requirement being the giving of one red rose every year to the King. They were given the right to keep swans on the river, a privilege usually granted only to members of the Royal Family.

Despite these several interesting possibilities, the most acceptable evidence resulting from the extensive twentieth century inquiries sponsored by Henry Ford of Dearborn[8] is that the

Approximate area shown on detailed map.

Opposite, detail map of southern Ireland. Some principal cities or towns referred to in the text: (A) Cork, (B) Queenstown (now Cobh), (C) Bandon, (D) Crohane, (E) Clonakilty. (D-1191)

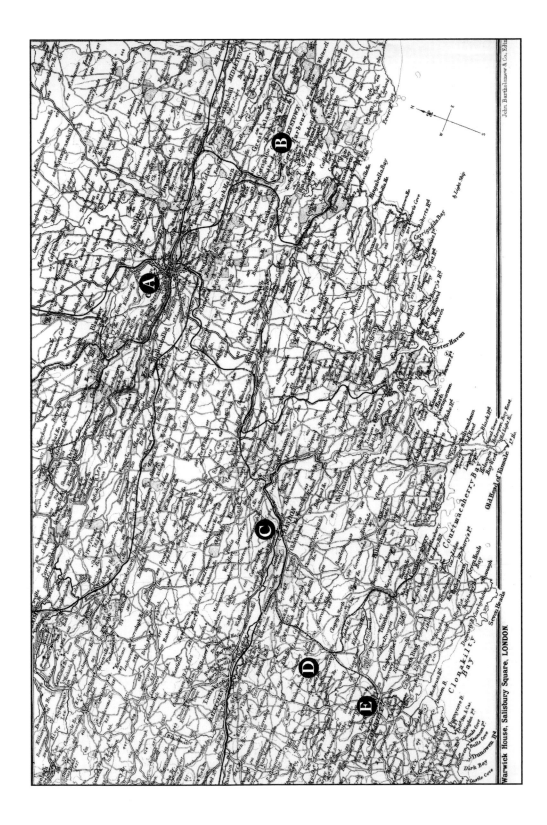

John Bartholomew & Co., Edin.

This dry-stone cottage near Crohane, Ireland, is thought to have been the Ford family home. This is perhaps where Samuel was born, and where he lived with his parents, William and Rebecca, and his four brothers. (833-50518)

Dearborn Fords were related to the seventeenth century Fords of Somerset and Devon in England. This was the evidence presented by Dr. Webster.[1] These Fords were freeholders and tenant farmers associated with the estates of Sir John Starwell.

ON TO IRELAND

"In 1585, Queen Elizabeth selected a number of English gentlemen who were to re-people Munster (one of the four Irish Provinces) with settlers from England. Among those gentleman was Sir John Starwell who was to bring to the County of Somerset as he found able and willing to come. It was also a historical fact that about 1601 a large number of the gentry of Somerset and Devon, mostly younger sons, went over to Ireland. From time to

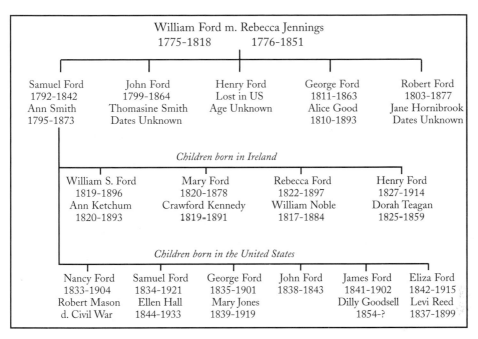

William Ford m. Rebecca Jennings				
1775-1818		1776-1851		
Samuel Ford	John Ford	Henry Ford	George Ford	Robert Ford
1792-1842	1799-1864	Lost in US	1811-1863	1803-1877
Ann Smith	Thomasine Smith	Age Unknown	Alice Good	Jane Hornibrook
1795-1873	Dates Unknown		1810-1893	Dates Unknown

Children born in Ireland

William S. Ford	Mary Ford	Rebecca Ford	Henry Ford
1819-1896	1820-1878	1822-1897	1827-1914
Ann Ketchum	Crawford Kennedy	William Noble	Dorah Teagan
1820-1893	1819-1891	1817-1884	1825-1859

Children born in the United States

Nancy Ford	Samuel Ford	George Ford	John Ford	James Ford	Eliza Ford
1833-1904	1834-1921	1835-1901	1838-1843	1841-1902	1842-1915
Robert Mason	Ellen Hall	Mary Jones		Dilly Goodsell	Levi Reed
d. Civil War	1844-1933	1839-1919		1854-?	1837-1899

Chart of Samuel Ford family showing his parents, his four brothers and ten children, four of whom were born in Ireland prior to their 1832 immigration to America. Rebecca Jennings Ford and William Ford and their son John Ford were great-grand-mother, great grand-father, and grand-father respectively, of Henry Ford (1863-1947) the industrialist.

time in succeeding years others came over to settle the nearly 600,000 acres granted in Munster. Queen Elizabeth was bound on her part to maintain certain forces for the security of the settlers."[1]

Early in the seventeenth century, an Anthony Starvell had property in the neighborhood of Clonakilty, Ireland, as had also a member of the Honner family. These two families were united by marriage in 1694 and by terms of the marriage settlement the Madame Estate came into the possession of the Starvell family. Early records show that the Fords were tenants of Starvells at Madame and of the Honners at Crohane, and indicate that these Fords were descendants of the Fords of Somerset and Devon, who came to Ireland to help people the confiscated lands.

Crohane, one Ford site, is readily found on a map of Southwest Ireland.[9] It is about four miles inland from the small coastal town of Clonakilty, about ten miles southwest of Bandon,[10] about 30 miles west of Queenstown (now Cobh). The Madame Estate is near the little village of Ballinascarthy.

It was difficult to find records of Fords on Madame or Honnor property for the early period in Ireland because of many church records having been burned in 1922 during the Irish riots. Valuable evidence was obtained, however, from a series of leases between Fords and Starwells. The earliest lease (1790) was to William Ford, Stephen Ford, and Robert Ford for a rent of £6 per year. Another lease in 1819 was in the name of Rebecca and John Ford for 23 acres, 1 rood, 10 perches* at a yearly rent of £29, 2 shillings, 10 pence. Both Rebecca and John appear to have used an "X" for their signature. A later lease (1843), made by Francis Starwell to John Ford as sole tenant of the farm, shows that rent had been reduced to £21, 6 shillings, 8 pence.

The William Ford of the first lease (1790) is thought to be the husband of Rebecca (Jennings) Ford. (See family chart.) This William Ford died about 1818, just before the second lease (1819). William and Rebecca are reported to have had five sons of whom Samuel, born in 1792, was the eldest. The John Ford named in the next two leases was the second eldest son (b. 1799). Other brothers of Samuel were Henry, George and Robert.

Samuel had been married more than a year when the 1819 lease was arranged by Rebecca and John. Samuel (age 27) had been married on January 25, 1818, by Rev. W. A. Lamb to Ann Smith (age 23), also of the Parish of Desertserges. Samuel was Anglican (Episcopalian) and Ann reportedly a Baptist. Their marriage is well documented, although before 1845 a "bond" was sometimes used by people to be married, instead of having their names read out in church, or "banns" published. The "bond" was, in fact, a "Letter of freedom" from the church stating that the contracting parties were free to marry.[1]

By 1819, Samuel and Ann (nicknamed Nancy) had had their first child, William. They are thought to have lived at Crohane, a mile or so from the Madame property. Three more children were born to the couple within the next eight years: Mary (1820),

---

*1 rood equals ¼ acre, 1 perch equals ¹⁄₄₀ acre.

Rebecca (1822), and Henry (1827). In 1829, it is said[12] that William, age 10, had an opportunity to come to America and stay with a family in Rochester, New York. It is not known whether this family consisted of relatives or friends. In 1832, Samuel, Ann, and the children left for America; and Samuel's brothers Henry and George joined the party.

They are thought to have been driven in a cart from Crohane to Bandon Station, County Cork, to entrain for Queenstown (Cobh) so as to sail to America.[11] It is said that Rebecca, then 56, furnished funds to Samuel for passage and to purchase land in America. Their passage would have been by sailing vessel because trans-Atlantic steamers were not yet operating. There was a steamer from London to Bombay as early as 1836, but Atlantic steamers did not commence until the *Sirius* from Cork, and the *Great Western* from Bristol in 1838.[13]

Brother John had been left in charge of the Madame acreage, until 15 years later when, during the 1847 famine year, he was evicted from it. That year John, his mother (at age 71), his wife Thomasine, and their children left Ireland to join Samuel's family in America.

REFERENCES

1. "Notes, Topographical, Historical and Genealogical on the Ford Family," compiled from various sources by Charles A. Webster, D.D., Acc. 23, Box 28, Ford Archives, Henry Ford Museum.

2. *Documents and Memorials of the Ford Family*, Francis Clare Ford, London: Harrison & Sons, Printers in Ordinary to Her Majesty, St. Martin's Lane, 1878. (Copy supplied by American Research Bureau, Washington, D.C. 1939) Acc. 23, Box 13, Ford Archives, Henry Ford Museum.

3. *Pedigrees of the Families of Ford of Devonshire* (also of Surry and Sussex, Stafford, and of Seaford), British Museum Library. Acc. 23, Box 29, Ford Archives, Henry Ford Museum.

4. Reference is made to Camden's Brittania, 1789 Edition.

5. *History and Biographical Sketch of Ford Family*. American Research Bureau, Washington, D.C. 1939. Acc. 23, Box 31, Ford Archives, Henry Ford Museum.

6. Letter from Frank Campsall to Edsel B. Ford, November 3, 1939. Acc. 23, Box 31, Ford Archives, Henry Ford Museum.

7. Charles H. Bartlett, Correspondence with Henry Ford. Letter dated December, 1936. Acc. 23, Box 13, Ford Archives, Henry Ford Museum.

Samuel Ford   8. Departmental Communication from R.H. Laird to E.G. Liebold and F. Campsall dated May 5, 1939. Acc. 23, Box 28, Ford Archives, Henry Ford Museum.

9. *A Pictorial and Descriptive Guide to Cork and Southwest Ireland,* Queenstown, the Backwater, Glen Gariff, Killarny, and the Southwest of Ireland, London: Ward, Lock & Co., Ltd. (1910).

10. *The History of Bandon* (Ireland) by George Bennett, Published by Cork, Henry and Coghlan, 1862.

11. Communication from RH. Laird to E.G. Liebold and F. Campsall dated May, 1940. Acc. 1, Box 1, Ford Archives, Henry Ford Museum.

12. Communications between the author and Myrtle (Ford) Fox, great granddaughter of Samuel Ford.

13. "The Progress of Steam Navigation," W.N. Brown, *The Mechanical News,* XXIII, May 1, 1893.

~~2~~ THE SAMUEL FORD FAMILY

Arrival in America, Michigan Territory, Purchase of Land, Wilderness Living

The earlist names on the Ford family tree[1] are those of William Ford and Rebecca (Jennings) Ford. Both were born in Ireland, William in 1775 and Rebecca in 1776. Not much is known about William, who died in Ireland in 1818, leaving Rebecca a widow, with sons Samuel (27), John (20), Henry (exact age unknown), and George (9). Samuel had married Ann Smith (23) on January 25 of that same year (1818). They were believed to have lived as tenant farmers near Crohane, in Cork County, until about 1829 when Samuel's oldest son William S(amuel) Ford, then age ten, is said to have been brought to the United States to stay with a family at Rochester, New York.[2] Three years later (1832) Samuel, his wife Ann (more commonly known as Nancy), William, and three children younger than William came to Dearborn. Samuel's brother, George, is also known to have arrived in Dearborn that same year, and brother Henry is thought to have left Ireland with the group.[3]

Date of arrival in the United States, port of entry, and exact means of getting here are as yet undetermined. There are at least two distinct versions handed down within the family. According to two sources,[4,5] these first Fords to come to Dearborn landed at either Philadelphia or New York and came westward by land. On the way, the one brother, Henry, is thought to have become ill and been left at the home of relatives in Pennsylvania to recover. This Henry was never heard of again by the Dearborn families. This story is embellished a bit by Olson[6] when he states that the routes taken by the Ford uncles (uncles of auto Henry) were from New York to Pennsylvania, to Pittsburgh, down the Ohio to Cincinnati, up to Dayton, canal boat by means of the Ports-mouth & Ohio Canal to Cleveland, and lake boat to Detroit.

Other sources seem equally certain that these earliest Fords came by way of Québec, Rochester, Erie Canal, and Lake Erie to

Detroit. Relatives of George Ford, who arrived in Dearborn the same year as Samuel, thought that George came by way of Québec.[7] Slightly later, the John Ford group came through Québec.[8]

Whether any of these versions applies to Samuel Ford's party is not certain. And to all this confusion is the added revelation that Samuel is listed as a veteran of the War of 1812.[12] He would have been twenty-one years of age. If this is indeed a fact, the year 1832 was not the first time that Samuel had been in the United States. This possibility is supported by evidence that Samuel's son, William, was in Rochester, New York, at age ten (1829),[13] and a statement by Clyde Ford[14] indicating that Samuel's younger brother, George, worked on the Erie Canal prior to coming to Dearborn in 1832.

MASS IMMIGRATION

There was a tremendous influx of Irish into the United States in the 1830s from the Counties of Cork, Mayo, Galway, Kerry, Limerick, and Tipperary. It is quite certain that Samuel's party embarked at Queenstown (Cobh), Cork County. Atlantic passengers in "steerage" furnished their own "provisions" which included food and cooking utensils. The ship furnished "berth, fire and drinking water."[15] During the 1840s thousands and thousands of Irish would be fleeing from starvation and disease. By the late 1830s, Irish had already replaced Anglo-Saxons as the main working class in America.

The National Archives Passenger Lists of immigrants arriving at Eastern ports during this period[16] show predominantly Irish and British immigrants in the twenty-to-thirty age group. Male occupations listed included: farmer, brewer, cooper, shoemaker, saddler, hatter, miller, tailor, tanner, apothecary, coachman, toymaker, mason, mariner, and a sprinkling of carpet weavers, cotton spinners, calico printers, warpers, silk winders, traders, jewelers, and a solitary "Gentleman." Of the female occupations besides "housewife," there were a multitude of "servants" (many, many by the name of Bridget), also dressmakers, seamstresses, and a few in the forty-to-fifty age bracket designated "spinster."

Sailing ships from Ireland and England at the time of Samuel's family's trip might be designated, "bark," "sloop," "brig," "schooner," or more frequently just "ship." In the 1830s some of the ships plying the Atlantic were the *Trusty, Favorite, Jupiter, Oceanus, Ganges, America, Brilliant, Lord Clive, British Prince,* etc. A little later there were such names as *Illinois, Indiana, California, Philadelphia, Tonawanda, Tuscarora, Rip Van Winkle,* and *Kalamazoo,* indicating that American as well as British ships were operating. The typical sailing ship crossing the Atlantic averaged about 300 tons whereas coastwise vessels, such as Newfoundland to Boston, were likely to be in the 70-to-200 ton range. Some

The Samuel Ford Family

William Ford m. Rebecca Jennings
1775-1818   1776-1851

John Ford	Henry Ford	Samuel Ford	George Ford	Robert Ford
1799-1864	Lost in US	1792-1842	1811-1863	1803-1877
Thomasine Smith	Age Unkown	Ann Smith	Alice Good	Jane Hornibrook
?-1847		1795-1873	1810-1893	Dates Unknown

William S. Ford	Mary Ford	Rebecca Ford	Henry Ford	Nancy Ford	Samuel Ford
1819-1898	1820-1878	1822-1897	1827-1914	1833-1904	1834-1921
Ann Ketchum	Crawford Kennedy	Wm. Noble	Dorah Teagan	Robert Mason	Ellen Hall
1820-1893	1819-1891	1817-1884	1825-1859	d. Civil War	1844-1933
Mary	Nancy	Alma	Eliza	Joseph	Francis
Sarah	Alice	James	Samuel	Fannie	Nellie
William	William	Martha	Mary		Anna
Rebecca	Samuel	Mary	Dorah		Frederick
Samuel	Henry	Catherine	Maria		
Susan	James		George		
John	George				
Charles			m. Mary Ford		
Emma					
Elizabeth			James		
Josephine			Thomasine		
			Oliver		
			Nancy		

George Ford	John Ford	James Ford	Eliza Ford
1835-1901	1838-1843	1841-1902	1842-1915
Mary Jones		Dilly Goodsell	Levi Reed
1839-1919		1854-?	1837-1899
Ida		Ney	Henry
Addison		Frederick	Edward
		Emory	Chester

manifests presented a long list of passengers carried in the steerage, separate from a very short list of those carried above. Many Irish, perhaps the majority who came to America during this period, landed at St. Johns or Halifax and transferred to ports in the United States. Boston, in particular, had more Irish coming from Newfoundland and Nova Scotia than directly from Ireland. It is said that immigrants were landing in such droves at Québec that the quarantine hospital was overflowing, and that many who died were buried en masse without identifying markers.[17] The passenger lists examined at our National Archives did not reveal entry of any of the Dearborn Fords.[18]

MICHIGAN TERRITORY

In 1832, Michigan was a territory but not yet a state. It had been part of the Northwest Territory organized in 1788. General Anthony Wayne, having defeated the Indians and British (1795), had been a popular hero and the County of Wayne was organized in 1796, "embracing the whole of the territory included between the present eastern boundary of the State of Michigan and the Mississippi River, extending as far north as the line of the British Possessions."[19] Wayne was then a vast territory, there was no other political subdivision, and the County was an unknown and unexplored wilderness. The seat of government was Detroit. In the year 1800 the Northwestern Territory was divided, forming the Territories of Ohio and Indiana. The former was admitted to the Union in 1802, and Michigan was included in the Territory of Indiana until the creation of a separate Michigan Territory in 1805. In 1815 Wayne County was reduced to the present counties of Lenawee, Monroe, Wayne, Washtenaw, Livingston, Oakland and Macomb, with portions of Shiawassee, Lapeer, St. Clair and Ingham. The final reduction came in 1822 when Wayne County took on its present limits.

The port of Detroit, the capital of Michigan Territory, in 1830 had a population of 2,200 permanent residents. It was largely French in custom, Catholic in religion — the citizens leading pleasant, harmonious lives from all accounts.[20] The primary business was furs. Agricultural methods were backward, and almost all necessary commodities, including food, were imported.

About then, the influx of land-hungry immigrants began. From New England came the Puritan "sober-sides" for better soil,

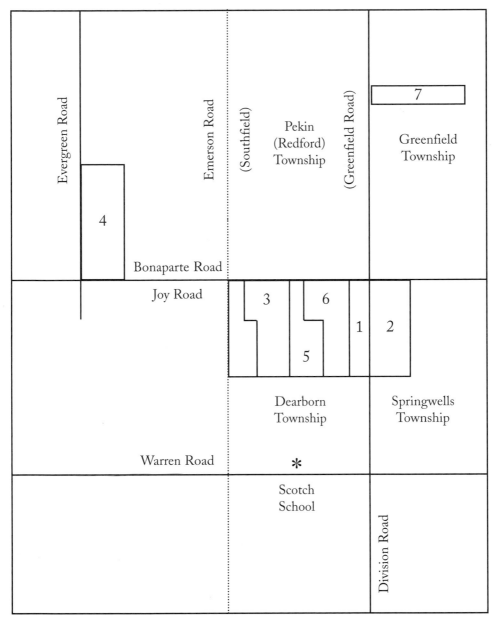

Early Ford Farms

1. *Samuel 1832*
2. *George (brother) 1832*
3. *William (son) 1840*
4. *John (brother) 1848*
5. *Henry (son) 1851*
6. *George (son) 186-*
7. *Samuel (son) 1862*

perhaps. Farmers of New York State could also sell their acreage and get much more land for their money in Michigan. The new Erie Canal was their connecting link. Buffalo was the jumping off place, Detroit the landing place. In addition, a giant wave of Irish immigrants, so great as to become the largest foreign born group in Detroit, were striving to escape their poverty and the religious turmoil in Ireland. News of the cheap, rich land in Michigan was reaching the troubled Irish in the personal letters sent back home,[21] and more were planning to come. As many as 2,000 immigrants arrived at Detroit in one week.[22]

Is it possible that Samuel had been here before? It is known that Samuel's wife, Ann, had relatives in Corktown soon after 1832, if not at that time.[23] A John Smith (1797–1878), of 150 Trumbull Street, is said to have been related to Ann. This John Smith's son, Henry Smith, married Samuel and Ann's niece, Mary Ford in 1856.[24] In any event, sometime prior to 1832, the Fords had heard of the Michigan Territory, of Detroit, and of the virgin timber lands available to immigration. Now, they too, were in Detroit to buy land, some of their money having been given to them by their mother, Rebecca, who was still in Ireland.[25]

The price of Michigan land had been fixed by law in 1820 (the "Ten Shilling Act") at $1.25 an acre when purchased directly from the government. The minimum purchase was 80 acres, and the Land Office at Detroit was selling nearly a half million acres of public lands each year. By 1836, four million acres were being sold in Michigan Territory — more than in any other area of the United States.

In 1785 the Continental Congress had passed the Grayson Land Ordinance which provided for division of the entire Northwestern Territory into "Townships" whereby each settler could purchase a specific parcel of land located in reference to a "Base Line" (east-west) of 42 degrees, 26 minutes and 30 seconds north latitude. (A segment of this line, now called Eight Mile Road, extends across Michigan to South Haven.) A north-south ordinate (Prime Meridian) of the survey was established at 84 degrees, 22 minutes and 24 seconds west longitude.[26] This approximates a line through Jackson to Cheboygan. Townships, being six miles square, were then divided into 36 one-mile "Sections," which in turn could be divided and described specifically as "halves," "quarters," etc.

*A photograph identified as Ann
(Nancy) Smith Ford, wife of
Samuel. Nancy lived until 1873,
whereas Samuel died in 1842. No
likeness of Samuel appears to exist.
(188-20826)*

Samuel Ford, on May 23, 1832, purchased 80 acres described
as the "East ¹/₂ of the N.E. ¹/₄, Section 1, Township 2 South, Range
10 East," which is the extreme northeastern corner of Dearborn
Township. Thus, Dearborn Township is two townships south of
the Base Line, and ten townships east of the Prime Meridian.
George Ford, Samuel's brother, on October 1, 1832, bought the
"West ¹/₂ of the S.W. ¹/₄ of Section 6, Township 2 S., Range 11 E.,"
the extreme southwestern corner of Greenfield Township.[27] These
titles issued by the new United States Government superseded the
many previous treaties, Indian dealings, and private trades which
often utilized trees, boulders, and streams as boundary markers.

The Samuel Ford party is said to have landed at Detroit by
boat. They likely came by schooner because there were few steamers as yet. Fare from Buffalo to Detroit was about $18 cabin and $7
steerage. Depending upon the weather, it could take as long as two
weeks for the trip.[28] At Detroit they are said to have stayed tem-

porarily at a combination hotel and outfitting establishment catering to immigrants. Here they acquired a yoke of oxen and a stoneboat load of goods.[29]

A stoneboat is a stout platform on log skids. It can be used both summer and winter, and is far less expensive than a cart or wagon. The platform being only a few inches from the ground, enables one to load and unload heavy objects such as stones, with comparative ease — thus the term stoneboat.

It is said to have taken the Samuel Ford family eight days to cut their way through the dense woods and transport their belongings to their property in Dearborn Township. How they precisely located this particular portion of wilderness is difficult to imagine, there being no roads or fences. However, the land had been surveyed in 1815. A few miles to the south through the woods lay the Sauk Indian Trail, with Bucklin's Mill on the Rouge, and Ten Eyck's Tavern which was one day's journey on the trail from Detroit by ox team. Neighbors, though miles away, had to be truly neighborly in those days. There were wolves and Indians to be reckoned with, as well as hunger and lack of shelter. The driving force behind these pioneers must have been the ownership of land. After generations of tenancy, the dream of being the landlord must have been overwhelming.

A camp of Indians nearby is said to have been helpful to Samuel's family when they arrived. Indians helped these pioneers construct their primitive cabin, showed them how to cook over an open fire, and sometimes supplied small quantities of corn and meat. In general they were friendly and helpful, but not always trustworthy. These Indians were gone ten years later.[30] Oxen and chains were used for heavy work such as dragging logs and stump pulling. Manpower with axes and saws finished the job. Marksmanship with a rifle helped with the food supply, and cooking kettle, spinning wheel, candle mold, punkwood and flints were essentials to the housewife. The original cabins seldom faced roads, inasmuch as the roads did not as yet exist.

PIONEERING

The year these Fords arrived (1832) was not a peaceful one. That same spring there were Indian uprisings near Lake Michigan, and this Black Hawk War frightened settlers around

Detroit. Militiamen from the Detroit area were assembled at U.S. Marshall Conrad Ten Eyck's tavern on Chicago Road, and marched as far as Saline before being told they weren't needed.[31] The Black Hawk War was serious enough, perhaps, to induce the Government to authorize the movement of the Detroit Arsenal about ten miles west to Bucklin Township, the site of a military reservation on the Rouge River. The new arsenal commandant, Lt. Joshua Howard, arranged for the Territorial Council to change the name from Bucklin to Dearborn in 1836.[32, 33] Another scare during that summer was an outbreak of cholera resulting in a serious epidemic and considerable panic in the whole area. Other nuisances to beset these pioneers were generally swampy land conditions, swarms of ferocious mosquitoes, thick underbrush, trails rather than roads, no bridges, no pure water, no matches, no glass for windows, and numerous other hindrances. These conditions are very ably described in *The Bark Covered House*.[34] The roles of the Indians, the wolves, the bears, the swamps and snakes are vividly depicted therein.

On the other hand there were many exciting happenings which must have given them encouragement when the news reached them. The residents voted in favor of statehood in 1832. Sawmills and gristmills were being established on small streams nearby. Military roads were being extended. *The Detroit Free Press,* established in 1831, reported news from Michigan's Capitol in Detroit. Flatboats were being used on the rivers to ship goods up the Huron to Ypsilanti, up the Rouge to Dearbornville, and up the Clinton to Mt. Clemens and Rochester.[35] Also, in 1831 the Chicago Road along the Sauk Indian Trail had been authorized, and clearing had been done as far as Saline. Eventually, a fast stage would reach Chicago in eight days, with the first overnight stop at Clinton. What was more impressive, in 1830 the Detroit and St. Joseph Railroad Company was incorporated. In 1834 the route was surveyed, and by 1836 several miles of track had been built. This railroad was to become a means of cash employment for Samuel's son, William.[36]

Michigan finally became a state in 1837. The new constitution permitted all white male inhabitants to vote if twenty-one or over, and were living in the Territory at the time the constitution was signed January 26, 1837.[37] Thus, Samuel and his sons must have become citizens without filing the usual naturalization papers in

District Court. There is no record of these particular Fords having filed for citizenship in Wayne County.[38] If they had come five years later, they would have had to "renounce forever all allegiance and fidelity to each and every foreign Prince, Potentate, State, or Sovereignty whatever, and particularly the Queen of Great Britain and Ireland" of whom they would have been subjects. (Victoria had become queen in 1837 at age eighteen.)

These pioneers worked hard to rescue the land from the wilderness. Wood was in the way, and much of it was cut and burned in the open. There was very little market for it, and no practical way to get it to one. Later they would be able to sell some "propeller wood" to the steamboat captains at Detroit. It was about five years before an ox cart was obtained for trips to town (Detroit), and about thirteen years before a horse and buggy would

be seen in the area. It would be driven by an itinerant preacher.[39] Horses had been considered too light and fancy to draw wagons through the mud.

The township became the principal unit of government for these people. Many of the responsibilities now handled by state and county offices were then handled by township officials. Taxes were levied and collected. Schools were organized, operated, and teachers certified. Roads were constructed and maintained almost exclusively as a function of the township.

By 1832, Dearborn Township meeting records[40] reveal much attention being given to the authorization of roads, and fences along these roads. Land for the road was taken equally from each landowner whose land adjoined the center line of the proposed road. Once a road was constructed, each landowner was then assessed a given number of days work which constituted a road tax to maintain the road, the time being commensurate with his amount of road frontage.

A section of the Ford Cemetery on Joy Road near Greenfield ca. 1925. The Samuel and Nancy Ford marker is at the far left. The taller of the two obelisks marks the grave of Mary (Litogot) Ford, mother of auto magnate Henry Ford. (833-71199)

Gravestone of Samuel and Nancy Ford in the Ford Cemetery. Inscription reads —

SAMUEL FORD
Died Nov. 12, 1842
Also his wife
NANCY
Died April 30, 1873
Aged-78 years, 3 months

TRAVELERS NOW AS YOU PASS BY,
AS YOU ARE NOW SO ONCE WAS I,
AS I AM NOW SOON YOU MUST BE,
PREPARE FOR DEATH AND FOLLOW ME.

Photo courtesy of Hubert J. Beudert.

It was nearly two years after Samuel's family arrived that an east-west road was authorized adjacent to their property. From Township Meeting Records there is: "Road No. 54, Beginning at the East side of the town at the corner stake of Sections one and 36 on the town line between Dearborn and Redford thence on said town line to the west line of said town. Given under our Hands on this 7th March 1834." This would appear to be the road that was first called "Ford Road" because of the Fords living on it; it later became "Bonaparte," and more recently "Joy Road." Samuel's road tax amounted to probably three or four days' work per year.

In the years 1834, 1835 and 1836, John and Amzi Ketchum were elected "Overseers of Highways and Fence Viewers" for the Township. In 1838 we first find Samuel Ford a "Pathmaster and Fence Viewer" for Road District No. 14; also an "Overseer of Highways" in 1839 and 1840.[41] The overseer of highways was the township road tax collector (road work supervisor) for his road district. As fence viewer, he aided in disputes involving the location and condition of fences, including what was to be deemed a legal fence.

There were no churches close by, and services were at first held in the homes, usually conducted by the head of the household. Samuel's son, William S. Ford, became instrumental in the eventual building of three Methodist church buildings, two in Dearborn Township. Samuel's oldest daughter, Mary, married Crawford Kennedy at Grace M.E. Church of Greenfield in 1843. Her husband had been born in 1819, on the Atlantic, during his parents' immigration from Ireland. Some of Samuel's family became active in Mariner's Episcopal Church in Detroit.[42] Samuel's daughter Nancy[43] was married to Robert Mason[44] on November 21, 1850, at Mariner's Church. Samuel's son Henry, with his wife, Dorah (Teagan) Ford, had their daughter Mary Ann baptized there on June 20, 1851. Their daughter Dorah was likewise baptized May 7, 1854. Sponsors were George Teagan, Ann Teagan, and Rebecca Ford. Samuel's daughter Rebecca (34) was married to William Noble (39) on December 17, 1856, at Mariner's Church. Samuel's brother George who lived until 1863, is said to have been seen driving each Sunday the eight miles from his farm to Mariner's with a team and wagon, wearing a tall black hat, and being seated in front beside his wife, Alice, and with the children riding in the box behind.[45]

There were as yet (1832) no free schools nor school taxes as such. A log school was sometimes built and "rate bills" issued to parents who agreed to have their children receive instruction. Each parent helped provide firewood, and boarded the teacher for a period commensurate with instruction received. Teachers received very little beyond bed and board. It was almost thirty years before the State provided for universal education.[46]

A territorial law had been passed in 1827, requiring that "every township containing fifty families, or householders, shall be provided with a good schoolmaster . . . for six months." It was six years later that Dearborn Township was organized into school districts: "At a meeting of the Commissioners of Common Schools in and for the Town of Dearborn convened at the house of Amos Gordon on Wed. 27th of Nov. 1833 for the purpose of organizing said Town into school districts Commencing at the North East corner of said Town Be it known that sections 1-2-11 and 12 Compose District No.1, . . .".[47] The neighborhood farmers of N.E. Dearborn Township organized what would be known as the Scotch Settlement School (District No.1) in 1838, and during the winter of

1840 DEARBORN TOWNSHIP CENSUS

Samuel Ford

Males	Females
2 (0-5)	- (0-5)
1 (5-10)	1 (5-10)
1 (10-15)	2 (10-15)
2 (20-30)	1 (20-30)
1 (40-50)	1 (40-50)

1850 DEARBORN TOWNSHIP CENSUS

	Age	Occupation	Real Estate	Birthplace
Nancy Ford	55	Housewife	$1500.	Ireland
Henry	23	Farmer		Ireland
Nancy	16	In School		Michigan
George	15	" "		"
Samuel	13	" "		"
James	10	" "		"
Eliza	8	" "		"

1860 DEARBORN TOWNSHIP CENSUS

	Age	Occupation	Real Estate	Birthplace
Nancy Ford	64	Housewife	$5000.	Ireland
George	25	Farmer		Michigan
Samuel	23	Farmer		"
James	19	Farmer		"
Eliza	17			"

1870 DEARBORN TOWNSHIP CENSUS

	Age	Occupation	Real Estate	Birthplace
James Ford	27	Farmer	$4000.	Michigan
Eliza	25	Keeping House		"
Nancy	74	At home (Blind)		Ireland

38

1839 built a frame school building on the corner of the Richard Gardner farm. This was on the south side of a trail which would become Warren Avenue, between what are now Southfield and Greenfield roads. The site was leased from Gardner for 21 years at a rent of 10¢ per year. The first classes are said to have been held for a period of three months during the summer of 1840. The teacher was Lovedy Ruddiman, age twenty-two, a daughter of William and Barbara Ruddiman.[48] The normal school year consisted of one month in the fall, three months in winter, and two months in spring.

The summer 1840 Dearborn Township Census[49] lists twelve persons in the Samuel Ford household. Samuel and Ann (Nancy) were in their forties. Son William had been married the previous December and was now building a cabin on his own property.[50] The other children were all home, other than Eliza who would be born two years later. All presumably lived in the original log cabin. Because William's new wife was Ann Ketchum, it is possible that Samuel's wife was then referred to as Nancy to avoid confusion.

These new arrivals to Dearborn eventually prospered because they brought with them fairly advanced agricultural methods and a vigorous, ambitious spirit. This mixing of the poor, ingenious Irish with the frugal, astute Scotch and the thrifty, methodical Germans created a very competitive but progressive neighborhood. Samuel is said to have been "very ambitious"[51] and very helpful to his younger brother, George. After ten years in Michigan, however, the rigors of wilderness living took their toll, and at the age of fifty-one (1842) Samuel was the first to die. His grave is on his own farm, the site of the Ford Cemetery at Greenfield and Joy roads.

Samuel, his son William S., his brother George, and their respective wives had been the real pioneers. Samuel, unfortunately, did not live to welcome his mother, Rebecca, and brother, John, and family, who came poverty stricken from Ireland in 1847.[52]

Samuel's mother, Rebecca, arrived with her son, John, in 1847 at age seventy-one. Rebecca Jennings was to live just four years in America.[56] It is said that when she died, there was no minister immediately available for a Protestant funeral service, and that she was buried in a shallow grave at the Ford Cemetery site with rites later administered by a passing priest. Because the cemetery was low, land was filled in around the grave, but later her body was moved to Grand Lawn. For a time, the small, private Ford

Cemetery was considered undesirable and it was thought that it might be abandoned.

After Grand Lawn Cemetery opened in 1908, several Fords, including Rebecca, were moved.[57] A yarn heard much later by the Samuel Ford great-great-grandchildren was that a derelict whose name was "Bismark" had died and had been buried in the Ford Cemetery by Henry Ford, and for that reason the Ford Cemetery was not a desirable place.[58]

The 1850 Dearborn Township Census shows Nancy as head of the Samuel Ford household, with son, Henry, working the farm, and the five younger children in school. By 1860, Henry, married, was on his own farm;[59] George, Samuel (Jr.) and James were listed as "Farmers" on Nancy's farm. The year 1870 is the last census which lists Nancy. She lives with her son, James, who eventually inherits the homestead.[60] Daughter Eliza is at home and not yet married. At age seventy-four, Nancy is old and blind. She died three years later, and was also buried in the family plot, just a few steps from where she had lived for over forty years.

Samuel and Nancy had ten children, and would have forty-seven grandchildren (see family chart). The 1925–40 family tree survey of the Samuel and Nancy Ford branch names close to 200 direct descendants. Very few of these people now live in Dearborn Township.

NOTES AND REFERENCES

1. The Ford family tree (a copy of which is on file at the Dearborn Historical Museum) was undertaken in 1924 at the direction of Mr. Henry Ford by Mr. Raymond Laird with the assistance of his wife, Mrs. Emma (Ford) Laird. Mr. Laird was employed in the Engineering Laboratories of the Ford Motor Company at that time, and performed many private, confidential assignments for Mr. Ford. An excellent effort was made by the Lairds. However, work on the tree was prematurely abandoned prior to 1940, leaving existing copies to suffer omissions, minor errors, and subsequent inappropriate modifications. See also *The Dearborn Historian*, 10, No.1 (1970).

2. Conversations with Mrs. Myrtle (Ford) Fox, great granddaughter of Samuel Ford.

3. Reminiscences of Clyde M. Ford, great grandson of Samuel Ford. Unsigned Typescript, Ford Archives, Henry Ford Museum.

4. *Ibid.*

5. Margaret (Ford) Ruddiman, "Memories of My Brother Henry Ford," *Michigan History*, Michigan Historical Commission, September, 1953. (Mrs. Ruddiman is a granddaughter of Samuel's brother, John.)

6. Olson, Sidney, *Young Henry Ford,* Wayne State University Press, Detroit (1963).

7. Conversations with Miss Olive Ford, great granddaughter of Samuel's brother, John Ford.

8. See Reference 2.

9. See Reference 7.

10. "The Henry Ford Family" interview by Dr. M.M. Quaife with Mrs. Esther (Flaherty) McDonald (granddaughter of Samuel's brother, John) Ferndale, Michigan, 1946. Burton Historical Collection, Detroit Public Library.

11. See Reference 7.

12. War of 1812 — *Commemorative Issue,* Michigan Heritage, Kalamazoo Valley Genealogical Society, Kalamazoo, Michigan, IV, No.1, 1962.

13. William S. Ford obituary, *Methodist Advocate,* August 6, 1898.

14. Interview with Clyde M. Ford, *Dearborn Press,* Sept. 8, 1943.

15. Stevenson, Frank, "Scotch Settlement," *Dearborn Historian,* 5, No. 1, 1965.

16. National Archives Microfilm Publications:

    Index to Passenger Lists of Vessels Arriving at Philadelphia, 1800–1906, Roll #45, FLY-FOX.

    Index to Passenger Lists of Vessels Arriving at New York, 1820–1846, Roll #32, FLJ-FOZ.

    Index to Passenger Lists of Vessels Arriving at Boston, August 2, 1831–September 29, 1832. (Not alphabetically arranged.)

17. Nevins, Allan, *Ford: The Times, The Man, The Company,* Charles Schribner's Sons, New York, 1954, p.33.

18. See Reference 16.

19. *Illustrated Historical Atlas,* Wayne County, Michigan, 1876. (Copy on hand at Dearborn Historical Museum.)

20. *Detroit,* Edited by Melvin G. Holli, New Viewpoint, New York, 1976.

21. "Migration to Michigan," *Dearborn Historian,* 12, No. 3,1972. (Focuses on a typical letter written from the Dearborn area to relatives in Ireland in 1839.)

22. Lewis, Ferris F., *Michigan Yesterday and Today,* Hillsdale Publishers, Hillsdale, Michigan, 1956.

23. See Reference 5.

24. It is thought that Ann (Nancy Ford) Smith may have had a brother in Detroit. A Mr. John Smith (1797–1878) of County Cork, Ireland, resided late in life at 150 Trumbull Street. Nancy's niece, Mary (1833–1882), daughter of George Ford, married John Smith's son, Henry Smith, also born in Ireland. The marriage was in 1856. Another daughter of George Ford, Eliza (1847–1913), married Thomas Smith, also of 150 Trumbull Street, in 1867. Thus, counting Thomasine, there may have been four marriages between the Fords and Smiths of County Cork.

25. See Reference 2.

26. Bald, F. Clever, *Michigan in Four Centuries,* Harper Bros., New York, 1954.

27. *First Land Owners of Wayne County, Michigan*, Michigan Heritage Publications, compiled by F. Gray and Ethel W. Williams, Kalamazoo, Michigan, 1964.

28. See Reference 22.

29. See Reference 2.

30. *Ibid.*

31. See Reference 26.

32. Haight, Floyd L., "Research on the Detroit Arsenal," *The Dearborn Historian*, 12, No.2 (1972).

33. Baut, Donald V., "The Detroit Arsenal Story — 1833–1875," Parts 1–7, *The Dearborn Historian*, 16 (1976), 17 (1977).

34. Nowlin, William, *The Bark Covered House*, Dearborn Historical Commission, 1973.

35. See Reference 26.

36. See Reference 2.

37. See Reference 26.

38. *Index to Petitions of Naturalization*, Records of County Clerk, Wayne County, Michigan.

39. See Reference 17.

40. *Transcriptions of the Municipal Archives of Michigan.* Minutes of the Meetings of the Townships of Bucklin, Pekin and Dearborn. May 28, 1827–April 13, 1857. Michigan Historical Survey Project, 1941.

41. *Ibid.*

42. *Mariner's Church 1849–1864*, Manuscript, Burton Historical Collection, Detroit Public Library.

43. See Reference 24.

44. See Reference 27.

45. See Reference 7.

46. See Reference 26.

47. See Reference 40.

48. See Reference 5.

49. *Dearborn Township Census*, Dearborn Historical Museum Files.

50. *Wayne County Michigan Land Records,* Early Land Transfers, Detroit and Wayne County, Michigan, Michigan W.P.A. Vital Records Project, Michigan State Library and D.A.R. Louisa St. Clair Chapter, 1940.

   William Ford and Anna Ford of Dearborn Twp. purchased from Amzi Ketchum and W. Barbary of Plymouth Twp. on April 10,1840, The East half of the N.W. quarter of Sec. 1, Twp. 2, S. Range 10 E. containing 80 acres in Wayne County. Recorded October 31, 1840. (County Records Vol. 19 p. 343)

   Henry Ford of Dearborn Twp. purchased from William Ford and w. Ann of Dearborn Twp. in Mar. 1851, a parcel of land beginning at the N. line of Sec. 1, Twp. 2, S. Range 10 E. in Wayne County. (County Records Vol. 41, p. 229)

Samuel Ford of Dearborn Twp. purchased from the Plymouth Plank Road Company in Dec. 1862, 20 acres of the S.E. Corner of the E. Half of the S.E. quarter Sec. 36, Twp. 1, S. Range 10 E. Witnessed by A.S. Cullen and Henry Ford. (County Records Vol. 48, p. 68)

George and James eventually share the original Samuel Ford property, although there seems to be no record of purchases.

51. See Reference 7.

52. *Ibid.*

53. O'Brien, Maire & Conor Cruise, *A Concise History of Ireland,* Beekman House, New York, 1971.

54. What interest, if any, John Ford may have had in the Life Leasehold when he was evicted in 1847, he may have sold for travel money, to one Jeremiah Kingston who is on the roll as "Representanve of John Forde" as late as 1877.

55. See Reference 7.

56. Grandmother, Rebecca, was formally referred to as "Mrs. Jennings." She is listed on cemetery records as Rebecca Jennings. This may be because she had three granddaughters here in Dearborn named Rebecca Ford, and Jennings was a distinguishing name.

57. On July 3, 1919, a son of Samuel's brother, namely George Ford, Jr. (1845–1925) purchased Lots 82 and 83, Sect. 4 of Grand Lawn Cemetery for $1,102.80. On October 16, 1919, a group of ten re-burials were recorded. These included "Grandma," Rebecca Jennings (1776–1851), "Father," George Ford (1811–1865), and "Mother," Alice Ford (1810–1893), all of whom had been moved from the Ford Cemetery by a Northrop Funeral Home.

58. Conversations with Rylma (Ford) LaChance, great, great granddaughter of Samuel Ford, and daughter of Clyde M. Ford.

59. See Reference 50.

60. *Ibid.*

ᵉⁱᵉⁱ 3 ᵉⁱᵉⁱ
THE GEORGE FORD FAMILY

The Family of Henry's Favorite Aunt, Alice,
Who Was Both Helped and Scared by the Indians

When it was planned to revise this book by adding a chapter about the George Ford family, immediately the question became, "Which George Ford?" There were five George Fords. This account describes the family of the very earliest George Ford in this locality, together with the family of his son, also named George.

Of the three Ford brothers who left Ireland for America, two arrived at Detroit in 1832, the younger being George (1811–1863). He had traveled with his much older brother, Samuel (1792–1842) together with Samuel's family consisting of Samuel's wife Nancy (1795–1873), two sons, William (1819–1898) and Henry (1827–1914), also two daughters, Mary (1820–1878) and Rebecca (1822–1897). During this period in Ireland, which was several years before the great potato famine, it is said there had been great unemployment in Europe and Great Britain due to the cessation of the Napoleonic Wars of 1805–1815. (A later group of Fords who came in 1847 including auto Henry's grandfather, John, left Ireland destitute because of famine conditions.)

There is evidence that these early Fords arrived at Québec City, Canada, and spent some time at Rochester, New York, where George is said to have worked on the Erie Canal when he was about eighteen years old.[1] Upon arrival at Detroit in 1832, no doubt the entire clan headed for 150 Trumbull Street where a brother of Nancy (Smith) Ford, Mr. John Smith, lived with his family. George, at 21, is said to have lived on Jefferson Avenue and worked as a hod carrier in Detroit before following the Samuel Ford family into the wilderness west of Detroit. It was during 1832 in Detroit that George married Alice Good (1810–1893), who had also recently arrived from Ireland. They had quite likely met at a social gathering in the Corktown district of Detroit where the Smith family lived.

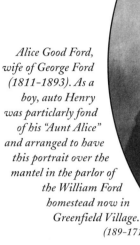

Alice Good Ford, wife of George Ford (1811-1893). As a boy, auto Henry was particlarly fond of his "Aunt Alice" and arranged to have this portrait over the mantel in the parlor of the William Ford homestead now in Greenfield Village. (189-1718)

Samuel, we know, purchased 80 acres of property on May 23, 1832, in the far northeastern corner of Dearborn Township. A few months later (October 1, 1832) George bought his first property — 40 acres described as the Southwest ¼ of the Southwest ¼ of Section 6, Township 2 South, Range 11 East at one dollar an acre. Although this was in Greenfield Township, the property adjoined Samuel's in Dearborn Township. There was no road separating them at that time. Another 40 acres — the Northwest ¼ of the Southwest ¼ of the same township — was purchased by George on July 23, 1833.[2] (See map on p. 47.)

It is said that after George had built a crude log cabin on his property, he sent to Detroit for Alice. He sent the local Indian Chief Tebow, who owned riding ponies, to bring Alice to the nearby Indian village. When Tebow and Alice arrived, all of the Indians chanted, "Tebow's new wife! Tebow's new wife!" This

Redford
Township

Greenfield
Township

Townline

3   Joy Road

1

2   Townline

Dearborn
Township

Springwells
Township (1873)

*

Scotch
School

Warren Road

1 - Samuel 1832   2 - George 1832   3 - George 1833

*George and Samuel
Ford Farms*

reception greatly frightened Alice until she saw George smiling in the crowd. And the ride with Tebow had been the first she had ever had on horseback.

This same Alice is the one who has been mentioned before as having been lost overnight in the woods due to a bear frightening her from the trail while returning from Detroit. A family search party found her the next morning.

Mabel Ford[3] wrote a short history of the George Fords which, in part, reads as follows:

> George Ford had to cut down trees from which he built his house. After it had been erected his young wife had to gather moss to chink in the spaces between the logs to make it weatherproof. Not far from the Ford's home was a large village of Indians. They were no longer on the war path. But the settlers were not too sure of that, and it was several years before they felt comfortable with these neighbors. One time Alice Ford saw the Indians. They had been skinning deer which they had slain in the nearby forest and their hands were red with blood. Mrs.

Henry Ford driving the horses and Clara holding her parasol in Dearborn's 4th of July carriage parade in 1924. They are dressed in old-fashioned (1860) costumes — Henry with false mustache and sideburns, and wearing George Ford's "stovepipe" hat which he had acquired from George Ford descendants. (0-15129)

Ford took one look at them and fainted. She told her children, years later, that she thought they were on a scalping party and had come to kill all the whites in the vicinity. However, if Mrs. Ford fainted at the sight of the Indians, that is the only occasion on record when she showed any weakness. She lived to the age of 82 and was never sick a day in her life until her final illness.

If the house was crude and the woods were full of Indians, pioneer life had its compensations. The fields abounded with wild turkeys which provided plenty of game for the bill-of-fare, and if the Indians could kill deer, so could the whites. The wolves, however, were a nuisance, and in order to save their pigs and cattle from these roaming marauders the Fords had to nail shut the doors of their barns at night — and for a long time had to take turns standing guard at night, gun in hand, so bold were the wolves.

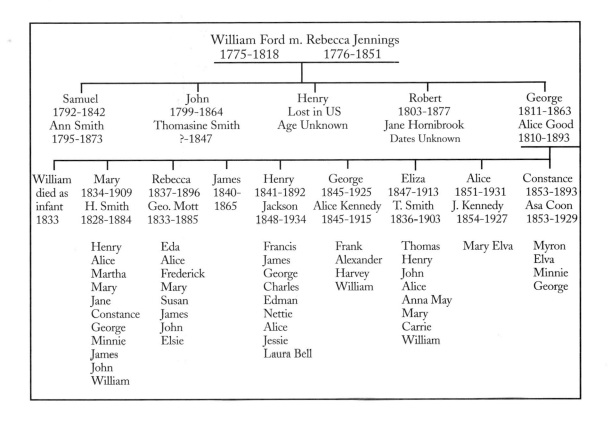

William Ford m. Rebecca Jennings
1775-1818   1776-1851

Samuel	John	Henry	Robert	George
1792-1842	1799-1864	Lost in US	1803-1877	1811-1863
Ann Smith	Thomasine Smith	Age Unknown	Jane Hornibrook	Alice Good
1795-1873	?-1847		Dates Unknown	1810-1893

William	Mary	Rebecca	James	Henry	George	Eliza	Alice	Constance
died as infant 1833	1834-1909 H. Smith 1828-1884	1837-1896 Geo. Mott 1833-1885	1840-1865	1841-1892 Jackson 1848-1934	1845-1925 Alice Kennedy 1845-1915	1847-1913 T. Smith 1836-1903	1851-1931 J. Kennedy 1854-1927	1853-1893 Asa Coon 1853-1929
	Henry Alice Martha Mary Jane Constance George Minnie James John William	Eda Alice Frederick Mary Susan James John Elsie		Francis James George Charles Edman Nettie Alice Jessie Laura Bell	Frank Alexander Harvey William	Thomas Henry John Alice Anna May Mary Carrie William	Mary Elva	Myron Elva Minnie George

George and Alice had their first child, William, in 1833; but this child died as an infant. A daughter, Mary, was born in 1834, and another daughter, Rebecca, in 1837. A son James, was born in 1840. The 1840 Greenfield Township census reveals George and Alice with three children — Mary, Rebecca and James. George was 29, Alice was 30, the children being six, three, and the baby (James) less than one. No value is given for their real estate at that date.[4]

Although these new settlers of the 1830s and 1840s were generally considerate of one another, some township rules and regulations were necessary. Among them were:

— No horses of any other town shall be free Commoners of this town.
— Stud horses shall be restrained after one year old. All stud horses over two years old to be prohibited from going at large under a fine of $12.00.
— Rams must be restricted from running at large after they are six months old under penalty of $2.00.
— Bears may not be allowed to run at large after six months old under penalty of $10.00 for each offense.

— A bounty of $2.00 to be paid for any wolf killed in the township by an inhabitant of the township.

By 1850 there were four more children in the family — Henry (age 11), George (5), Eliza (3) and Alice (1). Their property was now valued at $1,400 and George's mother, Rebecca, was living with them.[5] Rebecca (the automotive magnate's great-grand-mother) had come to America at age 71 with her son, John, in 1847 but stayed with George and Alice because they were already settled. It is very unlikely Rebecca was really 88 years old as the census indicated. From other records her age is calculated to have been 75 years. Rebecca, in a sense, was the mother of all the Fords

Photograph of the young George Ford Family taken about 1900. Alice and George are sitting at the right. From the left are the sons: Harvey, William, Frank and Alexander. (Photo courtesy of Charlotte Ford 0-15347)

1840 GREENFIELD TOWNSHIP CENSUS

George Ford

Males		Females	
1	(0-5)(James)	1	(0-5)(Rebecca)
-	(5-10)	1	(5-10)(Mary)
-	(10-15)	-	(10-15)
-	(15-20)	-	(15-20)
1	(20-30)(George)	-	(20-30)
-	(30-40)	1	(30-40)(Alice)

1850 GREENFIELD TOWNSHIP CENSUS

Name	Age	Sex	Occupation	Real Estate	Birthplace
George Ford	40	m	Farmer	$1400	Ireland
Alice Ford	40	f	Housewife		Ireland
Mary	15	f			Michigan
Rebecca	13	f			"
James	12	m			"
Henry	11	m			"
George	5	m			"
Eliza	3	f			"
Alice	1	f			"
Rebecca	88	f			Ireland

1860 GREENFIELD TOWNSHIP CENSUS

Name	Age	Sex	Occupation	Real Estate	Birthplace
George Ford	50	m	Farmer	$7000.	Ireland
Alice	48	f			Ireland
Rebecca	24	f			Michigan
James	22	m			"
Henry	20	m			"
George	15	m			"
Eliza	12	f			"
Alice	10	f			"
Constance	7	f			"

of both Dearborn and Greenfield. Rebecca died while with George and Alice in 1851. She was first buried in the Ford Cemetery, but in 1919 was moved to Grand Lawn Cemetery by her grandson, George. In 1856, Mary, the oldest daughter of George and Alice, married Henry Smith of the John Smith family on Trumbull Street in Detroit.

The George Ford family was in its prime in 1860. Seven children — four girls and three boys — assured a lively household.

51

1870 GREENFIELD TOWNSHIP CENSUS

Name	Age	Sex	Occupation	Real Estate	Birthplace
George Ford	24	m	Farmer	$8000.	Michigan
Alice	24	f	Keeping House		"
Alice	57	f	No occupation		Ireland
Alice	20	f	"		Michigan
Constance	14	f	"		"

1880 GREENFIELD TOWNSHIP CENSUS

Name	Color	Sex	Age	Occupation	Birthplace	Father	Mother
George Ford	w	m	35	Farmer	Michigan	Ireland	Ireland
Alice	w	f	33	Keeping House	Michigan	Canada	Ireland
Frank	w	m	9	Son	Michigan	Michigan	Michigan
Alexander	w	m	7	Son	"	"	"
Harvey	w	m	4	Son	"	"	"
Alice	w	f	69	Mother	Ireland	Ireland	Ireland
Alice	w	f	29	Sister (Dressmaker)	Michigan	Michigan	Michigan
Charley Hansen			21	Laborer			

1900 GREENFIELD TOWNSHIP CENSUS

Name	Birth	Age	Birthplace	Father	Mother	English read	write	speak
George Ford-Head	1845	55	Michigan	Ireland	Ireland	x	x	x
Alice -Wife	1846	53	Michigan	New York	Ireland	x	x	x
Alexander -Son	1872	27	"	Michigan	Michigan	x	x	x
Harvey -Son	1876	23	"	"	"	x	x	x
William -Son	1881	18	"	"	"	x	x	x
(at school)								

With a new house, their real estate value had jumped to $7,000. (The house was at what is now 15343 Joy Road in Detroit.) Every Sunday, George would hitch up his team and drive the family into Detroit to attend church. They belonged to the Old Mariners' Episcopal Church which is still standing in downtown Detroit. All of the children piled into the back of the big wagon and Mr. and

George Ford sons display horses used to deliver milk to Detroit. The barn has a date of 1884; the photograph was taken about 1890. From left to right (holding horses) are: Harvey, Alexander and William. At the far right in white shirt is their cousin George Coon — son of Constance Ford. (Photo courtesy Charlotte Ford 189.1844)

Mrs. Ford sat on the front seat with Mr. Ford wearing his high "stovepipe" hat.

In 1863, however, George died at age 52, and Alice had to carry on. Their son, James, the oldest, died in 1865 at an age of only 25 years. In 1867, their son Henry married Maria Jackson and became a farmer on his own in Greenfield Township. He and Maria were to have ten children. So it was the youngest son, George, age 17, who continued farming with his mother on the homestead property for the next fifty years.

Young George Ford married Alice Kennedy in 1870 at age twenty-four. They lived on the original farm on the southeast corner of Joy and Greenfield Roads, the farm being appraised at $8,000. Alice, his wife, was "keeping house" according to the 1870 census. Alice, his mother, was of course there — it was her farm. And his two sisters, Alice and Constance were at home. With three Alices in the household, there must have been utter confusion without agreed upon nicknames.

GEORGE FORD FARM OPERATIONS			
	George Ford (1811-1863)		George Ford (1845-1925)
	1850	1860	1870	1880
Acres improved	45	72	80	85
Acres unimproved	35	11	-	35
Cash value	$1400	$4500	$8000	$7000
Value of implements	$80	$150	$200	$200
Number of horses	3	8	3	5
Milch cows	6	6	5	4
Other cattle	2	7	4	4
Sheep	28	10	6	21*
Swine	8	8	8	18
Value of livestock	$229	$650	$600	$400
Wheat (bushels)	80	15	200	292
Indian corn (bushels)	100	100	100	500
Oats (bushels)	250	250	500	446
Wool (pounds)	30	na	na	105
Irish potatos (bushels)	40	450	40	100
Butter (pounds)	700	400	400	800
Eggs (dozens)	na	na	na	500
Hay (tons)	15	18	20	20
Wages paid	-	-	$100	$175
Total value of products	na	na	$900	$600

* George had purchased 82 sheep. He had sold fifty of these, dogs had killed eleven, leaving him with twenty one.

The year 1880 finds the younger George Ford with a full house, including sons Frank, Harvey and Alexander. George's mother Alice (69) is with them, and sister Alice (29) is listed as "dressmaker." Constance had married Asa B. Coon in 1876. George now has a hired man, inasmuch as the oldest of the three sons is only nine years of age. But according to Federal Census data, farm values had taken a considerable drop between 1870 and 1880 due to the financial panic of 1873.[6]

There would be a fourth son, William, born in 1881. Alice Ford, sister of George, in 1887, at age 36, married James Kennedy the brother of Alice (Kennedy) Ford, George's wife. And Alice (Good) Ford, mother of George, was to die during 1893 at age 82. She had four granddaughters named Alice.

Alice (Good) Ford was acknowledged by the automotive Henry Ford to be his favorite aunt. Especially after Henry's own mother died in 1876, he greatly admired his aunt Alice. He is quoted as saying that more wisdom flowed from her lips than any other person he ever knew.

Charlotte Ford, daughter of Alexander Ford and great grand-daughter of George Ford and Alice Good, recalls several incidents involving her family and the automotive Henry Ford:

> George Ford (1845–1925) was a relatively progressive farmer and had purchased the first McCormick binder in the neighborhood. Young Henry Ford, seeing the new machine, was so annoyed because his father, William, didn't also have one, he vented his disgust by tearing apart an old-fashioned sweep owned by his father.
>
> It was somewhat a custom among the Fords to get together potluck style at one of the homes for a Christmas Eve party. In the host's parlor was built a "Christmas House" of evergreen boughs. As guests arrived, presents for one and all were placed in the Christmas House, and when all guests had arrived the host passed out the presents from the Christmas House.

One Christmas when the Fords had gathered at the William Ford home, Alice (Kennedy) Ford gave her husband, George, a fine watch as a gift. Young Henry wanted to examine it. It was soon apart and George was very upset thinking Henry had surely destroyed it. But Henry, to everyone's surprise, put it together again with no damage done.

Another census, in 1900, had added an English literacy survey which the George Ford family seems to have passed with ease. In fact, the three older Ford boys attended Business College for a year, living with an aunt in Detroit. By 1900, Frank had left home to live in Detroit, but George still had three of his sons at home — two classified as "laborers." After George Ford (the younger) retired, he stayed with his son Harvey who owned a farm one-half mile north of the homestead. Son Alexander was the one who stayed on the original farm.

Harvey and Alexander took milk from their farms to Frank's place in Detroit from which the milk was distributed to customers in the city. Grocery stores seldom offered milk in those days. Milk and ice, as well as fish and fresh vegetables, were delivered on a daily basis door-to-door. To handle milk properly, Harvey and Alex cut blocks of ice from the Rouge River in winter and stored them in a large ice-house on their property. The ice was used in summer to cool the milk before and during delivery.

About 1920, the old farm was sold to Frischkorn Realty Company to be subdivided. George (1845–1925) had served on the Greenfield Township School District No. 9 for fifteen years. George Ford and all his children had attended the original one-room school which stood on what is now the corner of West Chicago and Hubbell avenues in Detroit.

In 1923, a new three-room school was built near Ford property and named the George Ford School in his honor. At this location (Orangelawn and Lauder streets), there is now a much larger George Ford School accommodating as many as 1,000 students. All of the George Ford property was annexed by the City of Detroit, October 6, 1925 — the same year this younger George Ford died.

REFERENCES

1. Interview with Clyde M. Ford, *Dearborn Press,* September 8, 1943.

2. *Wayne County Michigan Land Records.* Early Land Transfers, Detroit and Wayne County, Michigan. WPA Records Project, Michigan State Library and DAR Louisa St. Clair Chapter, 1940. See also, *Illustrated Historical Atlas,* County of Wayne, H. Belden & Company, 1876.

3. Mabel N. Ford was a great granddaughter of Samuel Ford and a neighbor of the younger George Fords.

4. Sixth Census United States Population Schedule — 1840. Michigan, Wayne County, Greenfield Township.

5. Seventh Census United States Population Schedule — 1850. Michigan, Wayne County, Greenfield Township.

6. Federal Non-Population Census Schedule of Products of Agriculture, 1850–1880. Michigan Department of State, Lansing, Michigan.

7. Accession 23, Box 28, "Genealogy," Archives, Henry Ford Museum & Greenfield Village.

4
THE JOHN FORD FAMILY

Including Highlights in the Lives of the
Grandparents and Father of Henry Ford

John Ford (1799-1864), grandfather of Henry Ford (1863-1947), was the second oldest son of William Ford (1775-1818) and Rebecca Jennings Ford (1776-1851). In 1819, the year following his father William's death, John Ford with his mother, Rebecca Ford, subjected themselves to a life lease of the Ford homestead on the Madame Estate in Ireland consisting of 23 acres of land and a small dry-stone cottage, as provided by Jonas Stawell of Kilbrittain, Ireland. Yearly rent was 29 pounds, 2 shillings, 10 pence. Both John and his mother appear to have used an "X" for their signatures.[1] A later lease (1843), made by Francis Stawell to John Ford as sole leaseholder, shows that rent had been reduced to 21 pounds, six shillings, 8 pence. A copy of the 1819 lease is quite legible and reads, interestingly enough, as follows:

> This indenture made the First Day of May in the year of Our Lord One Thousand Eight Hundred and nineteen Between Jonas Stawell of Kilbrittain County of Cork party the one part, and Rebecca Forde widow & John Forde farmer both of Maddam (sic) in the County aforesaid of the other part.
>
> Witnesseth, that the said Jonas Stawell for and in consideration of the Yearly Ren and Covenants herein after referred hath demised, granted, set, and to Farm Let; and by these presents, do demise, grant, set, and to Farm Let, unto the said Rebecca Forde & John Forde All that and those that part of the lands of Maddam now in their possession Situated in the barony of east division of east Carberry, and County of Cork Containing by a late Survey which is to be final & conclusive Twenty three acres one rood & ten perches excepet & always reserving out of this demise unto the Said Jonas Stawell his heirs & assigns, all mines, minerals, pits & quarries of Culm, Coal, Stone, Slate, sand & gravel, timber & trees, bog timber, turberries and all manner of game, with liberty for the said Jonas Stawell his heirs, assigns Servants & workers too . . . raise quarry and carry away the same without impeachment of waste, and also to hunt fish & Fowl theiron.
>
> To have and to Hold the said demised Premises, with The Rights, Members, and Appurtenances thereunto. The said Rebecca Forde & John Forde & also as herein after mentioned to their heirs and assigns,

from the twenty fifth Day of March last for & during the natural life of the Said John Forde a party hereto.

Yielding and Paying Therfore and thereout Yearly, and every Year during the said term unto the said Jonas Stawell his heirs and Assigns, the Yearly Rent or Sum of Twenty nine pounds two shillings and Ten pence Sterling to be paid by Half yearly payments on every Twenty fifth day of March & Twenty ninth day of September in each & every Year for the first Twenty years of said term and quarterly for the residue therof . . . AND if the said reserved yearly Rent, or any part thereof, shall happen to be behind or unpaid by the space of twenty-one days next after the days herein before mentioned for the payment thereof, then and so often as it shall happen, it shall and may be lawful to and for the said Jonas Stawell his heirs or assigns unto the demised Premises, or any part thereof, to enter and distrain. . . to re-enter and the same to have again, repossess and enjoy as in their former state.

In 1823, John Ford married Thomasine Smith, sister of Ann (Nancy) Smith who in 1818 had married John's brother Samuel. They were married by banns, which was public announcement in church of their proposed marriage. John and Thomasine were to have seven children born in Ireland: Rebecca (1824), William (1826), Jane (1829), Henry (1830), Mary (1833), Nancy (1834), and Samuel (1838).[3] Of this group of children, William was to become the father of Henry Ford the automobile genius. Apparently they had all been living contentedly in the little drystone cottage on the 23-acre plot of land. For 24 years John Ford and Rebecca Jennings Ford had complied with the life lease provided by Jonas Stawell. Likely because of the death of Jonas Stawell in 1835, a new lease involving only John Ford was arranged in 1843 with Rev. Francis Stawell.

By 1845 the devastating "black blight" had struck Ireland's potato crops in earnest. Potatoes had been the major sustenance of Irish farmers. In 1847, John Ford with his wife, Thomasine, his mother Rebecca Jennings Ford, and the seven children, ranging in age from nine to twenty-three years, faced eviction from their Irish home which had been occupied by members of the Ford family for over 200 years. [2,3]

By 1841 the population of Ireland had been increasing until it was well over eight million. However, due to the failure of the potato crops in 1845, 1846, and 1847, it was now under six million. During the great famine, it is estimated that a million Irish people emigrated — mainly to the United States by way of Canada — and a million more died in Ireland. Ireland was devastated.

The John Fords had no better choice in 1847 than to emigrate to America, and join older brother Samuel's family and the family of his younger brother George Ford. These two families had settled in America in 1832 and, by 1847, were owners of large and posperous farms on the outskirts of the City of Detroit in the State of Michigan. Along with the John Fords came the family of Robert Forde (1803-1877) with his wife, Jane Hornibrook, and their four children. The entire number set out for Quebec, Canada, from Cork, Ireland. The Fordes traveled steerage, and the small children are said to have had no shoes. Despite this poverty, the children could read and write because of having been tutored in Ireland.

Exodus from Ireland in 1847 was a very difficult adventure. Thousands of poor famished Irish were crowding the so called "coffin ships," each ship carrying as many as 400 passengers escaping from Ireland to America. Nearly 100,000 people sailed from Ireland to Quebec during 1847, with 33 shiploads arriving from Cork. Living in the crowded and septic conditions on the ocean for a month or more resulted in shipboard epidemics of cholera and typhus. It was estimated that twenty percent of Irish passengers arriving at Quebec had either died at sea or soon after arrival.[1] Thomasine is thought to have died of typhus either at sea or in Quebec's Quarantine Hospital located 48 kilometers downstream from Quebec on Grosse Ile. The hospital had treated 8,691 immigrants during 1847. Thomasine is thought to have been buried on Grosse Ile with 5,424 other Irish immigrants in mass graves now identified by a huge Celtic Cross.[3,7] While the Robert Fords settled near Quebec in Canada, the John Ford family continued on to Michigan, where it seems their names suddenly became Ford rather than Forde.

The John Fords, arriving in Detroit without Thomasine, no doubt first visited the John Smiths who were Thomasine's relatives residing at 150 Trumbull Street in Detroit. John Ford with his family is said to have been invited to move in with the farm family of George Ford (1811-1861). Rebecca Jennings Ford accepted the offer, and spent the rest of her life with the George Ford family. George was John's much younger brother who had come to the Dearborn area with Samuel Ford in 1832 when Detroit was surrounded by wilderness. By 1847, Michigan had become a State of the United States, considerable land around Detroit had been

*Celtic Cross
Memorial on Grosse
Ile erected in
memory of Irish
immigrants who
died before
reaching Québec.*
Photograph with per-
mission of Gilles
Durand, National
Archives of Québec,
Québec, Canada.[7]

cleared, dirt roads were becoming commonplace, and a plank road reached from Detroit to the little town of Dearbornville, a community ten miles west of Detroit consisting of about 60 families, seven stores, a blacksmith shop, and a physician.

In January of 1848, John Ford purchased 80 acres of woodlands in Redford Township about two miles west of the farms of George and Samuel Ford. The land, consisting of the W 1/2 of the SW 1/4 of Section 35, Township 1 south, Range 10 east, was purchased from Henry Maybury, an Irishman who had known the Fords in Ireland. John Ford paid $200 down, with a mortgage of $150. Maybury had purchased the same 80 acres from the Federal Government for $100 in 1834.[5]

John's eldest son, William (1826-1905), now 21 years of age was of considerable help in establishing a homestead for the family. William had been well tutored in Ireland, and was an accomplished carpenter. William is said to have brought carpenter tools from Ireland to America, and to have worked on the railroad building stations and sheds along the line going westward from Detroit toward Chicago. William's pay is said to have helped his father pay off the mortgage on the 80 acres purchased from Maybury. Some woods must have been cleared and a residence built on the property within two years because by August of 1850 the Redford Township census shows John Ford, farmer age 50, with real estate valued at $350. Mary Ford was then listed as age 17, and Samuel Ford age 13. William was not listed as he was probably working elsewhere.

John Ford's family was soon breaking up. Jane Ford (1829-1851) lived only four years in America. At age 22 she had married Henry Smith (1828-1884), a relative of her mother living in Detroit. Jane Ford died when an infant son was born to them in 1851. This was the same year that Rebecca Jennings Ford, staying with the George Ford family, died at age 75 years.

Rebecca, John's eldest daughter (1824-1895), was 23 years of age when she arrived from Ireland. In 1851, she married William Flaherty at Eagle River, Michigan. He had been born in Shanty Bay, Ontario, Canada. Together they lived in the town of Ontonagon, in Upper Michigan. There, between the years of 1852 and 1859, they had four children: John, Charles, Jane, and Thomasine. William Flaherty died in Shanty Bay, Canada, in 1861. Rebecca and the children then seemed to have migrated to

*Gravestone of John Ford
in the Ford Cemetery.
Inscription reads:*

*In memory of
JOHN FORD
DIED
March 22, 1864
Aged 65 Yrs.
May his soul rest with God
where trials and troubles
of the world are peace and
happiness*

Courtesy of Hubert J. Beudert

Detroit where her daughter, Thomasine, died in 1887. Rebecca died on August 28, 1895. Her son, John Flaherty, born in 1852, lived until 1914.

William Ford (1826-1905), John Ford's oldest son, married Mary Litogot (1839-1876) in 1861. Mary Litogot was an orphan living with Margaret and Patrick O'Hern, farmers near Dearbornville. William was 13 years older than Mary Litogot. They had eight children, of which five lived to become adults. The adults included Henry (1863-1947) the automotive genius, John, Margaret, Jane and William. (These children of William are each described in chapter entitled "The Family of William Ford, South.")

John Ford's second oldest boy, Henry (1830-1901), 17 years of age at the time of arrival in America also worked on the railroads for a while, but by 1851 had headed for the Far West and the gold fields of California. There, on August 26, 1857, this Henry married Catherine O'Leary. Between 1858 and 1873 they became parents of ten children. (More about the family of this Henry Ford is described in the chapter entitled "Henry's Uncle Henry.") Henry occasionally wrote to brother William in Michigan, but was not seen again in Michigan where the weather, Henry said, was far too cold. Because his son, Henry (1830-1901) had left Michigan for California, John Ford on September 1858 sold his Redford Township 80 acres, purchased in 1848, to his other two sons William (1826-1905) and Samuel (1838-1884). Each son paid $600 for 40 acres.

John Ford's daughter, Mary (1832-1882), was age fourteen when she arrived in Michigan in 1847. Mary appears to have been housekeeper for her father John Ford. In January 1855, a John Ford of Redford, Wayne County, is recorded as having obtained property described as $\frac{1}{4}$ of Section 25, T 9 N, R 1 E, Saginaw County, Michigan. This property was then apparently transferred to Mary Ford.[6] Mary, however, seems not to have left Redford because the 1860 Redford Township census lists John Ford as farmer age 60, with real estate valued at $2,000 and a personal estate valued at $500. Living with him were William Ford age 25, Mary Ford age 22, and Samuel Ford age 21.

In 1861, Mary Ford married her first cousin Henry Ford (1827-1914) who was a son of Samuel Ford (1792-1842) and now was a widower with six children living on a farm in Dearborn Township. (The story of this Henry Ford's previous marriage to Dorah Teagan is explained in the chapter entitled "Henry's Other Uncle Henry.") Mary was now 23 years of age and Henry 34 years of age. At the time Mary and Henry were married, it was agreed that John Ford (1799-1864) would move in with Mary and Mary's husband Henry Ford (1827-1914).

John Ford lived with his daughter Mary and son-in-law Henry (1827-1914) until John Ford's death on March 22, 1864 at age 65. Mary and Henry had four children between 1862 and 1874: namely James, Thomasine, Oliver, and Nancy. After Mary Ford died in 1882, Henry Ford, in 1884, as administrator of her estate, apparently allotted her Saginaw County, Michigan, property to families named Purdy and Reed.[6]

John Ford's youngest daughter, Nancy Ann Ford (1834-1920), was age 13 when she came to the United States from Clonakilty,

Nancy Ann Flaherty portrait (Photo 0-8269)

Ireland. Nancy married Thomas Flaherty (1829-1905) who had come from Wicklow, Ireland. They were married in Ontonagon, Michigan, when Nancy was about 20 years of age. Between the years 1855 and 1875, they had nine children: Robert, Thomasine, Richard, Ester, Mary, Thomas, Rebecca, Guy, and Annie. During most of this time they were living in Marquette, Michigan, but after 1905 when her husband Thomas died, she was often a visitor of the Fords living in the Dearborn area, including her nephew Henry Ford and his wife Clara.

An index of the John Ford branch of the Ford family tree[4] reveals that in the century following the death of John's wife, Thomasine, there were at least 54 descendants of John and Thomasine. There were 25 descendants named Ford, 17 named Flaherty, 3 named Gardner, 3 named Kingsford, 2 named Carter, 1 named Reed, 1 named Bayles, 1 named DeBons, and 1 named McDonald. Of these, there are four with the given name Thomasine.

As a result of marriages of Ford daughters, most of the descendants of the Fords of Dearborn and Greenfield now go by other names. Diluted approximately one-half by each generation, the Ford name is now carried by but a small fraction of these descendants. Likewise, people related to the automotive magnate, Henry Ford, are most likely to carry another surname than Ford. Applying very loose statistics, after, say, five generations, only about one in thirty descendants of William Ford and Rebecca Jennings would carry the Ford name. Some of the fairly close blood relatives of the early Dearborn Fords have had the following names:

Bagley	Gilson	Mott	Simms
Bayles	Hall	Moyles	Smith
Bench	Holmes	Newsome	Spence
Carver	Kennedy	Noble	Stephenson
Coon	Kingsford	Purdy	Sullivan
DeBons	Mason	Reed	Wetherbee
Flaherty	McAlpine	Richardson	Whitehouse
Gardner	McDonald	Ruddiman	Wolf

REFERENCES

1. "Notes, topographical, Historical and Genealogical on the Ford Family," compiled from various sources by Charles A. Webster, D.D., Acc23, Box 28, Benson Ford Research Center.

2. Nevins, Allan, *Ford: The Times, The Man, The Company,* Charles Scribner's Sons, New York, 1954.

3. Collins, Micheal J. *Clonakilty: A History, Cumann Seanchais Chloch na gCoillte,* 1999.

4. John Ford genealogy records, Acc. 23, Box 27, Benson Ford Research Center.

5. Frank Hill Papers, Acc. 940, E-H, Benson Ford Research Center.

6. Departmental communications between E.G. Liebold and Raymond H. Laird dated May and June of 1939, Acc. 23, Box 28, Benson Ford Research Center.

7. Parks Canada-Grosse Ile and the Irish Memorial National Historic Site of Canada. Internet 2003. Web Site: www.parkscanada.gc ca grosseile

---

Note: Genealogy table of JohnFord and Thomasine Smith appears on page 265.

✿✿✿ 5 ✿✿✿
REBECCA JENNINGS FORD

The Later Years in the Life of the Mother of All the Dearborn Fords

Rebecca Jennings Ford (1776–1851) and William Ford (1775–1818) were ancestors of all the Fords of Dearborn — that is, all the many Fords related to the famous automotive Henry Ford. In Ireland between 1792 and 1811, Rebecca bore five sons: Samuel, John, Henry, Robert, and George — no daughters to our knowledge. William Ford died in Ireland in 1818 and was buried in the Kilnagross churchyard a few miles inland from Clonakilty. Following William Ford's death, Rebecca and her second son, John, in 1819 took over the land lease covering twenty-three acres for which 29 pounds, 2 shillings, 10 pence were payable each year. This property, with its small dry-stone cottage, had been leased by the Ford family for several generations. Their landlord's family, who had been granted thousands of acres of land by Queen Elizabeth in the 1600s, lived in a castle at Kilbrittain nearly ten miles away.

This monument marks the burial sites of the George Ford family in Detroit's Grand Lawn Cemetery.
(Author's Photo)

Kilnagross church in Ireland is where William Ford (1775–1818) is buried, near the church wall by the center window. Shown on this misty May 1992 day is Hazel Ford Buttimer (facing camera) in conversation with Roxanne LaChance of Dearborn, a descendant of William Ford.

The first of Rebecca's sons came to America in 1832 from Crohane and Ballinascarthy in County Cork, Ireland. The group included her eldest son, Samuel, age forty-two, with his wife, Nancy, and their four children: two sons and two daughters ranging in age from five to thirteen years. Also with them was Samuel's twenty-one-year-old brother, George, who was unmarried. Samuel is said to have been given some money by Rebecca to help finance the trip to America. This was not a famine year in Ireland, but Nancy, Samuel's wife, had heard from her relatives, the Smiths in Detroit's Corktown, that a common person could own land in Michigan at small expense. That was not possible in Ireland.

Upon arriving at Detroit, both sons purchased forest land on what is now Joy Road — Samuel in Dearborn Township, George across the township line in adjacent Greenfield Township. (This township line later became Division Road and still later Greenfield Road.) Samuel bought eighty acres, and George purchased forty acres that year. George acquired another forty acres the following year. The Samuel Ford family quickly established itself in the remote woods of Dearborn, while George is said to have worked awhile in 1832 as a hod carrier in Detroit before building a log cabin on his wooded land. Before the cabin was finished, George married Alice Good, a recently arrived Irish girl of about his own age.

George and Alice had their first child, William, in 1833, but he died as an infant. A daughter, Mary, was born in 1834, another daughter, Rebecca, in 1837. James was born in 1840. The 1840 Greenfield Township census lists the three children plus George, age twenty-nine, and Alice, age thirty.

This background about the George Ford family is pertinent because seven years later, in 1847, the next contingent of Fords came to Michigan from Ireland. These Fords came because of the terrible famine conditions in Ireland. The lease, upon which the family had depended for generations and under which Rebecca and John had labored for twenty-eight years, was finally given up. The leader of this group coming to America was John Ford, brother of Samuel and George, and auto Henry's grandfather. John Ford's wife, Tomasine Smith, sister of Samuel Ford's wife, Nancy Smith, died before reaching Québec on the passage to this country. John's children were Rebecca, William, Jane, Henry, Mary, Nancy, and Samuel. This

On the Ford plot in Kilnagross churchyard is this black granite stone, which has now been placed to mark the graves of early Fords. On the left half of the book-like marker is the inscription pertaining to William Ford, great-grandfather of Henry Ford of Dearborn. The marker faces the pathway leading into the church.

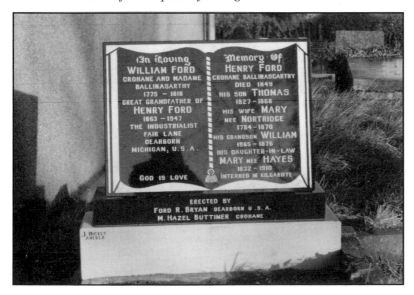

Among the many
individual
gravestones of the
George Ford family
is this one on the
grave of Rebecca
Jennings Ford.

William, age twenty-one, was auto Henry's father. Also coming with John and his family was Rebecca, the mother of Samuel, George, and John. She no longer had sons in Ireland at the age of seventy-one. Although her name was Rebecca, it seems that in America she was always known as Mrs. Jennings.

John Ford, with his large family, had no home upon his arrival in 1847 but promptly bought land and began to build one of logs, with his son William (Henry's father) providing considerable help. But where was Rebecca to stay? Her son Samuel had died in 1842, and Samuel's wife, Nancy, was managing that farm with her six children. So Rebecca elected to stay with her youngest son, George, and his wife, Alice, who were by this time well situated.

By the time Rebecca arrived, Michigan was a state, roads were beginning to be built, and the Indians were no longer a problem. She must have felt welcome because there were at least twenty-five of her grandchildren within a mile of the George Ford home, three of them named Rebecca, and also a one-year-old great-grand-daughter named Rebecca. But wherever she stayed, it would have been crowded. Just as in Ireland, Rebecca now lived with a large family in a very small cabin. But these were of logs on land owned by her own family, whereas the Irish stone cottage would always belong to someone else.

The families of both Samuel and George worshipped at Mariner's Church in Detroit, and Rebecca attended with the George Fords. There is very little recorded about Rebecca other

than her name on the 1850 Greenfield Township census and
Mariner's Church records because she only lived in America for
four years.

When Rebecca died in 1851, she was buried in the small
cemetery on Samuel Ford's property along with Samuel and, over
time, other Fords including George and Alice. But in the early
twentieth century, there was much concern regarding the perma-
nency and desirability of small private and parochial cemeteries
such as the little Ford Cemetery on Joy Road near Greenfield. On
July 3, 1919, Rebecca's grandson George (1845–1925) purchased
Lots 82 and 83, Section 4, of Grand Lawn Cemetery for
$1,102.80; and on October 16, 1919, ten reburials were recorded.
These included "Grandma" Rebecca Jennings, "Father" George
Ford, and "Mother" Alice Ford, all of whom had been removed
from the Ford Cemetery on Joy Road by Northrup Funeral Home
of Detroit.

A large upright marble stone bearing the name Ford now
dominates these lots in Grand Lawn Cemetery. Arranged in an arc
facing the stone are flat ground-level markers for twelve graves
including those marked "Grandma / 1776–1851," "Mother /
1810–1893," and "Father / 1811–1863." The names of Rebecca,
Alice, and George do not appear on the markers. The grandson's
own marker is "George/1845–1925," and his wife's marker is
"Alice/1846–1916."

Recently the burial location of William Ford, Rebecca's
husband, of whom we know essentially nothing but who is
nonetheless father of all the Dearborn Fords, was verified in
Kilnagross churchyard in Ireland. In January 1995, his grave was
marked with an appropriate stone. The inscription reads: "In
Loving Memory of William Ford, Crohane and Madame,
Ballinascarthy, 1775–1818, Great Grand-father of Henry Ford,
1863–1947, The Industrialist, Fair Lane, Dearborn, Michigan,
U.S.A."

REFERENCES

Rebecca Jennings Ford

Accession 1, Box 1, Fair Lane Papers, Henry Ford Genealogy. Benson Ford Research Center, HFM & GV.

Accession 23, Box 28, Henry Ford Office—General, Folder 4. Benson Ford Research Center, HFM & GV.

Burial records of Grand Lawn Cemetery, 23501 Grand River Avenue, Detroit, Michigan.

Conversations with Hazel Ford Buttimer. Crohane, Ballinascarthy, Clonakilty, County Cork, Ireland.

Nevins, Allan. *Ford: The Times, The Man, The Company.* New York: Scribner's, 1954, pp. 32, 34, 592.

❧❧ 6 ❧❧
THE ROBERT FORD FAMILY

A Brother of John Ford
Who Came on the Same Ship with John's
Family but Did Not Settle in Dearborn

The Ford family tree as drawn by Raymond H. Laird in 1925–26 has a main branch missing: the family of Robert Ford (1803-1877). There were four Ford brothers who came to America from Ireland in the mid-nineteenth century. They were Samuel, George, John, and Robert. John was auto Henry's grandfather. The families of Samuel, George, and John are well documented. The family of Robert, however, has incomplete documentation in the Ford Archives in Dearborn. There are but thirty unbound sheets pertaining to Robert Ford's family. None of Robert's family came to Dearborn, to our knowledge, although some were as close as Owosso, Michigan, between 1880 and 1910.

Although we know relatively little about the Robert Ford family, what information we have is quite interesting. Robert was born in Ireland in 1803, the son of William Ford and Rebecca Jennings. He is said to have worked as an "interior decorator" in Ireland. He married Jane Elisha Hornibrook in Cork, Ireland, on December 15, 1827. In Ireland, Robert and Jane had four children: Mary Ann, Henry, Robert, and Stephen. Mary Ann was born in 1831, and her brothers also were born in Ireland.

The entire Robert Ford family came to America with John Ford's family in 1847. The two families landed in Québec, Canada, but whereas John and his family moved on to Michigan and Dearborn, the Robert Fords settled near Québec. There, Robert and Jane's eldest daughter, Mary Ann, married an Irishman, Robert Bagley, in 1849 and, between 1850 and 1864, had seven

---

Previously published in the *Dearborn Historian*, Vol. 38, No. 1, 1998.

children in Standon, Canada, near Québec. These children later moved to upper Michigan and out west to Montana, Washington, and Oregon. Mary Ann died on November 29, 1909, and is buried at Owosso, Michigan.

But none of the three brothers of Mary Ann has been traced. So we are missing perhaps three-quarters of the Robert Ford branch of the family tree. And if it was difficult for Raymond Laird to locate these missing Fords in 1925, it is next to impossible now. So what follows here is a glimpse of some of the records of the Mary Ann Ford Bagley branch of the Robert Ford family. The prominent names are not Ford at all but include Bagley, Hall, Shepherd, and Moyles.

John Bagley, Mary Ann's eldest son, married Margaret Hazlett at Tacoma, Washington, in 1876. The couple had two children, Albert and Gertrude. John Bagley became vice president and general manager of the Tacoma Eastern Railroad, president of the Cascade & Mineral Lake Lumber Company, president of the Bagley Grader Company, and director of the National Bank of Tacoma. This same John Bagley at fifty-four years of age married Katherine Meecham in 1904. Another two children, Florence and Kathleen, were born of this second marriage. John Bagley died in 1920 and is buried in Tacoma.

Mary Ann's daughter, Jane Bagley, married George Hall in 1881 at Calumet, Michigan. Hall became a contractor, road and railroad builder, and councilman of the village of Laurium, Michigan. The Halls had seven children. In 1891, the family seems to have been struck by a devastating plague. Four of the seven children, between the ages of one and eight, died in less than a year. George Hall died in 1918, Jane in 1922.

George Hall, Jr., who survived the tragedy of 1891, grew up to marry Bertha Palmer of Exeter, Michigan, in November 1917 at Detroit. Young George took up his father's business of road building and contracting, with jobs in Bessemer and Negaunee, Michigan, before becoming an insurance agent in Calumet. There were three children in the family: William, Robert, and Alfred.

Gladys Hall, the second surviving child of the Calumet tragedy, graduated from the University of Michigan School of Music in 1907 and married John D. Kerr in 1911 at Laurium. Kerr was a successful lawyer. The Kerrs had no children, according to Dearborn records.

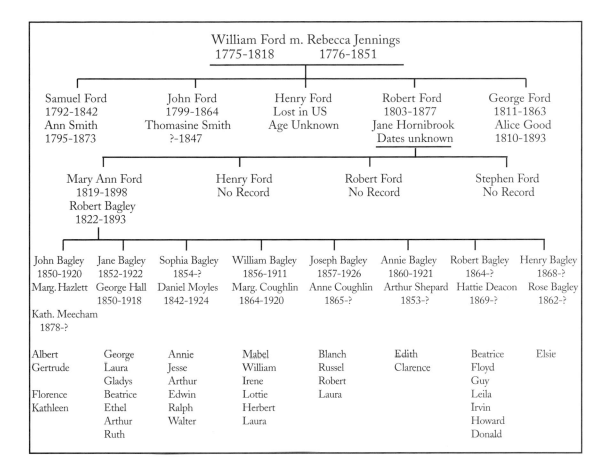

William Ford m. Rebecca Jennings
1775-1818   1776-1851

Samuel Ford	John Ford	Henry Ford	Robert Ford	George Ford
1792-1842	1799-1864	Lost in US	1803-1877	1811-1863
Ann Smith	Thomasine Smith	Age Unknown	Jane Hornibrook	Alice Good
1795-1873	?-1847		Dates unknown	1810-1893

Mary Ann Ford	Henry Ford	Robert Ford	Stephen Ford
1819-1898	No Record	No Record	No Record
Robert Bagley			
1822-1893			

John Bagley	Jane Bagley	Sophia Bagley	William Bagley	Joseph Bagley	Annie Bagley	Robert Bagley	Henry Bagley
1850-1920	1852-1922	1854-?	1856-1911	1857-1926	1860-1921	1864-?	1868-?
Marg. Hazlett	George Hall	Daniel Moyles	Marg. Coughlin	Anne Coughlin	Arthur Shepard	Hattie Deacon	Rose Bagley
	1850-1918	1842-1924	1864-1920	1865-?	1853-?	1869-?	1862-?
Kath. Meecham							
1878-?							
Albert	George	Annie	Mabel	Blanch	Edith	Beatrice	Elsie
Gertrude	Laura	Jesse	William	Russel	Clarence	Floyd	
	Gladys	Arthur	Irene	Robert		Guy	
Florence	Beatrice	Edwin	Lottie	Laura		Leila	
Kathleen	Ethel	Ralph	Herbert			Irvin	
	Arthur	Walter	Laura			Howard	
	Ruth					Donald	

The youngest of the Hall children of Calumet was Ruth, born in 1894. She graduated from the Oberlin Kindergarten Training School in 1915 and from the Laurium Commercial School in 1918. Ruth stayed at home until shortly after her widowed mother, Jane, died in June 1922. In September of that same year, Ruth married Peter Sandstrom, who is noted as having been a corporal of the 310th Ammunition Train, 151st Infantry. The couple was living in Mankato, Minnesota, when their daughter, Elizabeth Jane, was born in 1924.

Among prominent descendants of the Robert Bagley line are people by the name of Moyles. Sophia Bagley, born in 1854 in Québec, daughter of Mary Ann Ford and Robert Bagley, married Daniel H. Moyles, also of Québec, in 1877. This couple had six children born between 1883 and 1894 in Owosso, Michigan. These were Annie, Jessie, Arthur, Edwin, Ralph, and Walter. In

77

1925, when Laird requested information, Jesse, Arthur, and Walter lived in Tacoma, Washington; Edwin in Portland, Oregon; and Ralph in Cedar Falls, Washington. These children, in turn, listed seven of their own children in those locations.

The above notes are representative of the information contained on the thirty genealogical sheets collected from seventeen separate sources by Raymond Laird. There are a total of about 135 names listed. Most have dates of birth as of 1925 but not dates of death. Now, however, even the youngest listed would be nearly one hundred years of age and without a known address.

REFERENCES

Accession 1, Box 1, Fair Lane Papers, Henry Ford Genealogy. Benson Ford Research Center, HFM & GV.

Accession 23, Box 27, Henry Ford Office—General, Bagley Folder. Benson Ford Research Center, HFM & GV.

Accession 23, Box 28, Henry Ford Office—General, Bagley Correspondence. Benson Ford Research Center, HFM & GV.

7
THE WILLIAM S. FORD FAMILY

Oldest Son of Samuel, the Profusion of Fords in Dearborn Township, Family Interrelationships

This chapter deals primarily with the family of William S. Ford (1819-1898), and covers a long period of time during which several other Ford families were neighboring residents. In addition to many independent sources, the written memoirs* of Clyde M. Ford (1887–1948), a great-grandson of Samuel Ford and a grand-nephew of William S. Ford, are quoted extensively to provide highly descriptive accounts of several aspects of pioneer life in Dearborn Township.

It was one year and nine months after Samuel Ford and Ann (Nancy) Smith were married in the Parish of Desertserges, Ireland, that William Samuel Ford, their eldest child was born on November 24, 1819. He is known to have been born in Ireland, although there is some evidence that his father, before marriage, may have been in America.[1] William, no doubt, was born near Crohane, the family homestead.[2] As a child in Ireland he was bound to have witnessed a degree of poverty, and to have shared to an extent the economic and political worries of the Irish of that period.

William told his grandchildren[3,4] that he came to America when he was ten years old (1829), and stayed in Rochester, New York, for three years before coming to Dearborn with his parents in 1832. His parents did, indeed, buy land in Dearborn Township in 1832.[5] William also told one of his granddaughters that as a boy of fourteen (1833), he helped clear the trees and underbrush for the Michigan Central Railroad as far as Ypsilanti. William's being in Dearborn in 1839 is well documented. One of these early records is the marriage certificate of William S. Ford and Ann

---

*An original handwritten and signed manuscript of 206 pages, dated December 26, 1926. Dearborn Historical Museum Collection, Accession 81-86.7.

Ketchum "of Dearborn," dated December 4, 1839, giving the place of marriage as Detroit.[6]

Ann Ketchum (1820–1893) was the daughter of William Ketchum (1779–1824) and Mary Shurburn (1777–18—), both of Steuben County, New York State. John and Amzi Ketchum, who may have been brothers of Ann, had bought considerable property in Dearborn and Pekin townships in 1833.[7] The next spring after William and Ann were married, they bought seventy-nine acres from Amzi Ketchum.[8] This land consisted of the East Half of the N.W. Quarter of Section 1, Twp. 2, S. Range 10 E., and was located about one-half mile west of where William had been living with his parents, Samuel and Ann (Nancy) Ford. The summer, 1840, Dearborn Township census indicates that William was still living with his parents, Samuel and Nancy, and that his wife, Ann, was there too.

William was now twenty-one years of age, an experienced woodsman and farmer. He next built a log cabin in which he and his family would live for twenty-one years. These first cabins could have had dirt floors and bark roofs. Windows may have been covered with greased paper. Imported glass was a luxury. Their first child, Mary, was born December 31, 1840; to be followed by ten more children during the next twenty-four years (see family chart). All but one of these children (Josephine) would be born in this log cabin.

When William's father, Samuel, died in 1842, William's mother was left with eight children at home. William then became the mainstay of the Ford clan. The next oldest boy, Henry, was only fifteen years old. It was necessary for William to help his mother considerably until Henry could manage.[9]

When William's uncle, John Ford (1799–1864), came from Ireland in 1847 without his wife (Thomasine), but with his mother and seven children, it was William (28), Henry (20), and their Uncle George (1811–1863) who helped them get settled in Dearborn. The mother of these newly arrived children (Thomasine) had died at sea. The oldest boy was another William (1826-1904), age twenty-one, who became the father of industrialist Henry Ford.

Where this newest Ford family was fed and sheltered upon their arrival is not known for certain, but Nancy's family of seven and William's family of six, together, somehow accommodated these additional nine from Ireland. It is quite plain that the log

Ann (Ketchum) Ford and William S. Ford. Photograph ca. 1885. (188-20824)

cabins were crowded, and would become more crowded as the families grew.

By 1850, William and Ann are recorded in their own home with six children (see family chart). Children were a blessing to the pioneers. The boys, especially, were valued for their physical stamina in doing outdoor work. Girls were also put to work early with outdoor as well as indoor chores. We hear a great deal about the men clearing the land and building the cabins. However, the women's work of the cooking, cleaning, spinning, weaving, knitting, mending, washing, nursing, and teaching children to "read, reckon and pray," was equally vital. Ann knitted the woolen socks used as liners for the rough leather shoes made by William, and used by all. She operated a carding wheel, spinning wheel, and eventually several different size looms. Her comforters were woven of wool, filled with all wool batting, and tied with woolen, home-loomed yarn.

In clearing the land, large stumps were often left in the fields to rot. Limbs were burned, and trunks hauled to a sawmill if a road existed. Sheep were pastured among the stumps, and loose stones piled along edges of the cleared land formed low fences. The soil between the stumps could later be plowed to some extent using oxen, and corn planted in an irregular fashion. The first breaking of the soil was especially difficult because of the residual roots and

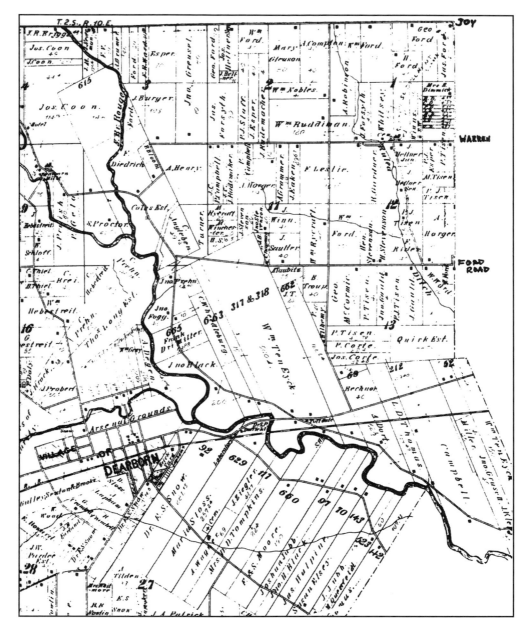

DEARBORN TOWNSHIP MAP
*1876 map of northeast Dearborn Township showing property of William Ford
(north) along early Ford Road. This road was later called Bonaparte, and now is Joy
Road. William Ford (south), father of industrialist Henry Ford, lived on South Road
which is now called Ford Road. (Courtesy Dearborn Historical Museum)*

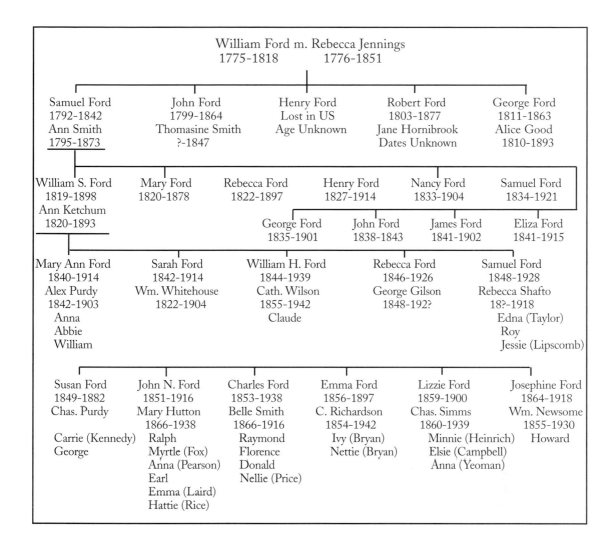

William Ford m. Rebecca Jennings
1775-1818   1776-1851

Samuel Ford	John Ford	Henry Ford	Robert Ford	George Ford
1792-1842	1799-1864	Lost in US	1803-1877	1811-1863
Ann Smith	Thomasine Smith	Age Unknown	Jane Hornibrook	Alice Good
1795-1873	?-1847		Dates Unknown	1810-1893

William S. Ford	Mary Ford	Rebecca Ford	Henry Ford	Nancy Ford	Samuel Ford
1819-1898	1820-1878	1822-1897	1827-1914	1833-1904	1834-1921
Ann Ketchum					
1820-1893					

		George Ford	John Ford	James Ford	Eliza Ford
		1835-1901	1838-1843	1841-1902	1841-1915

Mary Ann Ford	Sarah Ford	William H. Ford	Rebecca Ford	Samuel Ford
1840-1914	1842-1914	1844-1939	1846-1926	1848-1928
Alex Purdy	Wm. Whitehouse	Cath. Wilson	George Gilson	Rebecca Shafto
1842-1903	1822-1904	1855-1942	1848-192?	18?-1918
Anna		Claude		Edna (Taylor)
Abbie				Roy
William				Jessie (Lipscomb)

Susan Ford	John N. Ford	Charles Ford	Emma Ford	Lizzie Ford	Josephine Ford
1849-1882	1851-1916	1853-1938	1856-1897	1859-1900	1864-1918
Chas. Purdy	Mary Hutton	Belle Smith	C. Richardson	Chas. Simms	Wm. Newsome
	1866-1938	1866-1916	1854-1942	1860-1939	1855-1930
Carrie (Kennedy)	Ralph	Raymond	Ivy (Bryan)	Minnie (Heinrich)	Howard
George	Myrtle (Fox)	Florence	Nettie (Bryan)	Elsie (Campbell)	
	Anna (Pearson)	Donald		Anna (Yeoman)	
	Earl	Nellie (Price)			
	Emma (Laird)				
	Hattie (Rice)				

surfacing stones. However, the soil was rich and relatively stone-free in comparison to their Irish soil. Corn was an excellent subsistance crop. It would feed cattle, chickens, and when milled would be relished by the family as corn meal mush, Indian meal bread, and most enjoyably as johnny cake with maple syrup. Corn could be carried on one's back to a mill without benefit of a road. Later a horse would be used, with balanced bags tied to one another over the back of the horse.

In and around the cabin, activities were no less interesting. Wool was being cleaned and carded ready for the "big wheel." Flax fiber was being retted and scutched, ready to be spun on the "small

83

wheel." Johnny cake was being baked in the stone hearth oven. The outside butchering required help from almost everyone in sight, including the dogs. Ashes and animal fat would soon be mixed and heated in the large soap kettle. The hog grease would be used to grease paper for windows.

There had to be order and schedule to these activities. It was many years before the work would be simplified to: wash Mondays, iron Tuesdays, mend Wednesdays, churn Thursdays, clean Fridays, bake Saturdays, and to church Sundays. Sunday may have been a partial rest day for "Pa" and some of the children, but "Ma" still had her three meals to prepare. A neighborhood chopping bee on a Sunday afternoon might produce results equivalent to considerable work having been done. It is said that "Big Sam Ford" demonstrated that he could chop down the trees and split fourteen cords of wood in one day.[10] The men might clean their rifles, ready for the next turkey hunt where it was said "a good shot could bring down four turkeys if they held their heads together."

According to Clyde M. Ford:

> Some of the stories which I remember hearing are that in the very earliest part of the settlement, the one means of shopping, as far as the women were concerned, was to take their baskets of butter and eggs, or maple sugar, on their arms and set out on foot to the central part of Detroit to a store which stood on the corner of what is now Fort and Woodward Avenue, a distance of about ten miles over the trail which followed a small creek east of the Division Road to a point south where the trail took off on higher ground to the city of Detroit. On one occasion, one of the women, the wife of George (Alice) was frightened off the trail by what was probably a bear, and getting lost, so that she had to stay in the woods all night, until the next day when the men who had organized a searching party found her.
>
> This (walking) remained the only source of communication with Detroit until some of the younger boys had become large enough to drive an ox-cart. Uncle Henry (brother of William S.) was the first one to be able to do this. Uncle William was some eight years older than he, but his time had to be spent with the duties of the farm which involved the clearing of land and many other things calling for the hardest kind of work. The coming into use of the ox-cart was considered quite a convenience as it afforded an opportunity for all the women to go down-town shopping the same day which was done on a set day every week, and at least part of them took their turn at taking their produce to the far-off store in Detroit, where they traded it for groceries needed in their homes.
>
> During the period 1830–1847, perhaps because of transportation and storage problems, grain prices fluctuated wildly.

Some typical commodity prices were as follows:

Wheat flour/bbl	$4.50	(1830)
Wheatflour/bbl	12.00	(1837)
Wheat flour/bbl	8.00	(1838)
Wheat flour/bbl	2.25	(1840)
Corn/bu	4.00	(1839)
Corn/bu	.85	(1840)
Hay/ton	6.00	(1847)
Potatoes/bu	2.00	(1837)
Cider/bbl	2.00	(1830)
Sugar/lb	.14	(1838)
Salt/bbl	1.38	(1844)
Butter/lb	.15	(1844)
Cheese/lb	.06	(1844)

The ownership of land brought the inevitable tax bills. For the year 1844, the total State, County, and Township taxes on their seventy-nine acres and home amounted to only $1.95,[12] but by 1859 taxes had risen to $16.00, in 1863 to $23.90, and by 1889 taxes totaled $49.03. During the same period, fire insurance more than tripled from $2 to $7.

The year 1860 finds them with ten children still in a log cabin. The next year they would move into the "Big House." This house would be a large frame building on their original property, but now facing Bonaparte (Joy) Road. March, 1862, however, finds William working in the lumber camps in Kentucky and Tennessee to earn money.[13] A letter from Camp No. 3, south of Nashville, indicates he has earned $10 which he is afraid to send home through the mails. He describes the well advanced spring gardens and the high prices of chickens, turkeys, and corn bread — 50¢, $1, and 10¢ respectively. William's letter demonstrates excellent penmanship but poor spelling.

The Fords were very industrious as farmers. Some also became adept as carpenters, some as stockmen, and one a butcher. William S. Ford was considered a good leather-boot maker, as well as carpenter, as well as farmer. And with so many relatives nearby, they could not have been lonesome. As the children of the various Ford families grew up in close proximity, the problem of distinguishing one from another emerged.[14] There became "Big Sam," "Sam," "Uncle Sam" "Black Sam," "William's Sam," "Henry's Sam," "Red Head George," "George-on-the-hill," "George Over" (over the township line), "Foxy George," "Henry's George," "Uncle Henry,"

William S. Ford homestead on Joy Road, east of Southfield, built in 1861. Called the "Big House," it replaced a log cabin where William and Ann had lived with their eleven children. The photograph, taken about 1915 shows son John N(ewton) Ford (1851-1916) standing in front, and grandson Earl M(cKinley) Ford (1898-1987) sitting on the stair. (188-21515)

"Hank Ford," "William's Henry," "William's John," "William North" (William S. Ford), "William South" ("Auto Henry's" father), "Uncle Jim," "Henry's Jim," etc. — all contemporaries. On the family tree there are 9 William's, 9 Henry's, 7 Mary's, 6 John's, 5 George's, 4 Rebecca's and 4 Jame's. A good number of these eventually owned farms in Dearborn and adjacent townships. (See Dearborn Township Map on page 82)

Continuing with the memoirs of Clyde Ford:

> I remember hearing stories of the military post at Dearborn, of the drills put on by the soldiers, also the stories which came from the old tavern which stood east of the Rouge River at about opposite the entrance to Henry Ford's home. Outside of the trips to mill and town

meetings, there was not very much to do for them in the village of Dearborn, with the exception of a few social functions in the form of some dancing parties that used to be given from time to time in one of the old Arsenal buildings. Dearborn was a place which was some eight miles away, and at that time and afterwards meant, according to the mode of travel, a long ways to go. I have heard of my grandfather (George Ford 1835–1911) and one of his cousins who used to ride over on horseback to see some Indians who were part of the regular army. On Saturday afternoons and evenings they would put on feats of running and jumping much to the pleasure of the people gathered about. This used to take place back of what is now the Village Hall which was one of the old Arsenal buildings. These Indians afterwards were sent to the Civil War and it was understood that most of them were lost in one of the first battles.

As the trails began to give way to well laid out roads which were laid out to diverge from the center of Detroit, reaching out into the state, the line of travel for the Ford settlement became (eastward) over the Plymouth Road to The Howell Plank Road (Grand River), then to the center of the city, where they hauled their farm produce and also cord wood, the latter being at a time a good part of their income. I have heard it said that it would find a ready market at eight dollars a cord as it was the only means of fuel available. They also produced charcoal and the places where they used to have their charcoal pits can still be seen (1926). Charcoal would be produced by piling up logs in a heap, setting them on fire and then when they were well enough fired, throw dirt on them and keep them just so that they would char. They had to be watched so that the flames would not break out and burn up the logs, which was prevented by throwing more dirt on where the flames showed. So charcoal was part of their produce until as I have heard them say, "until the stove coal came."

Saturday frequently required a trip to the "Haymarket" which was on the present site of Tiger Stadium. Farmers took advance orders for hay, straw, grain and wood for which there was a ready market. In season there were also potatoes and apples to sell. In winter a sturdy bobsled would carry one cord of wood and several children perched on top.[15]

The main farmer's market in Detroit was on Woodward in front of the City Hall, and the wagons were frequently stuck in the mud. Grand River Road came to be a plank road as also did the Plymouth Road. At first planks extended only to Third Street. Planks were laid down on timbers which ran lengthwise of the road and were in their day a real road and served the purpose. They were built by private interests who were reimbursed by the toll collected at toll gates which were along the road at the rate of a few cents per mile. One toll gate stood on Grand River just west of the intersection of Grand Boulevard. As time went on, the condition of the roads became very bad, but they continued to toll without any effort being made to put the roads in condition. If there was ever a road hard to travel on, it was a plank road out of repair.

The Plymouth Road got into that condition and continued to get worse with the toll going on just the same, until there were no planks

*Above: Four sons of William S. Ford — from left to right, Samuel, William, John, and
Charles. John remained on the homestead. (0-6194)*

*Opposite page: Daughters of William S. and Ann Ford. From left, Josie, Sarah, Becky
(sitting), Emma [author's grandmother], and Lizzie (standing). Mary and Susan
were married and away from home. Photo ca. 1875. (188-20821)*

in sight, only mud; and the end of the collecting toll came one night when a rope was put around the old house which served as the keeper's quarters for the toll gate, and there were plenty of strong arms and backs on hand to pull the thing over. Later, a company was formed of the Fords and others who purchased a piece of land from which gravel could be had, and they built a new gravel road and maintained it by each drawing a certain number of loads of gravel per year. This continued until the County took over the road in 1910." Township records show William S. Ford being elected "Overseer of Highways for District No. 1" for the years 1847–49. These records also show this same William "liable for military service in 1849." There is no record of his ever having been conscripted.[16]

Stagecoaches operated by the toll road companies brought mail west from Detroit. One line running a mile or so north of the Dearborn-Redford Township border connected a series of post offices named "Yew," "Oak," "Beech," and "Elm." The Yew post office, about a mile northeast of William's farm was closest to the Ford settlement, and is listed as the address of William S. Ford in 1876.[17] The Dearborn post office was about five miles from William and Ann's farm. It is said that farmers took turns going to the post office and distributing mail to their neighbors once a week.[18] Later, railroad stations were strung across the land, and these became post office locations and cheese factory locations. Eventually the Flint & Pere Marquette Railroad (now C & O) crossed the William S. Ford property. According to Clyde,[19] "where the railroad crossed Division Road (Greenfield) used to be a station where the trains would stop, and used to afford the means of transportation to Detroit. The train brought the daily paper which was thrown off at Ford's Crossing. Previously there was a paper once a week — the *Wayne County Currier.* Ford's crossing in the evening was a meeting place for someone from every family. This continued until R.F.D. in 1901.

Before the first school was built, some instruction was provided by private teachers who conducted school in their own homes. A log school, then a frame building (1838), preceded the brick school (1861) now restored in Greenfield Village.[20] All were on Scotch Settlement Road (Warren) between Mill (Southfield) and Division (Greenfield) roads. The location of this Scotch Settlement School established the hub of the settlement. Scotch Settlement Road became central, with the road one mile north often referred to as "North Road" and the road one mile south as "South Road." William S. Ford (Samuel's son) was then "William North" and William Ford (father of the industrialist) was "William South."

William S. Ford was deeply religious; to the extent that some referred to him as "Holy Billy." He was a staunch Methodist, and often conducted family services at home. The early "Circuit Riders" made regular stops at his insistence; and later on, the minister had a reserved downstairs bedroom in the William S. Ford home. The only complaint heard from William was that the minister's horse ate an awful lot of hay.[21] William is said to have had a hand in the building of three church buildings during his lifetime. The first was a log structure, the second a frame building, and the third of brick. None of these buildings remain; the last having been torn down to make way for the Southfeld Freeway. The present William S. Ford Memorial United Methodist Church, established in 1898, is located on the north side of Warren, between Southfield and Greenfield, adjacent to the 1844 Evergreen or Scotch Settlement Cemetery. (Next to the Ford Cemetery, on Samuel Ford's 1832 farm, now stands St. Martha's Episcopal Church, funds for which were donated by Clara Bryant Ford.)

*William S. Ford Memorial Methodist Church located at Southfield and Joy roads in
Dearborn Township. This church was dedicated in December, 1898, four months after
the death of William S. Ford. The picture was taken about 1910. Back row, left to
right: Alfred Allison, Edward Hendry, Clyde M. Ford, Anna M. Ford; Center row:
Olive Hendry, Mrs. William Franklin, Mrs. Addie Rowley, Alma Noble, Myrtle M.
Ford; Front row: William Leslie, Mrs. Leslie, Christina Hendry, Mabel Simms, Stella
Gilbert, Anna Simms, three little Gilbert children, Evelyn Simms, Ruby Hendry,
Rev. Russell Hopkins. (Photo and identifications courtesy of Myrtle [Ford] Fox PO 6101)*

The Methodists were active in the Detroit area before any
other Protestant denomination. As early as 1818 they built a log
church on the banks of the Rouge River in what is now Dearborn.
It continued in use until about 1823. It was the first Protestant
church in Michigan except for one near Mount Clemens erected by
the Moravians in 1782.

William S. Ford is recorded as trustee of the First Methodist
Episcopal Church of Greenfield when it acquired property for a
church on the Plymouth Plank Road in 1860. This church was
about five miles from his home.[22] During the 1890s, William
solicited both farmers and businesses for funds to start a church

in his immediate neighborhood; some say in order to make it easier for his grandchildren to get to Sunday School.[23] It was supposed to have been an Episcopal church, but the Methodist's were the only denomination that would be the sponsoring organization.[24] In October, 1898,[25] the New Methodist Society dedicated the church building in memory of William S. Ford. (see photograph page 91)

William and his younger brother Henry (1827-1914) must have differed considerably in disposition. They each had built themselves exceptionally long wagons to haul logs. William's wagon, we know, was also equipped with bob sleds for winter use.[26] Buffalo hides kept them warm on long rides. There are stories that William used his wagon to transport pallbearers to and from funerals.[27] Henry, on the other hand, used his wagon to transport the baseball team, of which he was captain.[28] Henry's wagon, with a hay rack, is said to have hauled as many as fifty people, using two teams of horses to pull the load. One such long wagon also served as a band wagon. Henry played the fife, and his sister Mary's husband, Crawford Kennedy, is said to have been an excellent snare drummer, especially when well fortified.[29] This was the first band in Dearborn (1862);[30] it attended all patriotic occasions during the Civil War period, and took part in the second Lincoln campaign. Some 200 home guards, captained by Uncle George Ford had the benefit of the band at drill on Saturday afternoons.

Another wagon story involves Henry Ford, the industrialist, years later. It is said[31] that when William Ford (Henry's father) died — this would have been in early March of 1905 — that Henry was driving a team and wagon along Warren in front of the Scotch Settlement School when pupils, at recess, pelted him with snowballs. It was soon revealed that Henry was carrying the body of his father, in a casket, to the nearby church. The incident was recalled by children then in school, but probably not by those who threw the snowballs.

The 1870 census finds all of the William S. Ford family at home with the exception of two of the girls, Mary and Susan, who were married. (See photograph of children.) It should be noted that each of Samuel's sons stayed and farmed in the Dearborn area, and that several of his daughters married local land owners. However, the next generation did not fare so well. Of William's sons, only one (John N. Ford) stayed in Dearborn. He was able to buy his father's farm (see photograph of William S. Ford home-stead). None of the daughters of Williams S. Ford married men who remained in Dearborn. Land had become costly, and a mini-migration was necessary in order to get cheaper land or an occu-pation other than farming.

In the spring of 1888, William and Ann retired from farming and moved into Detroit, son John taking over the farm. Then, according to an 1889 newspaper clipping[32] an event of some prominence occurred in December of that year:

THE FIFTIETH ANNIVERSARY OF THE WEDDING OF MR. & MRS. FORD OF DEARBORN

Far over the waters of the Atlantic, on the bright isle of Erin, in the year 1819, there was born to a worthy couple a boy, the first born, but one of many children.

When he was about ten years of age, his father emigrated to our shores, and after stopping awhile in Rochester, New York, he came to Detroit in 1830, and a year later located a home in the woods, on what has since become the town-line, at the intersection of Redford, Greenfield and Dearborn, the farm being in the last named township.

In Steuben County, New York, in the year 1819, a lassie first saw the light, and her father with his large family, also came westward and located a farm a mile or so west of the first named, but a little later.

The young people here named were Wm. S. Ford and Ann Ketchum. Friendly neighborship in time grew into deeper affection and December 4, 1839, they were married. Mr. James Sheahan was at that time the proud possessor of the only team of horses in the neighbor-hood, and he had the honor of conveying the bridal party to the city, where the marriage was solemnized by Bishop McCosky in a house still standing on the corner of Lafayette and Wayne streets. They settled on a farm west of Mr. Ford's father, but in the same township. His parents kept the old home until their death and their youngest son James Ford (1841–1902) still resides there. The young pair took hold of life's work with strong hands and willing hearts and a beautiful home is the result of their war on the wilderness. Eleven children were born to them and all but one are still living. One daughter (Susan 1849–1882) died some years ago, leaving two children. There are, I think, nine grandchildren. All but three of the children are married. Last spring the aged pair resigned the farm into the hands of a son John (1851–1916) and removed to the city to take life easier. They were recalled to the old home on December 4, to celebrate their golden wedding. Brothers, sis-ters, children, cousins and friends to the number of one-hundred or more, offered congratulations, recalled olden times, and with music, conversation and merry jest sped the evening away. All their children but one were present. A bountiful repast was served to which all did full justice. Aunt Alice Ford of Greenfield and Mr. William Ruddiman, with old time gallantry, saluted the bride as he had done fifty years ago. The bride and groom wore bouquets of golden chrysanthemum and were as apparently youthful at heart and as devoted to each other as in their early days.

During the evening the bridal pair were called to the front, where Mr. Amos Otis, in a very neat and appropriate address, presented Mr. Ford with a fine gold watch and chain and Mrs. Ford a gold thimble, the gift of brothers and sisters. There was a beautiful dress, an elegant book and other gifts from the children, and a fine painting in a rich frame of gilt, the work and gift of Miss Anna Ford, a niece.

The guests dispersed at a late hour, mingling heartfelt good wishes for the future of the golden wedded pair with their adieus. The family relationships of the "Fords" comprise a large and highly respected element of the community.

At the end of the above article was a poem composed and read for the occasion by Mrs. T. Langley. This is thought to be the same Mrs. Langley who wrote rural society news, together with poetry, under the heading, "Thistledown" for the weekly *Wayne County Currier.*

Just four years later (1893), Ann, age seventy-three who had raised eleven children with that "stern countenance but kind heart,"[33] was laid to rest in Ford Cemetery. After Ann's death, William lived most of the time with John at the old homestead. Some five years later, after suffering a year with cancer, he died at the home of his son, John, on August 5, 1898. This was just a few months before the church which bears his name was dedicated.

NOTES AND REFERENCES

1. *War of 1812 — Commemorative Issue,* Michigan Heritage, Kalamazoo Valley Genealogical Society, Kalamazoo, Michigan, IV, No.1, 1962.

2. "Notes, Topographical Historical and Genealogical on the Ford Family," compiled from various sources by Charles A. Webster, D.D., Acc. 23, Box 28, Ford Archives, Henry Ford Museum.

3. Conversations with Myrtle (Ford) Fox, daughter of John N. Ford, granddaughter of William S. and Ann (Ketchum) Ford.

4. Papers of Anna (Ford) Pearson, now in the possession of Harriet (Pearson) Steinke.

5. *Wayne County Michigan Land Records,* Early Land Transfers, Detroit and Wayne County Michigan. W.P.A. Vital Records Project, Michigan State Library & D.A.R. Louisa St. Clair Chapter 1940.

6. Marriage Certificate between William S. Ford and Ann Ketchum dated 4th day of December, 1839. Acc. 23, Box 28, Ford Archives, Henry Ford Museum.

7. *Wayne County Michigan Land Records.*

8. *Ibid.*

9. Conversations with Myrtle (Ford) Fox, Reference 3.

10. Clyde M. Ford, "Article About Mr. Henry Ford," Dearborn Historical Museum Collection, Accession 81-87.6, December 26, 1926, p. 206. (Clyde Ford grew up on the Addison Ford farm on Joy Road near Greenfield. He was mayor of the City of Dearborn when it was consolidated with Fordson in 1929.)

11. *Ibid.*

12. Harriet (Pearson) Steinke Papers Acc. 1571, Ford Archives, Henry Ford Museum.

13. Original letter in Acc. 1, Fair Lane Papers, Box 33, Ford Archives, Henry Ford Museum.

14. Clyde M. Ford, Reference 10.

15. Margaret (Ford) Ruddiman, "Memories of My Brother Henry Ford," *Michigan History,* Michigan Historical Commission, Sept. 1953.

16. Michigan Historical Records Survey Project, "Minutes of the Meetings of the Townships of Bucklin, Pekin and Dearborn, May 28,1827 — April 13, 1857."

17. *Illustrated Historical Atlas,* Wayne County, Michigan, 1876. (Copy on hand at Dearborn Historical Museum).

18. Stevenson, Frank, "Scotch Settlement," *The Dearborn Historian,* Vol. 5, No. 1, 1965.

19. Clyde M. Ford, Reference 10.

20. *Ibid.*

21. Conversations with Myrtle (Ford) Fox, Reference 3.

22. Harriet (Pearson) Steinke Papers. William Ford is named as a Trustee of the Church in the acquisition of land by means of a quit-claim deed from one Ebenezer J. Penniman, March 8, 1860. Acc. 1571, Ford Archives, Henry Ford Museum.

23. Conversations with Myrtle (Ford) Fox, Reference 3.

24. Laird, Raymond, "I Worked for Mr. Ford," *The Dearborn Historian,* Volume 10, No. 1, 1970.

25. Gardiner, Elaine, "The Church is the People" 1814–1980, a history (unpublished) of the William S. Ford Memorial United Methodist Church.

26. Conversations with Myrtle (Ford) Fox, Reference 3.

27. *Ibid.*

28. Clyde M. Ford, Reference 10.

29. Conversations with Myrtle (Ford) Fox, Reference 3.

30. Pageant Program, "Carriages of Two Centuries," July 4, 1924, Acc. 1571, Box 1, Ford Archives, Henry Ford Museum.

31. Conversations with Harriet (Pearson) Steinke, daughter of Anna (Ford) Pearson, great granddaughter of William S. Ford.

32. Newspaper clipping in the possession of Carol (Ford) Templeton, daughter of Ralph Ford, great granddaughter of William S. Ford.

33. Conversations with Myrtle (Ford) Fox, Reference 3.

❧❧ 8 ❧❧
YANKEE SCHOOLMASTER

Charles Richardson, Teacher of Henry Ford,
Husband of Emma Ford, Grandparents of Writer

About 1870, a young man named Charles Richardson came from Connecticut to the Scotch Settlement of Dearborn looking for work and a career. The first farm at which he inquired was that of William S. Ford, and when William's daughter, Emma, saw him coming up the road she exclaimed jokingly to her sister, "Here comes my future husband!" This statement became fact.

Along with working on the farm of James Ford, Emma's uncle, Charles Richardson obtained the position of teacher of the Scotch Settlement School during a period when the future industrialist Henry Ford attended.

Records of the Richardsons date back eleven generations in Connecticut to 1653. Emma Ford's grandfather, Samuel Ford (1792-1842), came to Dearborn Township from Ireland in 1832.

CHARLES RICHARDSON

The north shore of Long Island Sound was wilderness in the mid sixteen hundreds when Amos Richardson and his brother were searching for a place to settle in the New World. Amos was born in England about 1623. It is quite possible that these two brothers, Amos probably the older, came by way of Massachusetts Bay Colony and then by boat along the ocean shore until they had found a spot where land was available, neighbors were religiously congenial, and the Indians not too unfriendly. The fact that their objective was to become land owners is recorded in Caulkins, *History of New London*, pages 98–99, as follows:

> Between Captain Mason's farm and Chesebrough's were several necks of land, extending into the Sound and separated by creeks. The neck east of Mason was allotted to Cary Latham, who in a short time sold it to Thomas Minor.

*Yankee schoolmaster,
Charles Richardson about
1880 when he was
boarding with James and
Dilly Ford, teaching the
Scotch Settlement School
and bidding for Emma
Ford's lunches at box
socials. (0-127)*

Beyond this were two necks or points, one of them called "pyne neck," with a broad cove between them; these were granted Isaac Willey, and sold by him to Amos Richardson.

Another still larger neck called Wampassock, and containing 550 acres of land, with a creek adjoining, was given to Hugh Caulkins. This was subsequently sold to Winthrop.

Next to Caulkins, and separated from it by a brook called Mixtuxet, was a tract of several hundred acres, allotted to Amos Richardson and his brother. A part of this division was known by the Indian name of "Quonaduck."

Later, a more specific location and date are provided from the same history (page 123):

"Nistuckset," a brook in Stonington forming a boundary of land at Quonaduck, granted to Amos Richardson, in 1653.[1]

The Richardsons were among the early settlers of Stonington, Connecticut, for when the town was incorporated as a town and a strip of 200 acres set aside for ministers' land and a small building erected for a church, a history states they did not use the building in cold weather but held their meetings at the home of Amos Richardson, who lived a short distance to the east of the church.

In the records of this First Congregational Church of Stonington may be found during the first hundred years of its existence, many Richardson names, among them Amos, Stephen, Salmon Treat, all forebears of Charles Richardson.[2]

The established ecclesiastical system was the Congregational. The Connecticut "Code" of 1650 taxed all persons for its support. The "Code" also required all parents to educate their children. In 1659 a property qualification of an estate of thirty pounds was required for suffrage. Assuming Amos qualified, he would have been considered a "freeholder," would have been addressed as "Mister" Richardson, could have worn silver buckles on his shoes, and most importantly could have voted.[3]

In 1662, a Royal Charter from Charles II created a corporation under the name of "English Colony of the Connecticut in New England of America." This charter defined the boundaries of Connecticut as being "from Massachusetts south to the Seas — and from Narragansett Bay west to the South Seas (Pacific Ocean).[3] This early charter of the Connecticut domain, together with the Western Reserve concept, has greatly affected succeeding generations of Connecticut people in their feeling toward Ohio and Michigan. To some in Connecticut, Michigan is still one of their back woodlots.

1850–1870

Evidence that Mr. and Mrs. Amos Richardson put down firm and vigorous roots is confirmed nine generations later when their offspring are estimated to be in the hundreds. The large majority resided in the Norwich, Stonington, New London areas of Connecticut.

Of this ninth generation was one Charles W. Richardson, son of William and Lucy Ann (Dawley) Richardson. There were nine children in all, three boys and six girls.[2] Charles was born on January 17, 1854, and raised with the other brothers and sisters on a farm near Patchaug. An inspection of this locality reveals a hilly, stony, sparsely settled area which could not have provided more than subsistence living from an agricultural standpoint. The stone farmhouse foundation is now barely discernible amid brush and weeds which abound over all of the farm land and a small adjacent cemetery where Charles Richardson's parents are buried. The author's impression is that the family practiced "diversified" farming, keeping cows, pigs, geese, ducks, chickens, likely a yoke of oxen, and thus worked primarily to raise feed for the same. Other than butter and eggs perhaps traded at a country store, the chief cash income was probably from hay, some of which made its way to New York City markets almost one-hundred miles away. Occasional twenty mile trips to the seashore at Stonington for clams were memorable outings for the whole family. Probably more memorable to the boys, however, was the endless rock picking. The remains of stone piles and stone fences still found in this vicinity attest to the labor of that occupation.

Any boy raised on a farm of this type, and experienced in trying to drive oxen and plow up and down these stony fields, would be generously lacking if he was not planning an alternate occupation. Law, politics, and teaching were all held in high favor by comparison. Some of the relatives were particularly proud of having been elected to the State Legislature. Thus farm life at Patchaug during the 1860–70 decade induced all three Richardson brothers to abandon the farm as a means of livelihood.

Charles Richardson attended academy a sufficient time to be qualified to teach common school. This was probably equivalent to having completed our present tenth grade, at which level one was eligible to pass a test for a teaching certificate. These tests were difficult by present standards, and dwelt heavily on government, history, grammar and arithmetic. At this point, Charles was in his late teens, qualified to teach, but apparently had no teaching position. To add to the disillusionment, his sweetheart, Josephine, is said to have ignored his attempts to gain her favor. So, like many others of his generation, he decided to head out West.

He had very little reason to set out for Michigan, in particular. He had no friends or relatives here to our knowledge. However, Southeastern Michigan was a popular destination for migrant Easterners during the middle of the 19th century because of the easy water transportation. He may have been just following the crowd. Not many details of his trip were divulged to his grand-children. He did mention, however, his having slept in a haystack at least one night on his way overland. In any event, it was not a luxury trip. He apparently did not avail himself of the advantages of the Erie Canal boats. Having a reputation of being both frugal and a fast walker, perhaps he thought he would make better time as well as spend less money by hiking across New York State to Buffalo. From Buffalo he said he took a steamer to Detroit.

In 1870, Detroit had a population approaching 100,000, and the city extended outward about three miles.[4] Still headed west, he began walking out Grand River Avenue toward the farms most likely to offer summer employment. He was large of build and accustomed to hard work and low pay.

Charles Richardson was walking west on what is now Joy Road, had just crossed the newly laid Pere Marquette Railroad tracks west of Greenfield Road, and was approaching the large farmhouse of William S. Ford, located on the south side of the road. One of William Ford's daughters, Emma, at that instant is said to have been looking out of the kitchen window and to have jokingly remarked to her sister, Rebecca, "Here comes my future husband." Charles did indeed stop at the William Ford house and inquire as to whether anyone in the neighborhood could use a hired hand. He was referred, by someone less frivolously inclined than Emma, to the farm of James Ford who had forty acres at the southwest corner of Greenfield and Joy roads. It is at the home of James Ford (Emma's uncle) that 1880 Dearborn Township census records list Charles Richardson as "farm hand," having probably arrived sometime after the August 11, 1870, census of that family.

EMMA FORD

Now that we have Charles Richardson safely ensconced with his legs under the dining table of Mrs. James Ford (Charles always had a good appetite), let us now investigate the lineage of Emma Ford.

Emma's grandfather, Samuel Ford (1792-1842), immigrated from Ireland to Michigan Territory in 1832 with his family and his brothers, Henry and George. It is thought that their forebears may have been English who were offered freeholds in Ireland in the late 16th century under Queen Elizabeth. During the 1830s a combi-

nation of economics and religious troubles induced many Irish to
come to America. Southeastern Michigan had cheap, rich land,
complete religious freedom, and prospects of a prosperous, civi-
lized life.[5]

Samuel bought the East ½ of the N.E. ¼, Section 1,
Township 2 South, Range 10 East, which is the extreme northeastern corner of Dearborn Township. This would now be the
southwest corner of Greenfield and Joy roads.[6]

In 1830, the census enumerated 31,640 persons in the Michigan
Territory. The number almost tripled in the next four years.
Territorial census counted 87,278 in 1834; 85,856 living in the
Lower Peninsula. The Erie Canal had opened and farmers came to
Michigan for cheaper land than available in eastern United States.

Southeastern Michigan was settling quickly and had applied for admission to the Union as a State in 1833.[4]

The Sixth Census of the Population, taken in 1840, indicates 12 people in the Samuel Ford household. Samuel and his wife Nancy, were in their forties, two sons and a daughter were in their twenties. One of these sons was William S. Ford, the father of Emma. Seven children under twenty were also tabulated but not named. At least three of these children were also old enough to have come from Ireland with their parents in 1832. The 1840 census indicated only the number of souls by various age groupings; whether "Male," "Female," or "Slave." There were no slaves recorded (despite the likely objections of the youngsters).[7]

By 1850, William S. Ford (age 31) had married Ann Ketchum who had been born in New York State. They had a farm valued at $1,200.[8]

The 1870 Dearborn Township Census gives a good accounting of the family of William and Ann (Ketchum) Ford, Emma's parents. At fifty-one, William and his wife had nine children ranging in age from twenty-seven to six years. There were four boys and five girls, none of whom had yet left home. Emma had two sisters older and two younger. Emma was fourteen and on August 14, 1870, the day of the census, was listed as "in school."[9]

In 1870, William S. Ford owned one-hundred acres at the southeast corner of Joy and Mill (Southfield) roads. This real estate was then appraised at $9,000, and the personal property at $1,500.[9] The house, a large, white frame structure, stood nearly a half mile east of the intersection. The homesite (the house was recently removed) is now a vacant parcel at the southwest corner of Joy Road and Grandmont Street in the City of Detroit.

This William Ford contributed materially to the founding of a church now named the William S. Ford Memorial Methodist Church which is located on the north side of Warren between Greenfield and Southfield. He is said to have donated land, and to have solicited the neighborhood for funds for the church.

SCOTCH SETTLEMENT SCHOOL

Charles Richardson did not forget that he was qualified to teach school. The tedious farm work as a hired hand was probably a constant reminder. Regardless of whether a single man did farm

William S. Ford homestead on the south side of Joy Road between Southfield and Greenfield roads where Emma Ford grew up. (0-5279)

work or taught country school, his pay was likely to be partly as room and board; if a teacher, he typically stayed with a member of the school board. The cash balance could be larger as a farm worker than as a teacher, especially in communities where farms were prosperous as they were in the Dearborn area. The higher farm pay was likely to be seasonal, however. The farmer considered it unprofitable to keep a hired man during the winter months. This situation made it advantageous for Charles to work on a farm during planting and harvesting seasons, and teach, if possible, winters. Another reason for the popularity of this arrangement was the fact that the older farm boys often skipped fall and spring school terms to help on their parents' farms. These big boys attended school only during the winter term and often made life miserable for their teachers during that period. Some women teachers gave up teaching the winter term. Some school boards made advance arrangements for a man to teach the winter term.

The James Ford farm was in the Scotch Settlement School District. Prior to one of these winter terms, Charles Richardson had been issued a teaching certificate by the Dearborn Township School Board, and was offered the position of teacher at the Scotch Settlement School. The red brick, one-room school building (now restored in Greenfield Village)[10] was located on the north side of Warren, between Greenfield and Southfield, very close to the present location of the William S. Ford Memorial Methodist Church.

The mechanics of teaching several grades simultaneously in one classroom were far from simple. Some relief was afforded if there were no pupils in a given grade. Scotch Settlement was relatively large for a single-room school. With twenty-four double desks, enrollment might have included all eight grades and approached forty pupils during winter terms.[10] Sometimes two grades would recite together to conserve time. However, with a minimum of four subjects per grade, the typical recitation period might be restricted to as little as ten to fifteen minutes throughout the six hour school day. From each period was subtracted the time shuffling from desks to recitation benches at the front of the room. Pupils not reciting were supposed to be studying. As often as not they were listening to recitations in expectation of hearing something laughable. A few of the larger boys, and occasionally a girl, would use their recitation as an opportunity to entertain the whole room at the expense of the teacher if possible.

Charles Richardson was respected as a knowledgable, no nonsense teacher. He had no "bad habits," a requisite of teachers in rural communities. He never did smoke, drink, nor use profanity; and if encouraged sufficiently would attend church, although it is doubtful that he was a true believer. Neither did he gamble, play poker, play pool, or dance — maybe because of his Puritan background, or maybe because of simple economics. Although young himself, he would not have fraternized with the older pupils, as teachers do now. He was usually hired to maintain discipline, and taught accordingly. He would have been kind to those who deserved it, hard on the bullies. Some boys having missed much school and not automatically passed with their age group, might be the teacher's age and yet be in classes with girls much younger.

These boys were extremely embarrassed at still being in school, and certainly did not love the system. Charles, therefore, had to be rough at times on some of the older ones to maintain order. These demonstrations probably put younger pupils in awe, if not in fear of their teacher. He taught pretty much by rote, which was the pedagogy of the period.

One of the pupils under Charles Richardson at Scotch Settlement was Henry Ford. Young Henry did not make a great impression on Mr. Richardson at the time. Henry and his friend, Edsel Ruddiman, were seatmates and had started school together on January 11, 1871.[10] Mr. Richardson's frequent comment years later was that, "Henry was a good boy in school." Henry apparently caused no trouble for this teacher. His seat near the back of the room was evidence that he did not need close watching. Henry was said to have shown more interest in "things" than in lessons from books. He was inclined to toy with mechanical objects beneath his desk during school hours. This did not annoy Mr. Richardson who had to deal with more obnoxious actions in the room than that. Henry Ford is described as having had no great lust for academic knowledge, but this attitude has been typical of boys in the more prosperous farm communities. After all, a landed farmer or blacksmith with little formal education was likely to be much more prosperous than the more learned teacher.

Charles' eastern training was not always to his advantage. In a class learning to read, a pupil once came to a new word. The dialogue is said to have gone as follows:

Teacher: "The word is hoss."

Pupil: "Hoss."

Teacher: "No, not hoss, it is hoss!"

2nd Pupil: "Is the word horse?"

Teacher: "Yes, of course, it is hoss."

Mr. Richardson seemed not to be able to pronounce a terminal "r." Even his signature became "Chas W. Richardson." All in all, however, Mr. Richardson used excellent diction, was precise in enunciation, and used no slang whatsoever.

CHARLES AND EMMA

During this period Charles was working hard, and without a doubt saving money (he constantly envisioned himself as on his

The Charles Richardson family, circa 1892. Left to right: Charles Richardson, daughters Nettie and Ivy, and Emma (Ford) Richardson. (Photo from author's collection 1660 Box 116)

way to the poorhouse — thus never was poor). He considered the farmers of the Detroit area as somewhat lazy. With the rich soil and ready market, they did not need to toil as farmers did in the East. They were fun-loving, and in his mind not very astute. As soon as Charles had saved some money he was able to lend it to local people at not only the going rate, but with a "bonus" in addition. This achievement greatly impressed his relatives in Connecticut, and convinced them of his success in Michigan.

Meanwhile, Emma Ford was not exactly languishing at home. There was always plenty of work on the farm for any number of children. And, the Fords were not so Puritan in their habits as were the Richardsons. The Fords, although modestly religious, joined in dances, thrived on box socials, corn husking bees, hayrides and skating parties. At just what time Charles and Emma began court-

ing is not known. Emma's autograph book, started in 1879 when
she was twenty-three, reveals a host of friends and admirers in the
Dearborn and adjacent areas. The 1880 census reveals Emma Ford
as being twenty-four years of age, living at home, and unmarried.[11]
The names of Charles Richardson and his brother, John, who was
visiting from Connecticut, do not appear in her autograph book
until February and May, respectively, of 1882.[12]

Charles did not dance, sing, or play the fiddle. But he did
enjoy socials, was large, fairly handsome, well dressed, and was an
excellent conversationalist in such situations. He was not inclined
to initiate or promote social events, but when he attended he usually managed to gain some attention. It is said that almost the only
time that he attended Sunday School was a period during which
he had been appointed Superintendent.

It was on April 5, 1882 that Charles and Emma were married.
Almost immediately the couple left for Genesee County where
they bought a small farm just north of Mt. Morris, Michigan, (Mt.
Morris was on the same Pere Marquette Railroad that ran through
Emma's father's farm). Emma's older sister, Sarah, had previously
married and moved to a farm at Pine Run, just a few miles from
Mt. Morris. Land, of course, was less expensive than in the
Dearborn area, and a true Yankee always paid in cash.

Charles soon began to teach as well as farm. Teaching must
have become his primary occupation because he soon moved into
the Village of Mt. Morris, onto seven acres, where he raised fruit,
"worked out" summers, and taught rural schools during the school
year. It is said to have been a common sight to see schoolmaster
Richardson on his "buckboard" racing to school — long red scarf
flying in the breeze, large lunch bucket at his feet, and a bundle of
hay for the horse tied on behind.

A daughter (Ivy) was born in 1883, and another daughter
(Nettie) in 1888. From time to time, Emma and the two daughters would take a train to Detroit where they would visit other
Fords in Dearborn and Delray. The horsecars and tower lights
made deep impressions on the girls.

The Richardsons became prominent in church and civic affairs
in the small community of Mt. Morris. Charles eventually became
Justice of the Peace and Village President. During this period also,
Mr. Richardson was industrious, frugal, and adept at lending money
on personal notes and mortgages. "Charlie" Richardson, as the

*Pictured here are Edsel Ruddiman, Charles Richardson and Henry Ford in front of the
Scotch Settlement School at a Greenfield Village reunion in 1935. (1660 Box 116 0-5276)*

townspeople referred to him, ran a tight household. He carried the
money, bought the groceries himself and passed out the nickels for
Sunday School.

In mid June of 1897, Emma (Ford) Richardson died at forty-
one years of age of tuberculosis, leaving daughters aged nine and
fifteen. She is buried in the Mt. Morris Cemetery. After about two
years, Mr. Richardson married Jennie Sweet of Webberville,
Michigan, who was an excellent stepmother to the two girls. Later,
when the children were grown (and there were fewer hands to pick
the fruit) Mr. Richardson and his second wife gave up the seven

acres for a house on Main Street. The two daughters of Charles and Emma Richardson had grown up to marry brothers (Harry and Frederick Bryan of Mt. Morris) both of whom became secondary school administrators.

In 1919, Jennie Richardson died of a series of strokes, and Mr. Richardson then broke up housekeeping and boarded first with Mt. Morris people and eventually with his two daughters. The daughters of Emma Ford maintained contact with their many Ford cousins at the Ford family reunions held each summer in Dearborn or its vicinity. One year Henry Ford's brother, William, brought cartons and cartons of Cracker Jacks for the children, and we children knew that he too must be rich. But it baffled us that he should be driving a Buick. Mr. Richardson seldom attended Ford reunions. He did, however, often travel to Connecticut summers, and to Florida or California for the winter. More than one winter was spent at Zephyrhills, Florida, with Charles Ford, one of Emma's brothers. When he traveled, he traveled by train with very good clothes and luggage. On letters from Florida to this grandson, a typical postscript was, "Tell your mother not to forget to collect the interest on that mortgage due about the time you get this letter." From age sixty-five to eighty-nine he lived largely on interest from mortgages.

In 1935, at the age of eighty-two, Mr. Richardson was invited by Henry Ford to attend a reunion of Mr. Ford's teachers at Greenfield Village. His immediate response was, "Let Henry come and get me, he has more automobiles than I have." In truth he was pleased to have been invited. Without much coaxing he allowed his eldest grandson, who owned a new Ford car, to escort him to the Village. There he was met and entertained by Mr. Ford and Mr. Ford's school seatmate, Edsel Ruddiman. The three revisited the restored Scotch Settlement School building, where Mr. Ford instructed his photographer to record their reunion.

Mr. Richardson, although only ten years older than Henry Ford, never cared to own nor drive an automobile. However, he was generous in later years in volunteering, "I'll pay for the gas" whenever there was a family discussion of an auto trip, whether he planned to go or not. He was a self-sufficient individual, spending much of his time in later years just rocking slowly in a chair, or reading a book. He seldom varied his sleeping hours, except to nap sometimes in the afternoon. He was normally up in the morning well before 6 a.m., waiting for breakfast which would be served perhaps hours later. He made no attempt to dominate the household, was as helpful as possible, and was very kind and generous to his grandchildren. He was usually off to his bedroom between seven and eight o'clock in the evening. After he was eighty he was especially proud of his age, and given to reminiscing when he encountered a receptive audience (probably also when he did not have an audience).

The evening of January 29, 1943, just a few days after his eighty-ninth birthday, while living with his daughter, Ivy, at Troy, Michigan, Charles Richardson passed away in his sleep. He is buried in the Richardson plot at Mt. Morris Cemetery, alongside Emma and Jennie.

REFERENCES

1. Caulkins, *History of New London* (Connecticut) pp. 98, 99, 123.

2. Private notes from Mrs. Ida Richardson, Norwich, Connecticut, including data from the Richardson Family tree as compiled by Ruth Richardson Bates.

3. Johnson, Johanna, *The Connecticut Colony*, Crowell-Collier Press, London, 1969.

4. Zunz, Olivier, "Detroit's Early Ethnicity," Rackham Reports, University of Michigan, 1975.

5. Nevins, Allan, *Ford: The Times, The Man, The Company*, Scribners, New York, 1954.

6. *Illustrated Historical Atlas*, County of Wayne, H. Belden & Co., 1876.

7. *Sixth Census of Population Schedule*, 1840, Michigan, Wayne County, Dearborn Township, Vol. 5, p. 268.

8. *Seventh Census of Population Schedule*, 1850, Michigan, Wayne County, Dearborn Township, pp. 273–289.

9. *Ninth Census of Population Schedule*, 1870, Michigan, Wayne County, Dearborn Township, Vol. 27, pp. 47, 58.

10. Metcalf, K., *Greenfield Village Exhibit Information*, Greenfield Village Guest Relations Dept., 1963.

11. *Tenth Census of Population Schedule*, 1880, Michigan, Wayne County, Dearborn Township, Vol. 29, p. 7.

12. Emma Ford's autograph book, 1879–1882.

❦❦ 9 ❦❦
EMMA FORD'S POETRY

Poem Portraying Each Member of the
William S. Ford Family

Emma Althea Ford, a daughter of William S. Ford and this writer's grandmother, enjoyed writing and publishing poetry. The following example describes the William S. Ford family about 1890 when Emma was in her mid-thirties, just a few years before she died.

GOING BACK IN MEMORY
TO CHILDHOOD DAYS

Ofttimes memory calls us backward
To the happy days gone by,
To the sunny hours of childhood
We remember with a sigh.

We remember, Oh, so fondly,
Those dear old days, forever past,
When trials, troubles, disappointments,
Upon our lives no shadow cast.

Childhood days, too quickly vanish;
Sunny hours how soon they pass;
And the dreams we dreamed in childhood
Droop and wither as the grass.

It is well to let our memory
Carry us back — away back again;
It will help to make us better women,
Help to make us better men.

Then let memory take us backward
Backward to the days of yore,
To the time when we were children,
All at home — at home once more.

Emma Ford Richardson

113

There was father, there was mother,
Mary, Sarah, Will and Bee,
Sam and Susan, John and Charlie,
Lizzie, Josie and Em — that's me.

God in His great loving kindness,
Showered blessings all around;
A merrier, happier family circle
In this fair land could not be found.

Little thought we then of sadness,
Little dreamed we then of care;
Light our hearts and gay our laughter
In our dear home circle there.

But old time, with all its changes,
Sends the home barques far and wide;
Some to struggle amid breakers,
Some drift onward with the tide.

Time rolls on as time will ever,
And the boys have grown to men;
The older girls are grown up women,
Then the change in home began.

Ivy Bell Richardson

Mary married and now is living,
With husband and grown children two,
In a pleasant little village
On the river Kalamazoo.

Sarah, dear generous-hearted Sarah,
Answered oft to the call of need;
Her's a life of self-denial,
A noble, though trying life indeed.

Time for her had many changes,
Like waves by strong winds blown;
Married now, she is nicely settled
In a neat little home of her own.

Will, in all his vigorous manhood,
His good fortune tried to find;
Discouraged, he at last returned
To the home he had left behind.

Now in his home in Kent County,
With his dear wife and boy around;
Should you ask, he will answer quickly
Oh yes, I my fortune have found.

Bee has gained an education,
And joined the army of teachers grand,
Who year by year are widely spreading
Education through our land.

Sam was always a home body,
He never sought or cared to roam;
He married and on a farm they settled,
Just one mile from the dear old home.

Children three the Lord has given,
A merry, laughing trio they;
May they return in tenfold ratio
Their parents' love for them to-day.

Susie, a successful teacher,
Married many years ago;
What she endured in her brief wifehood,
God and Susie only know.

Death, that pale and silent boatman,
Came unbidden to her side;
Grasped the oars, her pale hands folded,
Bore her safely o'er the tide.

And the angels at the gateway,
Stooped and wiped her tear-stained eyes;
Welcomed her with songs of triumph,
To her Home in Paradise.

Glancing at the family record,
As my eyes do onward roam;
John alone of all that household,
Is living at the dear old home.

Does he heed the many changes?
As the days and weeks speed by;
For he has now a family record,
Just we three: May, baby and I.

Nettie Richardson

Charlie always frail and slender,
Never cared for farming life;
Has made his home within the city,
Mid its noisy toil and strife.

Em, she married a down-east-yankee,
Right from the blue-law-state was he;
Now Em bakes beans and tends two babies,
Up north in County Gennesee.

Lizzie's home is in the City,
With husband dear, and baby girl;
Little Minnie, may God bless her,
And keep the darling pure as pearl.

Josie youngest of the family,
She the baby, therefore the pet;
She is still at home with father and mother,
They feel they need their baby yet.

On a quiet street in the city,
Away from the noise and whirl;
Dear father and mother are living,
With their baby boy and girl.

May God bless our father and mother,
Day by day may we hold them more dear;
May each child feel it is his duty,
To cherish and love them while here.

For it is not the love and the kindness,
The pleasures we give and get,
But the cruel slights to the loved ones,
That we will have cause to regret.

May we all do our life work so nobly,
That God in his wonderful love
May seat us in His family circle,
In His beautiful home above.

Written by Mrs. Charles Richardson,
Mt. Morris, Michigan

10
HENRY'S UNCLE HENRY

The Henry Ford Who Mined Gold and Raised a Family in California

Henry Ford of auto fame is often said to have been named after his "Uncle Henry." This introduces the question of which Uncle Henry, because he had two. One was his father's younger brother, Henry Ford; the other was his father's sister's husband, Henry Ford. The information to follow concerns the uncle most often considered the one so honored, but the reader should be warned at the outset that the question is by no means incontestably resolved.

Henry Ford, the younger brother of William Ford (father of the auto magnate), came to Dearborn from Ireland in 1847 at age 17,[1] one of seven children ranging in age from nine to twenty-three years. Unlike William who was twenty-one when he arrived, savored the ownership of land, and apparently enjoyed the occupation of woodsman and farmer, brother Henry was dissatisfied with such meager financial returns and in 1851 left Dearborn for California and the gold fields of the West.

Both William and Henry had earned some cash laboring on the roadbed of the Michigan Central Railroad being built toward Chicago, doing the hard work for which the Irish were noted. When Henry left Dearborn, just a few months after California had become a state, railroad transportation was available only as far west as Hannibal, Missouri. The line from Hannibal on the Mississippi westward to St. Joseph on the Missouri was then under construction, and it is quite possible that Henry did some railroad work on his way to California. But he managed to reach California — probably on foot — years before the Union Pacific and Central Pacific completed their historic connection to and from the West Coast in 1869. Descendants of Henry Ford in California cannot say how he arrived. They do say, however, that many from the East Coast are known to have traveled by boat to Panama, by horseback cross the Isthmus, and again by boat to San Francisco. But many who came by that route succumbed to yellow fever.

117

*A photograph of the
long abandoned mine site
which was on Henry
Ford's original claim
near Bath. The man in
the foreground is
"Uncle Harry," a relative
of Alice Ford. 0.6696*

In California, Henry is reported to have arrived in 1856 at
Iowa Hill in Placer County, a gold mining district in the hills of
the Sierra Nevada range. About this time he acquired a mining
claim in the settlement of Bath on the Forest Hill Divide, also in
Placer County.[2] Records show that he married a Catherine
O'Leary on August 25, 1857, in San Francisco. Catherine was of
the same Irish nationality but of the Catholic persuasion, and
Henry then became a Catholic. And for an Irish Protestant to have
married an Irish Catholic at that time implies that Catherine was
undoubtedly quite attractive. They must have soon returned to
Bath because the first of ten children was born in Bath in 1858.

Workings at Henry's California claim could not have been especially "easy pickings" because in 1864 he wrote to William here in
Dearborn from Fort Hogem, Idaho, as follows:[3]

William Ford
Idaho Territory
Forth Hogum   May 4, 1864

My Dear Brother, your letter of January 4th was received by my
wife March 24th and She Sent it rightaway to me the gretist Pleasure
immagenated to Hear that you and your wife and the children were
well and in good Health as these few lines leaves me at Present thank
god For his Mercis to us all Dear Brother i Have bean a way From
Home From my Dear Wife and little children Prety near a year and it
Seems to me as tho i Had bean ten years but i Hear From Her every
month She has bean Asking me to Come Hoam every letter i receive
From Her She and the children are well and getting a long
Comfortable i intind to go Down to Californe this Fall and if i can Sell
out my Claims Hear i might go Soner i long to go back to See my Wife
and Dear little Children a gain as you now now your Self that it is very
Hard For a man to Be a way From His Famyly but i Hope this will be
the last time Dear Brother you wanted to Know if i was going Back to
See you All any more but there is no brother in the world that would
like any better to go Back and see you All than i would but the winters
is so Cold Back there and long and i like the Climate in Californe So
well an a Count of no Snow in the winter and Pleasant in the Summer
i Shall not be able to give you a Disid Answer until i See my wife this
Fall i am Getting old and tired of mining and Shall Settle Down Prity
Soon i have got a mining Claim Down in Calaforne that Has Cost me
two thousant Dollers But i Cannot Sell it For near what it is wort on a
Count of these new Discoveries maid in these teritorys of Washington
and ideho the Peaple all Has left Calafiforne For these new Discoveties
but i Shall leave Prety Son i Hope and go Back to michigan a See you
once more Dear Brother william i wish you would let me know How
my Poor Father is and wo is ceapmg House For Him and How He is
getting a long and if He nead any mony and if So Send me word right
a way because i will Send Him Some and let me now all the news there
and if i know who your wife Dear Brother it is geting late and my Hand
is getting tired So good By only give my Kindest Regards to your Wife
and children and to one and All my Frinds Back there ac.cept a Paurt
your Self My wife Joins me in Sending you all our Kindes regards
Direct As before to Bath

i remain your Affetanete Brother
— Henry Ford

Quite a bit can be gleaned from the letter. William was trying
to keep in touch with his brother in California, and in his January

4th letter had no doubt mentioned the good health of his wife and the five month old baby (auto Henry), although there is no acknowledgment on the part of Henry of the baby's name being the same as his. Henry, in California, had apparently not known Mary Litogot whom William had married in 1861, nor of the death of their first child that same year. So correspondence could not have been frequent. The condition of their father, John Ford, was worse than Henry suspected, because John had died March 22, 1864, two days before Katherine had received William's letter. Their younger sister, Mary, who had been "ceaping House for Him," married her own first cousin, Henry Ford (the other "Uncle Henry") in September, 1861, and taken John into her new home at that time. When John died, his farm (at Joy Road and Evergreen) was divided between William and another brother, Samuel, here in Dearborn. It would be a while before Henry would be made aware of all this — perhaps years.

Henry did return to Bath from Idaho quite soon according to letters[4] from an elderly Mr. Evans of Duncan, British Columbia, who had been a friend of the Ford family in Bath during the 1860s. Mr. Evans wrote to the famous Henry Ford of Dearborn in 1937 as follows:

May 17, 1937

Henry Ford Esq.
Dear Sir:

I have long thought of writing you a few lines and you would wonder why, seventy years ago I worked with your uncle Henry Ford of Bath in the same mine so that takes us back some years. In those days we were nearly all Batchlors, and of course there would be a few young girls around and we boys had to have white shirts and white Linen coats, so we had to beg of the very few women who were there to wash them and do them up, so I got your aunt (Katherine Ford) to do up mine, and I can assure you they were done up well, I have never seen her equal. After all these years I have so many pleasant recolections of Mr. and Mrs. Ford, I believe I am the only grown up of those days who is alive today. I am now ninety-one, a resident of British Columbia but often my mind journeys back to the land of sunshine and fruit and flowers, and my memory oftentimes lingers with the Ford's, so I thought I would tell you how I prize those memories.

Yours Very Truly,
John N. Evans

In Dearborn, Henry Ford's secretary replied, asking a question:

June 14, 1937

Mr. John N. Evans
R.M.R.   No. 4 Duncans
British Columbia, Canada
Dear Sir:

Your letter of May 17 to Mr. Ford has been received, which we shall be glad to refer to him at the earliest opportunity.

Our records are not quite complete as to the birth date of Uncle Henry Ford. Do you remember the date of his birth or do you know anyone who could furnish this to us?

Thanking you for writing and awaiting your further information, we are

Yours very truly,
C.A. Zahnow
Secretary's Office

The birth date question was not answered in Evans's reply,[5] but more about the Fords of Bath is revealed:

The Outfitting Shop which the brothers, George and William, operated in Forest Hill (California) in the late 19th century. Wagons could be fixed, horses shod, tools and rations supplied to prospectors. George was an expert wagon wheel maker. The photographer has everyone at attention, and it is possible that Henry Ford is standing on the stoop. 0.6695

June 27th, 1937

Henry Ford Esq.
Dear Sir:

Your letter Re: Henry Ford of Bath, Placer Co., California, Re: date of his birth at hand, I doubt if I can give you any information as to his birth, but you ought to be able to get it from his children. I believe several of them reside in or near Forrest Hill, Placer County, California — when I knew them "70" years ago, when they were children — some not then born and now they are old men and women. I believe George Ford and Mrs. John Henning (Becky) are in or near Forrest Hill. They lived in Bath When I knew them, a small town about a mile and a half from Forrest Hill, now its what they would call a Ghost town, the original name of Bath was Sarahville, when a post office was established it was changed to Bath. Another Sarahville existed in California.

Now failing the children, try Auburn the County Town of Placer County you may find in old registers something to show you. I worked alongside of Henry in the Golden Gate Mine in which he was part owner. I think it was 1866 or 1867. They then lived on a street or Road we then called Bulls Run, it was soon after the Civil War, I left California in 1870. But my recollection of that land of sunshine, fruit and flowers are of the most pleasant and Happiest days of my life and the memories of my old friends are the outstanding ones of my life, today I am the last of them in my 92nd year.

Yours truly,
John N. Evans

Henry and Catherine had five daughters and five sons (See chart). One of the sons, George, was a miner and blacksmith; Albert was a storekeeper; and William, a bachelor, was employed by the Ford Motor Company for a few months during the 1920s, but because of our cold climate and unfriendly people, returned to Forest Hill to work in the blacksmith shop with his brother George.[6]

Henry is said to have mined on various claims for about forty-five years, but never became rich. His sons, George and William, and his grandson, Elmer Ford, also spent considerable time in winters seeking gold. It is said that Henry sold his original claim near Bath because he "broke his pick" with a neighboring miner in a dispute over water rights, and that the person who bought the claim subsequently mined several million dollars worth of gold from the property.[7]

There is little substantial evidence that Henry Ford ever came back to Michigan, although the following unsigned and undated note exists.[8]

William Ford m. Rebecca Jennings
1775-1818   1776-1851

Samuel Ford	John Ford	George Ford	Henry Ford	Robert Ford
1792-1842	1799-1864	1811-1863	Lost in US	1803-1877
Nancy Smith	Thomasine Smith	Alice Good	Age Unkown	Jane Hornibrook
1795-1873	?-1847	1810-1893		Dates Unknown

Rebecca	William	Jane	Henry	Mary	Nancy	Samuel
1825-1895	1826-1905	1829-1851	1830-1901	1832-1882	1834-1920	1837-1884
Wm. Flaherty	Mary Litogot	Henry Smith	Catherine O'Leary	Henry Ford	Thom. Flaherty	Nancy Kennedy
?-1861	1839-1876	1828-1884	1829-1912	1827-1914	1829-1905	1844-1890

Mary	Rebecca	Henrietta	William	John	Anna	George	Albert	Alice	Jeremiah
1858-1838	1859-1914	1861-1910	1864-1931	1865-?	1865-1870	1868-1952	1869-1928	1870-1950	1873-?
Jesse Bayles	JR Henning	JD DeBons	Bachelor			Alice Snyder	Alice Staigler	AC Bequette	
18?-1906	1862-?	1863-1920				1876-?	1879-1940	1867-1951	

Carlton		Cathrine				Arthur	John Henry	Peter	
1878-?		1902-?				1896-1906	1915-1965	1905-?	
Rex						Elmer	*Her Children*	Gladys	
1880-?						1899-?	Dorothy	1908-1965	
Alice						Cathleen	1900-?	Albert F,	
1882-1908						1902-1913	Robert	1911-1971	
Vernon						William H.	1906-?	Aileen	
1884-1922						1903-1921		1913-1916	

Henry Ford Family
— California

Mr. Fords uncle, Henry Ford after whom he was named and his father's brother left for Calif. in 1847. The night before leaving Detroit he stopped at the Perkins Hotel corner Grand River and Park Street, and occupied room No. 4.

This Uncle lived out West for years in mining and other business, raised a family etc. Forty years later he returned and finding it necessary to stop overnight in Detroit went to the Perkins Hotel and was shown the same room No. 4.

By 1900, William Ford had retired from farming in Dearborn, had moved to Detroit, and in July of that year traveled with his son, John, by train to California to visit his brother, Henry. In a July 22nd letter back to Clara and "Maggie," daughters with whom he was living in Detroit, he thus described his experiences:[9]

Dear Clara:

I received your welcome letter. I am glad to hear from you, we are all very well here, and we have a very pleasant and good time of it. We

*George Ford at his anvil
(ca. 1900) as a young man.
George operated his
blacksmith shop until 1945
when he was seventy-seven
years old. He lived to be
eighty-four. 0.6687*

*Elmer Ford, son of
George Ford, with his saddle
horses and dog in the
California hills.*

got here on the 4 of July. I rote to Maggy the day following my letter
and Johns letter was mailed the same day and I have not heard from
Maggy yet. We are at brother Henrys yet waiting for a letter from
Maggy from home.

. . . We have drove round a great deal to see the mountains the
mines and the sawmills, In one mine we went two miles under ground
in the tunnel We could see the gold very plenty in the rock and . . . they
were blasting with the same kind of cartridge that Henry blew up the
stumps; this tunnel is over fifteen hundred feet below the surfase; one
day we went to see a sawmil and the big pine trees it was very warm
about 95 in the shade, and about two minutes walk you could have a
good snowbaling as soon as I hear from maggie we will start to
Sanfrancisco we will see more of this state and can tel you all more
about it I am sorry about mother's accidence I hope its not very serious
I hope george McCormick will be very soon well again, give my regard
to Any McCormick tel her I am enjoying it out hear very much it is
very warm out hear from 95 to 98 in the shade in the sun 120 to 128,
there is a fine cool brees at night we have a little fire in the stove and
we can sleep very comforty
I hope to hear from you all soon —

I remain your loving Father
William Ford

*The Forest Hill grave
marker of Henry Ford,
his wife Catherine,
and son Jeremiah,
presumably their last
child who died as an
infant. Stones of
Rebecca, Henrietta,
Annie and Johnnie
further grace this
well-kept plot located
in a primordial
setting. 0.6675*

Albert Ford's grocery in Auburn about 1910. Albert with his business partner Clarke Bequette were soon recognized as "probably the largest grocery and feed merchants in the county."

Albert, on the right, with his helpers in front of his Auburn store.

The letter said nothing about Henry's health. Henry was to die the next May (1901) and be buried in the Catholic Cemetery at Foresthill in the family plot where the children, "Johnie," "Annie" and "Jeremiah" had been buried. Just a few years later (1905), William, who had been living with his daughter Jane taking care of him, died in Detroit.

It seems that nephew Henry Ford of Dearborn visited Foresthill at least twice. His first trip, in 1913, was announced in the Auburn, California paper as follows:[10]

HENRY FORD PANS OUT GOLD ON FORESTHILL VISIT

— Detroit Manufacturer Visits Relatives at Auburn and Mountain Town; Leaves for South.
Auburn (Placer Co.) February 11 — Henry Ford, Detroit automobile manufacturer left here to-day on his return trip to Southern California after a visit with distant relatives here and at Foresthill.
At the latter place he had the experience of panning out a few particles of gold in approved miner's fashion.
The father of the present manufacturer once visited with a brother, Henry Ford, uncle of the present Henry Ford, at Foresthill. William and George Ford of Foresthill are cousins, as is Al Ford of Auburn.

The same visit was described later in another local paper:

Foresthill, Placer Co. — Henry Ford, the name synonymous with the automobile industry was puzzled when he arrived here and saw the waters of the American River running wildly through the canyon. Turning to his second cousin Elmer Ford, as they chugged along the high ridges of the river in one of his horseless carriages, Henry asked: 'Why hasn't someone, done something to harness the power of the river?'
Ford arrived in the Mother Lode for two reasons. He had relatives here and, like thousands of other persons, was interested in gold mining operations in the canyons nearby. He drove from his vacation home in Los Angeles[11] to visit his cousins, children of his late uncle and namesake, Henry Ford, who died in 1901
Al Bequette, Placer County superintendent of schools and also a second cousin of the manufacturer, remembers him as a 'sophisticated appearing man perched high in a Model-T Ford which sported flashing white spoked wheels.' Bequette's mother was the former Alice Elizabeth Ford, daughter of Henry Ford of Foresthill.

A letter from Auburn merchant, Albert Ford, to "Dear Cousin Henry" in January, 1919, invites the Dearborn Fords to visit.[12]
From Albert's letter:

*Henry's
Uncle Henry*

*William Ford,
the one who came to
Detroit for a short
time, pictured with
his niece,
Gladys Bequette,
daughter of Alice
(Ford) Bequette.
Photo ca. 1925.
0.6691*

I saw in the papers you were wintering in our state so thought I would drop you a few lines to say that we would all be glad for to have you make that promised visit to Bath as this is an open winter and the Roads in good shape.

We have not heard from Michigan for some time and this has been such a year of sickness that one is quite lucky to escape.

How is Aunt Ann, have always thought she would come out to Calif as she said she liked this country very much. Don't suppose Wallace will ever stroll so far from his home — one of his girls writes us occasionally to tell us they are well but haven't heard from her for some time.[13]

Bill and George are trying their luck at mining in one of father's old mines. It's quite risky but has quite an attraction for all native Californians as anytime you might stumble onto a pocket, and it sure stirs that old spirit that lured the old miners like father on to the end of their lives without much returns.

I still stick to the Grocery business which the war surely put to the bad as all the Regulations seemed to be directed at the food man while big business got by with a wink. Hope that I have not got tiresome, and

you will take a few minutes to scribble a line to let us know you
Remember your Calif Cousins.

> Remain
> Albert Ford
> E Auburn
> Calif
> Jan. 29–1919

There is no evidence that auto Henry visited his cousins that
year, although in 1927 he is said to have been in Auburn to obtain
pictures and information concerning the family. They say that was
the last time they saw him.[14] Clara Ford apparently never paid
them a visit.

In August 1928, when Model-A Fords were still in short supply, Alice (Ford) Bequette wrote to Dearborn to get preferred
delivery on a 4-door sedan for her two "boys" (Peter and Albert)
who had work at some distance requiring a dependable automobile. They obtained one through a Sacramento dealer in two weeks
rather than the three to four months otherwise required.[15] Alice
wrote again to "Dear Cousin Henry" in June, 1939, to report the
death of her sister, Mary Bayles of Sacramento. The last correspondence on file from California seems to be in September, 1945,
when Alice Bequette sent a letter to Henry Ford introducing her
son Albert Francis Bequette, a school teacher recently married,
with two children, and being discharged from military service.

There are many direct descendants of miner Henry Ford now
living prosperously in the communities of Foresthill, Auburn, and
elsewhere in California. Very few carry the Ford name, however.
Whereas this "Uncle Henry" was caught up in the Gold Rush of
155 years ago, his alleged namesake here in Dearborn found his
"Acres of Diamonds" right in his own backyard.

NOTES AND REFERENCES

1. Records from Ireland indicate that Henry was born in 1830, while data from
   his gravestone indicate 1835. Other evidence favors the 1830 date.

2. Bath has been abandoned as a village and is no longer on the map. It was a
   few miles east of the present town of Foresthill, previously spelled Forest
   Hill.

3. Original letter is in Fair Lane Papers, Acc. 1, Box 1, Archives, Henry Ford
   Museum & Greenfield Village. Gold was discovered at Pierce, Idaho, in

1860. Fort Hogem was founded in 1862 on Grimes Creek about thirty miles north of Boise. By 1863 it had a population of 2,743. It was first named Pioneer City, but as succeeding waves of miners arrived it became Fort Hogem. By 1868 the easy ore had been removed and, as the population dwindled, Pioneer City became Pioneerville, and as such is on modern maps of Idaho.

4. Correspondence with John N. Evans is in Acc. 23, Box 28, Archives, Henry Ford Museum & Greenfield Village.

5. The exact date of birth of Henry Ford is recorded as February 5, 1830, in the Register Book of Baptisms as attested to by Frederick Guy Walker, Rector of the Parish of Kilamalooda, Ireland, and reported to William Ford in a letter dated September 11, 1882. Acc. 1, Box 1, Archives, Henry Ford Museum & Greenfield Village.

6. In conversation with Alice Leavitt of Foresthill, niece of George Ford, William is described as having been a soft-spoken man who came to Detroit and worked at the Ford Motor Company. But like his father, "Uncle Billy" disliked the Michigan climate, and finding the city people unfriendly, soon returned to Forest Hill. Doris Ford, of Auburn, adds that Henry Ford of Dearborn paid William's fare back to California.

7. Correspondence with Charles Hills of Auburn, California, quoting Doris Ford.

8. Typed note in Fair Lane Papers, Acc. 1, Box 1, Archives, Henry Ford Museum & Greenfield Village.

9. Original letter in Fair Lane Papers, Acc. 1, Box 1, Archives, Henry Ford Museum & Greenfield Village.

10. Clippings in possession of Robert Ford of Auburn, California, step great-grandson of Henry Ford.

11. The "vacation home in Los Angeles" is thought to be that of Mr. & Mrs. George Brubaker. Mrs. Brubaker was Clara Ford's sister, Eva Bryant.

12. Original letter in Acc. 1, Box 135, Archives, Henry Ford Museum & Greenfield Village.

13. Aunt Ann (Nancy, 1834–1920) at age eighty-five in 1919, was a sister of William and Henry and the last of her generation. Wallace was son of Henry's brother Samuel who inherited half of John's farm in 1864. Wallace was living on the homestead. The girls were Olive and Mabel Ford.

14. In 1927, auto Henry was active in collecting genealogical data on the Ford family. Data sheets for each of his California first cousins were filed by Alice (Ford) Bequette, youngest daughter of Henry Ford, and are now in the Ford Archives. There are also many unidentified photographs, some of which could be California relatives. The photos with this article, however, were obtained from family members in 1984.

15. Correspondence of Alice (Ford) Bequette, Acc. 23, Box 28, Archives, Henry Ford Museum & Greenfield Village.

11
HENRY'S OTHER UNCLE HENRY

The Well-Known Henry Ford Who Farmed in Dearborn and Married the Auto Magnate's Aunt Mary

For seventy-five years the most prominent Henry Ford in Dearborn had no inclination to drive an automobile, but he did drive an ox cart. He had arrived from Ireland in 1832 at age five, the second oldest boy in the Samuel Ford family.[1] When the Fords arrived in Detroit in 1832, it is said that there were but three brick buildings in the city, the majority of the buildings being of logs. More Indians than white people walked the streets.[2]

Samuel's land — all woods — had been surveyed in 1825 as part of the Northwest Territory. There were no roads — only trails between the trees. Surveyor's markings were often difficult to find and land boundaries were frequently in dispute. This first Ford land consisting of eighty acres was purchased in 1832 from the United States Government at a cost of $100 — the standard price of ten shillings per acre. The land grant bears the signature of President Andrew Jackson. The property was in Section 1 of a township named "Bucklin" for a William Bucklin who had offered to serve as Township Clerk without pay for having the township named after him. The Township of Bucklin became the Township of Dearborn in 1836 after the Commandant of the Detroit Arsenal which was located in Bucklin Township asked that the township be renamed "Dearborn" in honor of General Henry Dearborn of Revolutionary War fame.

This boy, Henry Ford, living in the far northeast corner Dearborn Township, had no formal school to go to, but attended lessons two miles west at the home of Mrs. Charles Ward. About 1842 — too late for Henry — a log schoolhouse was built, to be called the Scotch Settlement School. Along with his private schooling, Henry is said to have been the first of the Fords to drive a cart from

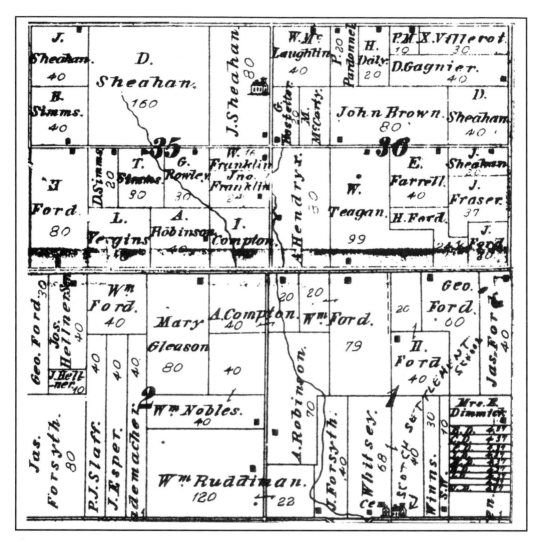

Section 1 and 2 of Dearborn Township, and Sections 35 and 36 of Redford Township where Henry Ford owned three farms in 1876. His home was on the sixty acres in Section 1. (Courtesy Dearborn Historical Museum)

Dearborn into Detroit. His parents, Samuel and Ann (Nancy) Ford owned oxen and had obtained a cart. But because both Samuel and older brother William needed to work hard to clear the land, Henry, about ten years old, was assigned to drive the neighborhood ladies through the woods and into town on a given day each week to shop and barter for necessities.[3]

Henry's father, Samuel, was a hard worker, as was William the older brother. But the war with the wilderness took its toll, and Samuel, barely fifty, died in 1842. William, the brother, had already married in 1839 and had two children in his own cabin on another eighty acres almost a mile away. This left Henry, now fifteen, to work the homestead eighty acres with his mother. Younger brothers, Samuel (eight) and George (seven), of course helped, as did daughter Nancy (nine). The others were still younger. (See chart.)

When the next family of Fords arrived from overseas in 1847, including auto Henry's grandfather, John, this Henry Ford welcomed them and helped them get settled in their own cabin about a mile-and-a-half farther out the trail,[4] "farther into the bush" as they later lamented. (This location would now be Joy Road at Evergreen.)

Just across the line from Henry's home and in Redford Township lived the Teagans, George and Ann, with several children including a daughter Dorah, born in Ireland two years before Henry. Henry and Dorah were married October 2, 1847. Their first child, Eliza Jane, was born in July, 1848. With many families of ten-twelve children, it was commonplace to find a mate of suitable age next door. Two or even three brothers would sometimes marry sisters of the same family, resulting in a multitude of double cousins. And close cousins would often intermarry in those days before the principles of genetics were well understood and preventative laws established.

The 1849 minutes of a Dearborn Township meeting show Henry Ford (age twenty-two) among men listed as being liable for military duty.[5] Henry, with his parents and older brothers and sisters, all of whom had been British subjects, automatically became citizens of the United States in 1837 when Michigan became a state. But Henry was never called to serve. Although he was a good shot with a gun, he was only regimented to play the fife in the Dearborn Band and captain the local baseball team. Strangely enough, the 1850 Dearborn Township Census shows Henry at age twenty-three still farming on his mother's farm, whereas Dorah his wife and his daughter Eliza are not listed with Henry in the Nancy Ford household.

In March, 1851, Henry Ford purchased a parcel of land from his brother William S. Ford, the land beginning on the North Line of Section 1, Township 2, South, Range 10 East in Wayne County. (County Records, Vol. 41, p. 229). He built his cabin a quarter-mile or so south of the Town Line because the property was low near the Line. A long private drive led to his home. Henry's first forty acres (S.W. ½, N.E. ½, Sect. 1, Dearborn Twp.) was valued at $350 in 1856. His State, County & Township taxes amounted to $1.93. His school taxes were a whopping thirty-three cents.[6]

At the Annual Meeting held for the Township of Dearborn on April 6, 1857, Henry Ford was named an "Overseer of Highways" for Road District No.1. This meant that he was to see that each farmer did his share of work to keep the roads in good condition. With an ox or a horse, the man's time was doubly credited.

DEARBORN TOWNSHIP CENSUS

1840

Samuel Ford

Male	Female
2 under 5	0 under 5
1 (5–10)	1 (5–10)
1 (10–15) Henry	2 (15–20)
2 (20–30)	1 (20–30)
1 (40–50) Samuel	1 (40–50) Ann (Nancy)

1850

	Age	Occupation	Property	Birthplace
Nancy Ford	55	Housekeeper	$1,500	Ireland
Henry	23	Farmer	$400	Ireland
Nancy	16	In School		Michigan
George	15	In School		Michigan
Samuel	13	In School		Michigan
James	10	In School		Michigan
Eliza	8	In School		Michigan

1860

	Age	Occupation	Property	Birthplace
Henry Ford	33	Farmer	$4,000	Ireland
Samuel	10	In School		Michigan

Dorah	7	In School		Michigan	*Henry's Other*
Maria	4			Michigan	*Uncle Henry*
George	2			Michigan	
Nancy Kennedy	17	(Housekeeper)		Michigan	

1870

	Age	Occupation	Property	Birthplace
Ford, Henry	40	Farmer	$8,000	Ireland
Mary (Ford)	38	Housekeeper		Ireland
Samuel	20	At Home		Michigan
Maria	14	In School		Michigan
George	12	In School		Michigan
James	9	In School		Michigan
Thomasine	4			Michigan
Oliver	1			Michigan

1880

	Age	Occupation	Property	Birthplace
Ford, Henry	53	Farmer		Ireland
Mary	46	Wife (Keeping House)		Ireland
Samuel	26	Working on Farm		Michigan
George	22	Working on Farm		Michigan
James	18	Working on Farm		Michigan
Thomasine	14	At School		Michigan
Oliver	11	At School		Michigan
Nancy	7	At School		Michigan
Milally, Michiel	62	Farm Laborer		Michigan
Falaris, Catherine	15	Servant		Michigan

Henry's farming operations were tabulated by the 8th Michigan Census of Agriculture-1860[7] as follows:

Acres Improved — 20	Livestock Value — $135
Acres Unimproved — 30	Wheat — 35 bushels
Value of Farm — $3,000	Rye — 15 bushels
Value Implements — $75	Indian Corn — 100 bushels
Horses — 0	Oats — 80 bushels
Asses & Mules — 0	Peas & Beans — 15 bushels
Working Oxen — 1	Irish Potatoes — 90 bu.
Milch Cows — 3	Butter — 400 pounds
Other Cattle — 1	Hay — 6 tons
Sheep — 5	Animals slaughtered — $72
Swine — 5	

Although Henry lists no horses, his mother, Nancy, on the next farm lists five horses, some of which Henry no doubt borrowed. Nancy also had an ox to spare, and sufficient bees to provide seventy-five pounds of honey and eight pounds of beeswax for

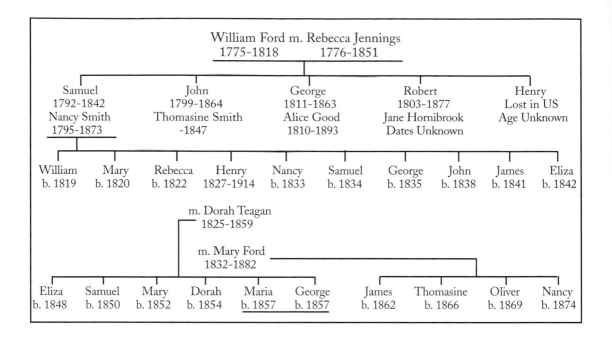

William Ford m. Rebecca Jennings
1775-1818   1776-1851

Samuel	John	George	Robert	Henry
1792-1842	1799-1864	1811-1863	1803-1877	Lost in US
Nancy Smith	Thomasine Smith	Alice Good	Jane Hornibrook	Age Unknown
1795-1873	-1847	1810-1893	Dates Unknown	

William	Mary	Rebecca	Henry	Nancy	Samuel	George	John	James	Eliza
b. 1819	b. 1820	b. 1822	1827-1914	b. 1833	b. 1834	b. 1835	b. 1838	b. 1841	b. 1842

m. Dorah Teagan
1825-1859

m. Mary Ford
1832-1882

Eliza	Samuel	Mary	Dorah	Maria	George	James	Thomasine	Oliver	Nancy
b. 1848	b. 1850	b. 1852	b. 1854	b. 1857	b. 1857	b. 1862	b. 1866	b. 1869	b. 1874

candles. Henry's older brother, William, had six horses, two working oxen and eighteen sheep yielding eighty-seven pounds of wool in 1860. Nancy's farm was worth $5,000 and William's $4,000 when Henry's was valued at $3,000.

Dorah (Teagan) Ford died on September 12, 1859 at age thirty-four. Henry then needed someone to keep house and look after the remaining four children including the two year-old twins Maria and George.[8] Mary Ann had died at age two in 1854, and Eliza Jane had died at age nine in 1857. Fortunately, Henry was able to get his niece Nancy Kennedy (sixteen), daughter of his older sister, Mary, to help. (See 1860 Census.) This arrangement lasted until Henry found his new wife "down the road a piece" — his first cousin Mary Ford who had come over from Ireland with the 1847 Fords at age fourteen. Mary was now twenty-eight and Henry was thirty-four. (This Mary Ford was sister to the William Ford who would become father of auto Henry in 1863. Thus Mary would become an aunt and our Henry Ford become an uncle by marriage to auto Henry.)

Henry and Mary were married September 26, 1861, in a double ceremony along with Nancy Kennedy, the housekeeper, who married Samuel Ford, a younger brother of the Mary Ford our

Henry Ford was marrying. They were all closely related and living within a mile or so of one another. This was "Ford Country!" Mary had been caring for her father, John Ford age sixty-two, a widower since 1847. And part of the arrangement was that John would retire, sell his farm home to the newly married Samuel, and go with Mary to Henry's home. Put simply: Nancy and Mary exchanged homes.[9]

At the time auto Henry was born, July 30, 1863, his father William Ford must have been quite appreciative of how Henry Ford, his first cousin and now his brother-in-law, was providing a home for his sister Mary and his father, John. Naming his first son Henry and his second son John before naming his third son William, suggests that perhaps this William Ford might have named his son Henry because of our Henry Ford's having so honorably embraced his family at that particular time. William and Henry had worked together building a house for Patrick Ahern in 1861. John Ford was to be living with Henry and Mary at the time of his death in 1864.

Henry and Mary owned sixty acres at the time of their marriage. Their property was assessed at $900 and taxed at $13.47 of which $1.29 was school tax. Henry's daughter, Dorah, died in 1863 at age nine. This left only Samuel of his first four children by his first wife, Dorah Teagan. Infections about which we now seldom worry were taking their vicious toll. Mary and Henry by purchases in 1867 and 1868 acquired the entire eighty acres of the original John Ford farm. Samuel sold his forty acres in 1867, and Jacob Esper who had purchased William's forty, sold to Henry the following year.

Many of the Fords attended Mariner's Church in Detroit. Entries in the church records from 1850 to 1856 record baptisms of the children, Mary and Dorah, as well as marriages of Henry's sisters, Nancy and Rebecca. George and Ann Teagan, parents of Dorah, were often sponsors at these ceremonies. After traveling became easier, the Henry Fords attended the Dearbornville Episcopal Church although it was quite a distance. When Grace M.F. Church was built in 1862, at what is now West Chicago and Wyoming avenues, Henry helped by doing carpenter work on the frame structure. Again, in 1875, he joined with a local group to found St. Paul's Episcopal Church on the Grand River Plank Road only two miles or so from his home.

NOTICE[10]
There will be a meeting held at Mr. Geo. Bristow's on Wednesday,
March 24th, (1875) at seven o'clock P.M. to form a vestry for a new
church to be built on Mr. Mouhot's Farm on the Grand River Road
Signed By - James Bossardet
Melvin S. Bryant
George Mouhot
Henry Ford

At the aforesaid meeting, the following named persons were elected wardens, to wit, George Mauhot, Wm. Bench, and Samuel Ford. Building Committee, Henry Ford, Melvin S. Bryant, George Mouhot, James Bossardet. For Treasurer, George R. Bristow, and Mr. J.H. Martindale was elected secretary.

Henry Ford had the reputation of being an expert barn builder.[11] He could swing the broad-axe with the best. He selected his black oak trees, felled them, hauled them from the woods with his ox, trimmed the trunks into beams of proper length with the necessary bevels and mortices, bored the holes and made the pins. He then assembled the neighbors for the barn raising—erecting a framework stout enough to last a hundred years. This Henry helped build the house in which his famous nephew was born. Some of his workmanship exists today in Greenfield Village.[12]

In February, 1870, Henry Ford, Samuel Ford, George Ford, Peter Esper, Francis Ward and Jacob Burger were all issued a court order under penalty of $10,000 to "... absolutely desist and refrain from felling or cutting down or causing to be felled or cut down any timber or trees standing or growing on said mortgagee premises or any part thereof or from drawing off any wood or timber from the same now thereon or drawn away therefrom ..." The complainant, a Mathew Burchard of Detroit — a former neighbor — held a mortgage on property in the western half of Section 3. It is likely that at least one of the accused had a fair idea of who had misappropriated the wood. It is reassuring, however, that William S. Ford, "Holy Billy," the writer's great-grandfather, was not subject to said bill of complaint.[13]

One will note that in 1870 the Henry Ford household appears quite ideal, with the parents at a healthy age, son Samuel helping on the farm, three of the children in school and two not yet ready for school.

Henry was especially fond of johnny-cake with maple syrup,[14] which recalls the old story of the farmer who took his corn to the mill on a horse. Ingeniously he kept the weight evenly divided over the back of the horse by tying two sacks together — one with the corn and the other with a stone of similar weight as a balance. His son, when assigned to the same task, instead divided the corn, putting equal amounts of corn into the two bags with such good results that the father gave him a sound talking to for being such a young upstart.

By 1880, Henry and Mary had outdistanced both William and also James who was now working Nancy's farm. The "1880 Production of Agriculture" report[15] covering the year 1879 offers the following statistics regarding Henry's farming business:

Acres tilled — 150
Pasture — 30 ac.
Woodlands — 188 ac.
Land & Bldgs. — $18,100
Implements — $200
Livestock — $1,000
Bldg. repairs — $20
Produce value — $2,715
Grassland mowed — 70 ac.

Butter made — 1,500 lbs.
Sheep on hand — 8
Lambs dropped — 5
Sheep sold — 2
Sheep shorn — 8
Fleeces — 45 lbs.
Swine — 22
Poultry — 700
Eggs produced — 750 doz.

Henry Ford about 1885. (0-2445)

139

Hay harvested — 80 tons
Horses — 5
Milch cows — 9
Other cattle — 20
Calves dropped — 10
Cattle sold — 7
Cattle slaughtered — 1

Indian corn — 15 ac., 750 bu.
Oats — 11 acres, 385 bu.
Wheat —12 ac., 400 bu.
Potatoes — 4 acres, 240 bu.
Apples — 7 ac., 100 bu.
Wood sold — 30 cord, $140

Compared to Henry and Mary's $18,100 property, William's was $12,000 and James's (Nancy's) was $9,200. This speaks well for Henry and Mary's progress.

Henry Ford's farm buildings and contents were insured in 1881 for fire and lightning by Farmers' Mutual Fire Insurance Company, and according to the policy, could be insured for no more than three-fourths of actual value. Items were listed as follows:[16]

Frame Dwelling House, 1½ Stories, Kitchen,
    Woodhouse   Sec.1 $500
Household Furniture, Wearing Apparel & Provisions   Sec. 1   300

Log Barn, Sheds Attached	Sec. 1	100
Frame Horse Barn, Shed Attached	Sec. 1	200
Frame Barn, 34x45	Sec. 1	300
Frame Granary	Sec. L	40
Frame Dwelling House, 1½ Stories, Kitchen Attached	Sec. 35	200
Frame Barn	Sec. 35	300
Hay Barn and Shed	Sec.35	150
Frame Barn, 44x34	Sec. 36	300
Hay and Grain in said Buildings		800
Horses, Cattle and other Live Stock		100
Farm Implements		100
		$3,390

There was no specific insurance carried on Carriages, Wagons, Harness, Musical Instruments, Books or Pictures.

The 1880 U.S. Census reveals a large and apparently prosperous household with three sons working the farm, three children in school, a hired man and a household servant. But Mary did not benefit for long. She died in 1882.

When Mary died there were four children at home. Maria had married three years earlier and moved away from Dearborn. George and James stayed on the farm with Henry for another ten years and Oliver for thirty years. But it was Thomasine who was with Henry until he died thirty-two years later on September 5, 1914. Thomasine, named after her maternal grandmother who tried but never reached the United States,[17] was forty-eight when her father died. But on Christmas Eve the following year, she took herself a husband — a Mr. Penner.

For seventy years or more, Henry had often fished with his neighbors from the banks of the meandering Rouge River, all the way from Town Line (Joy Road) down to Chicago Road (Michigan Avenue). About the last we heard of Henry in his old age was of his walking from farm to farm near his home with his dip net, to get the bunch to drop their work and go fishing along the Rouge for broad mullet. When they elected to continue working he reminded them, "you used to always go, and nobody in the community ever starved as I know of."[18]

Almost everyone mentioned in this story is buried in the Ford Cemetery on Joy Road near Greenfield. And it's quite conceiveable that the Henry Ford who helped clear the land before a cemetery was ever needed, would not mind your paying him a visit if you're quiet about it.

NOTES AND REFERENCES

1. Bryan, Ford, "The Samuel Ford Family," *The Dearborn Historian,* Vol. 22, No. 4, Autumn, 1982.

2. "Septuagesimal Celebration," St. Paul's Memorial Church, May, 1945.

3. Ford, Clyde, "Memoir," Acc. 1068, Dearborn Historical Museum, (1926).

4. *Ibid.*

5. "Minutes of the Meetings of the Townships of Bucklin, Pekin and Dearborn," Michigan Historical Records Survey Projects, May 23, 1827–April 13, 1857.

6. Dearborn Township Tax Rolls for 1856, Dearborn Historical Museum (Microfilm).

7. "Production of Agriculture in Dearborn Village in the County of Wayne — Produce During the Year Ending June 1, 1860." *8th Census of Agriculture — 1860 of Michigan,* Original at Michigan Historical Commission Archives, Lansing, Michigan.

8. There is some confusion concerning the birth dates of Maria and George. Family records indicate they were both born November 1, 1857. Census figures for both 1860 and 1870, however, show Maria two years older than George.

9. With nearly every generation of each Ford family having a Nancy, a Mary, a Rebecca, a William, a John, a Samuel and a Henry, the writer as well as the reader is hard-pressed to keep them straight.

10. Op. cit. 2.

11. Op. cit. 3.

12. Hood, Ann, Biography of Henry Ford" (Auto), Acc. 653, Archives, Henry Ford Museum & Greenfield Village.

13. "Injunction—State of Michigan—In the Circuit Court for the County of Wayne," dated February 1, 1870. Acc. 1699 Archives Henry Ford Museum & Greenfield Village.

14. Op. cit. 3.

15. 1880 Production of Agriculture, Original at Michigan Historical Commission Archives, Lansing, Michigan.

16. Insurance Policy dated December 19, 1881, Acc. 1699 Archives Henry Ford Museum & Greenfield Village.

17. Bryan, Ford, "Family of William Ford, South," Dearborn Historian, Vol. 28, No. 2, Spring 1986.

18. Op. cit. 3.

12
THE FAMILY OF WILLIAM FORD, SOUTH

Auto Magnate's Family,
Arrival in America, Farm Life,
Brothers and Sisters through Adulthood

This is an account of that branch of the Dearborn Ford family to which Henry Ford the auto pioneer belonged. There being two prominent William Fords in the vicinity, double first cousins of one another, the one living north of the Scotch Settlement Road (Warren Avenue) was often called William Ford-North, and the one living south of the Settlement was called William Ford-South.[1] William Ford-North was William Samuel Ford whose family has been described in Chapter 7.[2] William Ford-South, the subject of this story, has the distinction of being the father of Henry Ford the auto pioneer.

In Cork County, Ireland, the grandparents of this William Ford leased land from a Jonas Starvell, landlord of the Madame Estate, a few miles inland from the coastal town of Clonakilty. It is thought that the Fords had been "yeomen farmers" associated with the Starvells for many generations, both in Ireland and previously in England during the reign of Queen Elizabeth I.[3]

In May, 1819, William's father, John Ford, then twenty years old, together with William's grandmother, Rebecca Jennings Ford, a widow age forty-three, entered into a lease with Starvell for a twenty-three acre plot of land, a plot which may have been used by the Ford family for several generations. This lease was binding for the duration of John's life, and called for a yearly rent of twenty-nine pounds Sterling, which if not paid within twenty-one days of the date due would allow Starvell to retake the land and seize personal property such as oxen, cows, pigs, etc., in lieu of payment.[4]

The possession of this lease jointly with his mother may have enabled John Ford to seriously consider marriage to Thomasine

Smith, the sister of the older brother Samuel's wife, Nancy.[5] Indeed, John and Thomasine were married by published banns on February 14, 1824.[6] The family lived in a small dry-stone cottage on this plot of land subject to the life lease for the next twenty-eight years. In 1825 a daughter, Rebecca, was born to John and Thomasine, and in 1826 William — the focus of this chapter.

In 1837 the family consisted of ten members: grandmother Rebecca Ford, father John, mother Thomasine, William, sisters Rebecca, Jane, Mary, Nancy, and younger brothers Henry and Samuel. Although they were apparently all housed in the small stone cottage and barely eking out a living from the twenty-three acres, it is understood that the children were tutored to read and write, and that William was trained as an apprentice carpenter while in Ireland.[7]

Some years earlier (1832), two of William's uncles with their families had gone to America and settled in Dearborn Township, Michigan. They had often written of their adventures and of the readily available, fertile, wooded land. But John Ford did not budge from the homestead in Ireland. Instead, he signed another lease with Starvell in 1843 at the reduced rent of twenty-one pounds per year, the lease now being granted for the combined lives of both John and William who was only seventeen. Just four years later, however, the disastrous potato failure and famine conditions in Ireland are believed to have resulted in the decision of these Fords to move to America.[8]

William was loaned two pounds Sterling by his cousin, Henry of nearby Knockea, to help him in America.[9] The John Ford family joined with the family of John's brother, Robert, to cross the ocean. Robert Ford had a wife and four children. They are said to have all traveled steerage from Queenstown (Cohb) to Quebec.[10] The one casualty was Thomasine who became ill en route and died either at sea or at The Quebec Quarantine Hospital. Robert's family decided to stay in Canada, whereas the remainder of John's group continued on to Dearborn; by what route is not certain. This was a one-way trip. None of these Fords ever returned to Ireland to our knowledge.

In Detroit the John Ford party may have stayed briefly in Corktown where relatives of Thomasine lived at 150 Trumbull Street.[11] From Detroit there was no simple way to find the other Fords in the woods of Dearborn Township. Somewhere north of

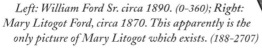

Left: William Ford Sr. circa 1890. (0-360); Right:
Mary Litogot Ford, circa 1870. This apparently is the
only picture of Mary Litogot which exists. (188-2707)

the Chicago Road it is said that the party became lost until in a clearing of stumps they met a young man who directed them on to the Ford neighborhood.[12] Whereas Nevins[13] relates that upon their arrival, there must have been great rejoicing, fiddle music and dancing, this writer believes that the mood would have been more somber because of the loss of Thomasine, and the further problems of establishing themselves in this strange land with so little money. The Fords were serious minded people. John Ford and family had suffered great hardships both in Ireland and on the trip to America. It is certain that they were grateful to find and be reunited with their relatives.

The following January (1848) John Ford was able to acquire eighty acres in Redford Township, a mile or so west of the farms of his brothers Samuel and George. Samuel, however, had died in 1842 and it was Samuel's wife, Nancy, Thomasine's older sister, who was managing that farm.[14] John purchased his land from Henry Maybury, paying $200 down with a mortgage of $150.[15] In the meantime, William was attending the Scotch Settlement School as one of the older boys.[16]

Now William, twenty-two, his father, forty-nine, and his sister Rebecca, twenty-three, would be carrying the load. A log cabin was built. Rebecca, the oldest child, managed the household. William with his younger brother, Henry, helped their father clear the land. A main source of income during the first few years was cordwood from the forest, sold to the railroads, the charcoal makers, and Detroit householders. William's training in carpentry also enabled him to get work on the Michigan Central Railroad which was extending its tracks to New Buffalo and needed stations, sheds and freight houses along the way. This extra cash no doubt helped William's father pay off the $150 mortgage on the farm in December, 1850. Just one year later, William's married sister, Jane, died when she was only twenty-two. That same year brother Henry, becoming restless at the age of twenty-one, headed for California and the gold fields.

William worked on his father's farm as farm hand and as carpenter for several more years. One of his occasional employers was Patrick O'Hern[17] who owned a ninety-one acre farm at Division and South Roads (Greenfield and Ford Road). In working for the O'Herns, William took a liking to the O'Hern's teen-age foster daughter, Mary, who was thirteen years younger than William. She had been born Mary Litogot in 1839, and became an "acknowledged child" of the O'Herns when she was three years old.

In 1858, John Ford retired, selling his farm to his two sons, William and Samuel, each paying $600 for forty acres. William's sisters, Rebecca and Nancy, were now married and had moved to Michigan's Upper Peninsula. His sister, Mary, continued as housekeeper until September, 1861, when Mary chose to marry her widower cousin, Henry Ford, taking John into her new household. On the same date as Mary's wedding, records show the wedding of Samuel to Nancy Kennedy.[18] This latter couple stayed on the John Ford farm.

William, perhaps anticipating the break-up of the family, had made his move a few months prior to these weddings. He had

married Mary Litogot on April 21, 1861, and had immediately moved into the brand new house he had been helping Patrick O'Hern to build. William was thirty-four and Mary twenty-two years old when they were married in the home of Thomas Maybury of Detroit, with Rev. Edward Dimrocke of St. Peter's Episcopal Church officiating. Both William and Mary later became members of Christ Episcopal Church of Dearborn.[19] A son was born in 1861. This child died as an infant. On July 30, 1863, a second son was born and given the name Henry.[20] This Henry became famous for his automobiles.

Although the Civil War did not directly affect William Ford as he was still a British subject, two of Mary's brothers, John and Barney Litogot, were serving in Company K of the Twenty-fourth Michigan Infantry, largely a Wayne County regiment. John, one year younger than Mary, was killed at Fredericksburg on December 12, 1862. He had been serving as a "substitute" for a man who had paid him $1,000. The war must have been quite worrisome to Mary.

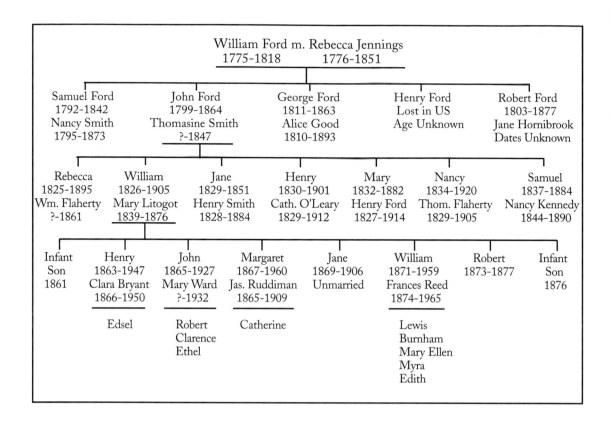

Within three years after their marriage, William and Mary had deeds to the O'Hern properties, subject to leases allowing the O'Herns to live on the premises for the rest of their lives.[21] This arrangement was practical because the O'Herns had no heirs other than Mary. And William, denouncing his British citizenship, became a citizen of the United States in 1864. Within another year, William had sold for $2,500 the forty acres purchased from his father in 1858, and had bought eighty acres to the west on South Road from George Moir for $4,000.[22] In 1867 still more acreage was purchased, this time forty acres to the east of the homestead from Jonathan and Mary Brown for $4,100, subject to a mortgage of $1,950 which was released in 1868.[23] William now had a total of 211 acres.

At two-year intervals, the additional children, John, Margaret, Jane, William, Jr., and Robert were born to William and Mary. However, on March 29, 1876 Mary died following yet another childbirth. Mary was buried in the Ford Cemetery where William erected the tallest memorial on the premises. Mary was only thirty-seven, William was fifty, and Henry the oldest child was not yet thirteen years old. Margaret, age eight and the oldest daughter, was a good helper, but could not run the household and also attend school. Margaret O'Hern, the grandmother, had died six years earlier, and grandfather Patrick O'Hern, age seventy-two, was helping as best he could with outside chores. William therefore persuaded his niece, Jane Flaherty, daughter of his sister Rebecca, to come with them and keep house until Margaret could take charge in another few years. The family sorely missed their mother who had favorably molded the character of each of the older children in particular. Henry, especially, has extolled the virtues of his mother many, many times.

According to Margaret,[24] William was a strict disciplinarian, but not harsh. He had a sense of humor and enjoyed a prank now and then. He liked the land, the occupation of farming, and was a progressive farmer. With the help of Patrick O'Hern, Henry and John, wood was cut, taken to town and sold as firewood. Later the stumps were hauled out and the area thus cleared for farming and crops. William Ford had regular customers for his wood, his hay and other farm produce. They were never hungry. Even in winter there was always a variety of canned fruit — also a well stocked "root cellar" where apples, potatoes and other root vegetables were stored. The family was taught not to be extravagant.

William Ford was a tolerant father. He allowed cards to be played in the evening on the dining room table, but if the games became too noisy and there was bickering, William, lying on the couch in the sitting room, would say "Time for bed." They all knew that meant no more cards for that evening. The pipe from the kitchen stove went through an upstairs bedroom to the chimney, thus keeping that bedroom warmer than the others. That bedroom Henry occupied, thus providing him with a warm retreat for tinkering well into the night.

It seems that William, for a period, assigned the morning outdoor chores so as to give the least difficult to the first boy to arrive outside. William, Jr. ("Will"), has told the story[25] of once getting down to the kitchen a bit ahead of Henry, and filling Henry's boots with applesauce from the kitchen stove to slow him down a bit. That morning Will got the easy job usually given to Henry. It is also told that son Will once took his grandfather O'Hern's rifle into

the fruit cellar and accidentally discharged the weapon with the ramrod in the barrel. The ramrod narrowly missed brother Robert.

One day William, Sr., and young Will had taken a load of potatoes to Detroit. They were returning from the City, and William was counting his paper dollars on the wagon seat when a gust of wind blew a few of the notes from the wagon. William remarked to his son that, considering the state of the government, he didn't know whether they were worth chasing. On special occasions when the circus came to town, William took all of the children to see it. He enjoyed it as much as they did.

In the fall of 1876, William attended the Philadelphia Centennial Exhibition where, among other things, steam powered farm machinery was lavishly displayed. It was that year, also, that young Henry had seen his first steam traction engine in the Dearborn area and "became all steamed up," as his brother Will describes it. Both William and Henry were impressed with the possibilities of steam power on the farm. William Ford was not a backward farmer. He employed hired help and invested in then modern equipment such as corn planter, grain harvester, etc. On their land were the usual crops of a general farmer, namely, wheat, oats, corn, potatoes, and timothy hay, some to be sold and some to feed the horses and cattle. Sheep grazed stumplands, pigs fed on skim milk and middlings, chickens lived on insects and spilt grain. With the fall pumpkins, the winter wood cutting, the spring maple syrup, life could not be called monotonous; but on the other hand there was a lot of hard work.[26]

The very next year (1877) the youngest son, Robert, died at age four. The other children were attending school at Scotch Settlement or Miller. Their home being on the boundary of the two districts allowed them to attend either school. At various times, William Ford was on the school board of one district or the other; and he served as jury foreman. He was also road commissioner of Springwells Township, and in 1877 was Justice of the Peace. William was well informed by means of the *Wayne County Courier*, the *Michigan Farmer* and it is said, a New York newspaper. He liked to read and discuss current events with his neighbors, especially with George McCormick who lived just down the road. William Ford was a member of a committee to investigate the feasibility of electric street cars for Detroit and Springwells. The city of Cleveland, Ohio, had replaced their horse-drawn cars with electrics. The Committee visited Cleveland, returning with a favorable report, and eventually the horse-drawn cars between Springwells and Detroit were replaced by electric cars.

Patrick O'Hern died in 1882. Young Henry Ford had already spent some time working in the city and was back home pondering life, working with steam engines, and helping with farm work. William, the three boys, and often a hired man were handling approximately 230 acres, growing grain and hay, raising cattle and sheep, as well as cutting wood for timber and fuel. For a time William boarded horses for Detroit people.[27] Could it be that

Henry became at odds with horses about this time? *Detroit Free Press* — Nov. 20, 1883 —

> Henry Ford driving a horse drawing a manure wagon was seriously injured about 4 p.m. on Sunday, November 18, by the animal running away and collapsing the wagon. The horse was stopped by a fence.

In 1887, William offered son Henry the use of the Moir eighty-acre farm of mostly woodland in an attempt to keep him from returning to the City and the occupation of mechanic. William felt that farming was a more independent and rewarding occupation. Henry, seeing an opportunity to use a steam engine to harvest considerable timber, accepted the offer and moved into the Moir farmhouse in 1888 after his marriage to Clara Bryant. Margaret, John, and Jane redecorated the old farmhouse as a wedding present. Henry built the "Square House" on this property in 1889, but by 1891 he was back to the City and the mechanical trade as we all know.[28]

Some Fords in front of the homestead in 1896. From left: Jane, Margaret, Clara with Edsel and William, Sr. Henry took the photograph. (0-479)

About the time Henry and Clara moved to Detroit, John and William, Jr., were operating a milk and egg route in the city of Detroit, and supplied Henry and Clara. John also attended business school in Detroit, probably the same Goldsmith, Bryant and Stratton Business University where Henry had studied earlier. Margaret, for a year, attended the Detroit Home and Day School, a boarding school at 564 Cass Avenue, better known as the Liggett School for Girls.[29] She returned home to the farm on weekends. William, Jr., is said to have enrolled at Cleary College, a business school at Ypsilanti, Michigan; but after two weeks he became disgusted and walked back to Dearborn. In 1895, John married Mary J. Ward and built a home on Chase Road, one-half mile east of William's place. John and Mary's first child, Robert, was born in 1896, and "Bob" Ford later (1932) became the "World's Largest Ford Dealer."

The year William, Sr., reached age seventy (1896), he made his will[30] which allocated the Moir eighty acres in Dearborn Township to Henry; the homestead, fifty-one acres in Springwells Township to William, Jr.; the forty acres immediately to the east of the homestead to John; the forty acres across from the homestead to Margaret; and the twenty acres adjoining Margaret's on the east to Jane. Henry and John were already on the assessment rolls in 1896, the year the will was signed. William, Jr., who married Frances Ann Reed on October 27, 1897, apparently occupied the homestead about that time and began paying taxes on the homestead before 1900.[31] The daughters received their portions of the estate following William's death (1905), at which time there were also to be $500 cash transfers from Henry to the girls to compensate for their receiving less land. Henry had been appointed executor by his father.

With the homestead in the hands of William, Jr., in late 1897, William, Sr., with Margaret and Jane moved into Detroit, renting a house at 582 West Grand Boulevard. About this time Margaret was taking lessons in embroidery which was to serve her well as a lifelong pastime. Jane, who was not too well, helped with the housework and shopping. Clara sometimes joined them to attend the theatre, or to take a trip to the country.

In July of 1900, William, Sr., no longer working the farm, traveled by train to California to visit his brother, Henry. From there, William wrote back to his daughter, "Maggie," and also to his daughter-in-law, Clara, describing the gold mines and sawmills in the mountains northeast of Sacramento in Placer County, California.[32]:

> We have driven around a great deal to see the mountains, the mines and the sawmills. In one mine we went two miles underground in the tunnel. We could see the gold very plenty in the rock and seems that they were blasting with the same kind of cartridge that Henry blew up the stumps. This tunnel is over fifteen hundred feet below the surface. One day we went to see a sawmill and the big pine trees It was very warm about ninety five in the shade and about two minutes walk you could have a good snowballing.

William's penmanship was excellent, but there were some mistakes in spelling. In this same letter William seemed particularly concerned about the health of his good friends George and "Any" McCormick, Dearborn neighbors, but there is no mention of the health of his brother, Henry, who died the following year and was buried in The Catholic Cemetery at Forest Hill, California.

On November 7, 1900, Margaret Ford and James Ernest Ruddiman, son of pioneer William Ruddiman, were married.[33] They were to live in the Ruddiman farm house located on sixty acres, a part of the original 1837 grant from the government (now the corner of Warren and Southfield roads). The wedding took place at 582 West Grand Boulevard. James Ruddiman had attended the Scotch Settlement School with the Ford children, was well known in the Dearborn community, and had served as Township Treasurer during 1894 and 1895.

After Margaret left the 582 West Grand Boulevard address, Henry, with Clara and Edsel, who had been renting at 1292 Second Avenue, then moved into the upper floor of the same building with William and Jane. According to Clara's diary, they were all settled by January 9, 1901.[34] The next move for William and Jane came in January of 1902, when they moved to 338 Hendrie Avenue (Detroit) where Henry and Clara had rented an adjoining terrace at 332 Hendrie. Each party paid $16 per month.

The Detroit City Directory of 1904 lists:

William Ford, home, 338 Hendrie
Henry Ford, Pres. Ford Motor Company, home 332 Hendrie
John Ford, farmer, home west side Horger, south of Ford Road, Springwells

William D. Ford, engineer, home southwest corner Holden, (Tireman) and Scotten Avenue.

Mary Ward and John Ford about the time of their marriage in 1895. (0-1122)

William Ford, Sr., was at 338 Hendrie when he died on March 8, 1905 at age seventy-eight. He is said to have suffered from paralysis for some time. The funeral was conducted at the home of his daughter, Margaret Ruddiman, on Emerson (Southfield) Road, Dearborn, with Rev. Stephen W. Frisbie of Detroit providing the eulogy. Burial was in the Ford Cemetery.[35]

Henry and Clara moved away from the Hendrie address quite soon after the death of William, Sr. Just what became of Jane who had been living with her father is not clear. In September of the following year, records show a large medical bill from a Christopher Campbell, M.D. of 318 West Grand Boulevard. The bill had been sent to "Miss Jane Ford, 177 Joseph Campau Ave.," and was paid on October 10, 1906.[36] Jane died on November 26, 1906 at age thirty-seven. Jane is recorded as having died from hemiplegia. She is buried in the Ford Cemetery.

None of the William Ford children left the Detroit and Dearborn area. John stayed closest to the homestead, building a home for his own family at 5265 Chase Road in the 1890s, and

William Ford, Jr. ("Will")
photographed about the time
of his marriage to Frances
Reed in 1897. (0-1026)

operating a dairy farm for approximately twenty years on the forty-one acres inherited from his father. In 1922, all but the three-acre homesite was subdivided and known as the "John Ford Subdivision." John was a partner in the Castle & Ford real estate firm, and was active in Springwells, Fordson, and Wayne County governmental affairs. He was a member of the Fordson City Council at the time of his death in September, 1927.[37]

Margaret lived on the Ruddiman farm from the time of her marriage in 1900 until 1909 when her husband, James, died. That winter of 1909–1910 she and her daughter, Catherine, lived with Henry, Clara and Edsel Ford, in their new home at 66 Edison Avenue in Detroit, Henry then assisted Margaret in building a house at 120 Glynn Court, just four blocks north of Edison. Catherine attended Duane Doty School, and then the new Northern High School. For a while in the 1920s, Margaret and her daughter resided near Boston, Massachusetts, returning to Detroit in 1928. In 1931 they moved to Longacre Avenue, part of the sub-divided Ruddiman land grant. Later, Margaret and Catherine took up residence at 154 River Lane in Dearborn.[38] Margaret died at that address on February 27, 1960.

William, Jr., and his family continued to live at the homestead for about six years after his marriage in 1897. He was on the farm

*Left: Margret Ford Ruddiman, circa 1900. (0-3184);
Right: One of the Ruddiman boys, likely James Ernest
Ruddiman, circa 1890. (0-6622)*

when Division Road (Greenfield) was extended south from Scotch
Settlement (Warren) toward Michigan Avenue. In 1901, William,
Jr., was likely the one who was required to move the farmhouse
some one-hundred feet or so toward the east to make way for the
new road. William, Jr., was mechanically inclined like his brother,
Henry. As early as 1899, W.D. Ford's business stationery denoted,
"Dealer in All Kinds of Farm Machinery." Will is said to have had
greater interest in farm tractors than Henry.[39]

Contrary to the 1896 will, in February of 1902, William Ford,
Sr., sold the homestead property to Henry Ford for $4,000.[40]
William, Jr., apparently moved to Detroit in 1903 where he is listed in 1904 as "engineer." Later (1911–1912) he went into the
threshing business out near the old settlement, and about 1914
became superintendent of the Ford Farms owned by Henry. This
was where the Ford tractor was being developed. After also being
employment manager at the tractor plant for a few years, he again
went into agricultural implement sales business for himself.

In 1916, William, Jr., returned to live in Dearborn Village where he built a home that was then at 21551 Garrison Ave., and became a very popular Village President and Chief of Police in 1919–1921. He was to remain in the agricultural implement business, becoming again associated for a time with his brother in the distribution of Fordson Tractors and accessories. William, Jr., retired in 1949 and moved to his farm on Pleasant Valley Road, Brighton, Michigan. He died in 1959.

NOTES AND REFERENCES

1. Ford, Clyde M., "Article About Mr. Henry Ford," Dearborn Historical Museum Collection, Accession 81-86.7, Dec. 26, 1926. pp. 206.

2. Bryan, F.R., "The William S. Ford Family," *Dearborn Historian*, Vol. 25, No. 2, 1985.

3. Webster, Charles A., "Notes, Topical, Historical and Genealogical on the Ford Family," Acc. 23, Box 28, Archives, Edison Institute.

4. Ibid.

5. Bryan, F.R., "The Samuel Ford Story," *Dearborn Historian*, Vol. 22, No. 4, Autumn, 1982, pp. 111–126.

6. See Reference 3.

7. Ruddiman, Margaret (Ford), "Memories of my Brother Henry Ford," *Michigan History*, Michigan Historical Commission, Sept. 1953.

8. See Reference 3. Jeremiah Kingston succeeded John Ford on the Madame acreage. Kingston is described in a Rent Roll of 1877 as the "representative of John Ford." This implies that John Ford may not have been actually evicted, and may instead have sold his interest in the farm to Kingston. The proceeds of the sale may have paid the family's passage to America. Jeremiah Kingston is believed to have been a son of Thomas Kingston, rent warner on the estate of Madame.

9. Letter by Charles Bateman dated 1924, Acc. 23, Box 28, Archives, Edison Institute.

10. Conversations with Miss Olive Ford, great granddaughter of John Ford.

11. It is thought that Thomasine (Smith) Ford had relatives in Detroit. A John Smith (1797–1878) of County Cork, Ireland resided at 150 Trumbull Street. Thomasine's daughter, Jane, married John Smith's son, Henry, in 1856; and a niece, Eliza Ford married Thomas Smith also of 150 Trumbull in 1867.

12. Stevenson, Frank, "Scotch Settlement," *Dearborn Historian*, Vol. 5, No.1, 1965.

13. Nevins, Allan, *Ford: The Times, The Man, The Company*, Charles Scribner's Sons, New York, 1954, p. 54.

14. After John had lost his wife, Thomasine, and had brought his family to Dearborn and found Thomasine's sister, Nancy, now a widow with a prosperous farm and home, he must have at least toyed with the idea of marrying Nancy.

15. John Ford of Greenfield Township purchased from Henry Maybury of Detroit on Jan. 15, 1848, the W $1/2$ of SW. $1/4$ of Sec. 15, Twp. 1 South, Range 10 East. From County Records, Vol. 32, p. 254.

16. See Reference 7.

17. Bryan, Ford R., "Patrick Ahern, Henry Ford and Fair Lane," *Dearborn Historian*, Vol. 22, No.1, Winter 1982.

18. John Ford family genealogy records, Acc. 23, Box 27, Archives, Edison Institute.

19. See Reference 7.

20. It is frequently published that Henry (the tycoon) was named after his "Uncle Henry." Which of his two Uncle Henrys was so honored is not revealed. Was it his father's brother Henry (1830–1901) who deserted the family and went to California, or was it his Aunt Mary's husband, Henry Ford (1827–1914) whom auto Henry has identified in photographs as "Uncle Henry?" And Henry could have been named after his father's generous cousin, Henry Ford, of Knockea, Ireland, who in 1847 loaned money to William for use in America.

21. Documents concerning ownership of Ahern-Ford property, Acc. 1, Box 3, Archives, Edison Institute.

22. Ibid.

23. Deed, Jonathan and Mary Brown to William Ford, N.E. $1/4$ of N.W. $1/4$, Sec. 18, Springwells Township (41.5 acres) for $4,100. dated April 1867. (See abstract of John Ford Subdivision, Dearborn Historical Museum.)

24. See Reference 7.

25. Ford, Burnham, Reminiscences, Acc. 65, Box 27, Archives, Edison Institute.

26. Aird, Hazel B. and Ruddiman, Catherine, "Henry Ford — Boy with Ideas."

27. Ruddiman, Edsel A., Reminiscences, Acc. 65, Archives, Edison Institute.

28. Copies of leases indicate that William Ford rented the Moir farm between 1871 and 1876 to Matbias Assenmacher for $200 per year, and from 1901 to 1904 to Joseph Fichner for the same payment.

29. Correspondence with Miss Catherine Ruddiman, grand-daughter of William Ford.

30. Copy of will of William Ford, Sr. dated June 10, 1896. Acc. 1, Box 33, Archives, Edison Institute.

31. Springwells Township Assessment Rolls, Dearborn Historical Museum.

32. Handwritten letter from William Ford dated July 22, 1900. Archives, Edison Institute.

33. Ruddiman, Edsel A., "Genealogy of the Leslie and Ruddiman Families," Entry 99, Page 48 (1948), Dearborn Historical Museum.

34. Clara Ford's Diary, Acc. 1, Boxes 18-24. Archives, Edison Institute.

35. Obituaries of William Ford, Sr., Detroit newspapers, Mar. 9, 1905.

36. The Joseph Campau address is listed in the Detroit City Directory for 1906 as a boarding house operated by Ernest G. and Ida Gearhart.

37. John Ford obituary, *Detroit Times,* September 28, 1927.

38. Ruddiman, Catherine, "The William Ruddiman Family and The Ruddiman Farm House," Dearborn Historical Museum, May, 1984.

39. See Reference 25.

40. Copy of deed by William Ford, Sr. to Henry Ford, fifty-one acres, (Homestead property) for $4,000. Deed dated Feb.1902. Acc. 1, Box 3, Archives, Edison Institute.

13

PATRICK AHERN

Auto Henry's Foster Grandfather,
Henry's Close Relationship, and
Correct Origin of Name Fair Lane

The reason Mr. and Mrs. Henry Ford of Dearborn, Michigan, chose the name "Fair Lane" for their Dearborn residence has been somewhat obscure. The name Fair Lane is usually associated with the Irish County of Cork, and also with Henry Ford's father, William, who immigrated from County Cork in 1847. Recent research at the Ford Archives, Henry Ford Museum, investigating the Ahern family with whom William and Henry Ford lived for many years, reveals a definite connection between Patrick Ahern and Fair Lane. Fair Lane was an area in the northwest section of Cork City, a district which in the early 1800s was a respectable residential neighborhood. Before that it was probably literally a lane. Both Aherns and Fords lived in Fair Lane. Some of those Fords could possibly have been distant relatives of industrialist Henry Ford of Dearborn. But our interest is especially aroused when we learn that Patrick Ahern was born and raised in Fair Lane, and that Patrick Ahern was the only grandfather that Henry Ford really knew and loved. It is a long and intriguing story.

There is evidence that Patrick Ahern was born in Fair Lane, Cork, in 1804.[1] His father was Daniel Ahern and his mother was Catherine Neil. He had a brother, Cornelius. The brothers worked as butchers in the English Market, a large municipal meat market in Cork. When about twenty-six years old, Patrick joined the British Army, while Cornelius stayed in Cork and is said to have died there.[2] After Patrick's enlistment in England, the British Army shipped him to Quebec where he and some others quite promptly became absent without leave.[3] This group made their

A portion of an 1893 map showing "Fair Lane" and the Cattle Market district of Cork. (Courtesy Cork Public Museum)

way to Detroit unapprehended, where Patrick learned of work at the Detroit Arsenal, then under construction in Dearbornville.

Sixty-eight men were on the Arsenal payroll in June, 1834, where Patrick Aharn [sic] is shown as having worked twenty-four days at the posted rate of 87½ cents per day, for a total monthly pay of $21.22. Whereas most of the men signed for their pay, Patrick made his mark which was duly witnessed by the payroll clerk. Patrick continued his work at the Arsenal as "laborer, excavating and grading" during July and into August of 1834. He is not listed in later months nor following years.[4]

Patrick's name, apparently Aherne in Ireland, began to vary on documents from Aherne to Aharn, Ahern, O'Hern, O'Herin, O'Hara and other variants, perhaps because of his desertion from the British Army, but more likely because he could not write his name. Being Catholic, he may have had little intention of fighting for the British government, but may have seen the army as a means

This copy of a tintype (ca. 1850-55) was copied at the request of Henry Ford in 1924, and labeled "Mr. Ford's Grandfather." It is quite possible that it is Patrick Ahern. Henry Ford doted on his grandfather Ahern with whom he grew up, but there is little mention of his grandfather John Ford (1799-1864), whom Henry (1863-1947) could not have remembered. (0-1709-B)

of getting to America. Patrick, in Michigan, was saving money, making friends, and, in particular, had met a comely spinster by the name of Margaret Stevenson, an Episcopalian who may have been about twelve years older than Patrick.

Property records show that a John Stevenson, born in Ireland, settled in Dearborn Township in 1831, and filed a location claim in September, 1833, for forty acres in Greenfield Township, on the northeast corner of the intersection of what is now Ford and Greenfield roads (Dearborn Ford Woods Park). This forty acres was deeded by John Stevenson (1804–1889) and his wife, Susan (1809–1875) to Margaret Stevenson in consideration of $50 (the government purchase fee) on July 4, 1834.[5] Just eleven days later, July 15, 1834, Margaret and Patrick were married,[6] and it was on Margaret's land that Patrick built a log cabin.

*This picture, a copy of a tintype,
ca 1855-60, is labeled "Mr. Ford's
Grandmother," and is believed to be
Margaret (Stevenson) Ahern, Henry
Ford's foster grandmother. Mr. Ford's
grandmother Litogot died about 1840,
and his grandmother Thomasine Ford died
at sea in 1847. Grandmother Ahern lived
with the William Ford family until Henry
was seven years old (1870), and is most likely
to have been the grandmother photographed.
(0-6299)*

Soon after their marriage they are said to have adopted a girl, Fannie.[7] It is not certain how long Fannie lived with them, but Fannie O'Heran [sic] is shown in early records of the Scotch Settlement School.[8] Apparently Fannie had left by 1842 when Patrick and Margaret heard of an orphan girl in her third year, whose mother had died and whose father, a carpenter, was killed either by a fall from a roof,[9] or from falling through the ice of the Rouge River while hauling logs with oxen and sleigh.[10] This orphan girl was Mary Litogot, daughter of William Litogot of Wyandotte, Michigan. She had two older brothers, Saphara (1833–1878) and Barney (1838–1873), and one brother, John (1840–1862) who was a year younger. There is more than one story of how the Aherns first heard about Mary Litogot. In any case, it seems that Mary was the second girl adopted[11] by the Aherns.

It is 1841 before there is a record of Patrick's buying land for himself[12]. He began buying in bits and pieces. His first purchase was

in Dearborn Township, a parcel of one acre for $10 "lawful money."
Then in 1842 he bought ten acres more for $75. Both of these lots
bordered Greenfield Township, and the smaller piece adjoined
Margaret's forty acres. Then in 1845, for $313.28, he bought the
N.W. $\frac{1}{2}$ of the NW. $\frac{1}{2}$ of Section 18, Town 2 South, Range 11
East, amounting to forty acres, from a Benjamin Walker of the U.S.
Army who had obtained it from the government in 1830. Walker
took a mortgage for $145, which Patrick paid off in 1846. This is
the forty acres directly south of Margaret's property where they had
built their log cabin. (This is the land on which Patrick later built a
new frame house in which Henry Ford the industrialist was born.)
State, County, and School taxes on Margaret and Patrick's ninety-
one acres for the year 1845 amounted to $3.62, and were paid by
Patrick O'Herin [sic] on Jan. 9, 1846.[13]

The 1850 Michigan Census[14] reports:

	Age	Occupation	Real Estate	Birthplace
Patrich O'Hern	45	Farmer	$1,800	Ireland
Margaret O'Hern	48	—	—	Ireland
Mary O'Hern	10	—	—	Michigan

By 1847 the second contingent of Fords had arrived (Chapter
4), also from County Cork, Ireland.[15] They settled on what is now
Joy Road.[16] The father was John Ford. The mother, Thomasine,
had died at sea, and the oldest son was William Ford, age twenty-
one. This William Ford was well acquainted with hard work and
poverty in Ireland. His family had been evicted from their twenty-
three acres of leased land near Clonakilty and had come to
America via steerage. William had been an apprentice carpenter in
Ireland, and brought his carpenter tools with him on his voyage to
America.[17] He immediately set to work helping his father, and during the next few years also was employed by the Michigan Central
Railroad in the western part of the state. Carpenters were in
demand to build stations, platforms, and water tanks along the
line. William's younger brother, Henry (1830–1901), was more
adventuresome, and took off for the gold fields of California and
Idaho, never to return. From there he later wrote back to William
saying he could never endure the cold climate of Michigan.[18]

During the 1850s, William continued to work both at home

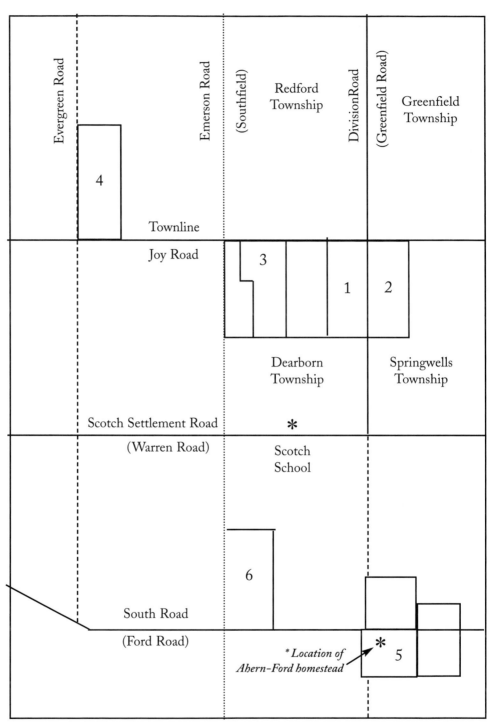

19th Century Ford Farms: 1. Samuel 1832; 2. George 1832; 3. William (North) 1840; 4. John 1848; 5. William (South) (homestead) 1864; 6. William (South) 1865.

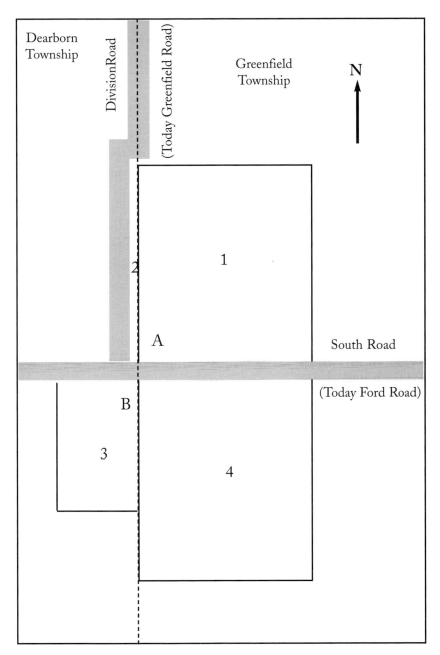

Dearborn Township

DivisionRoad

(Today Greenfield Road)

Greenfield Township

N

1

2

A

South Road

(Today Ford Road)

B

3

4

Ahern Property: A. Log Cabin, ca. 1834; B. New House, ca. 1861.

Acquired by	Date	Acres	Price
1. Margaret Stevenson	1834	40	$50
2. Patrick Ahern	1841	1	$10
3. Patrick Ahern	1842	10	$75
4. Patrick Ahern	1845	40	$313

and as hired hand, at both farming and carpentry. In 1858, William's father, John (age sixty), retired from his farm on Joy Road and went to live with his eldest daughter. At this time John sold his eighty acres, forty acres to William,[19] and forty acres to a much younger son, Samuel (1837–1884). Son Henry in California seems not to have figured in the transaction. William paid his father $600 for his forty acres, and was very proud of at last being a land owner;[20] so much so that his first property tax receipt for $5.70 for the year 1859 was framed and still exists in that frame.[21]

However, at this point, William (now thirty-four) did not build a house on his own land, but rather had his eyes on Patrick Ahern whom he admired, and on Patrick's foster daughter, Mary (now nineteen), whom he admired even more. William had worked for Patrick occasionally, and now was helping him build a sizeable house on the property Patrick had purchased in 1845.

Either the 1860 census taker may have been hard-of-hearing, or Patrick must have had a terrifying brogue, as the 1860 record of the Ahern family is as follows:[22]

	Age	Occupation	Real Estate	Birthplace
Patrick O'Harran	50	Farmer	$4,000	Ireland
Margaret O'Harran	60	—	—	Ireland
Mary O'Harran	16	—	—	Michigan

About the time Patrick's new house was being finished, William Ford married Mary Ahern, on April 25, 1861.[23] According to Nevins,[24] immediately after the wedding the couple moved into the log cabin occupied by the Aherns, and quite soon thereafter the four moved into the large new house. (The new house, incidentally, was on the Dearborn-Greenfield Town Line, and had to be moved in 1901 when Division Road (Greenfield) was constructed southward.) The house was a two-story structure with parlor, kitchen-living room, and eventually five bedrooms. In referring to this house, after having moved it to Greenfield Village, Henry Ford is said to have remarked apparently with considerable emphasis, "You see that home across the street there? That's my mother's home. My father just walked into that place. That belonged to my mother. That was my mother's home. It was her home and my father just walked into the place."[25]

A son was born to William and Mary in January, 1862. This

An 1876 artist's sketch of the farm which Patrick Ahern sold in 1864 to son-in-law William and foster daughter Mary for $1,000 subject to a lease allowing Mary's foster parents, Patrick and Margaret Ahern, to live on the premises for the rest of their lives. The small building, left foreground, is the cabin in which the Aherns had earlier lived. (Courtesy Dearborn Historical Museum)

son died as an infant.[26] On July 30, 1863, a second son, Henry, was born in the Ahern household with no great fanfare. On September 26, 1863, about two months after Henry Ford's birth, a warranty deed was drawn, conveying Margaret O'Hearne's (sic) forty acres with the old cabin to William Ford and Mary, in consideration of $400. By the next year Patrick had reached age sixty, and his retirement was imminent. On Feb. 15,1864, Patrick Hern (sic) and Margaret Hern deeded the new house, together with the fifty-one acres on which it stood, to William Ford for $1,000. About three weeks later, March 7, 1864, William received $500 in return for a lease which granted Patrick O'Hearn (sic) and his wife Margaret this same property to be used, "for the term of their natural lives."[27] All accounts seem to indicate that this arrangement succeeded for all concerned.

At this point in time, the one year old Henry Ford, the future industrialist, is living in the house now owned by his mother and father, and shared by both foster grandparents. This is the year (1864) when Henry's grandfather, John Ford died; and his grandmother, you remember, had died at sea. So when Henry Ford later spoke of his grandfather or grandmother he was speaking of the Aherns. (The author uses this spelling because Henry Ford insisted in his interview with Ann Hood that "Ahern" was the correct spelling.)

William Ford was probably the typical hard-working, land-hungry farmer of those times. On June 7, 1865, William and Mary sold the forty acres on Joy Road, which William had bought in 1858 from his father for $600. This he sold to Jacob Esper for $2,500.[28] A $500 two-year mortgage from Esper and his wife to William Ford eased the transaction for Esper. With this money and some more, William was able on July 12, 1865, to buy eighty acres in Dearborn Township from George Moir for $4,000. This property is located at the northeast corner of Ford Road and Southfield. One week later, William Ford declared his intention to become a citizen of the United States.[29]

In a strangely worded legal document on March 26, 1867,[30] the forty acres where the original log cabin was built is now deeded by Patrick O'Hearne (sic) to "William and Mary, his wife, of the same place . . . for $400. . . ." "This Grant being of the same land devised by Margaret O'Hearne to said Mary before she was married to said Ford, and this deed is on consideration of the love and affection of said Grantor to said Grantees, it being expressly understood and agreed that said Grantor Patrick O'Hearne retains the full use and possession, occupancy, Rents and profits of said land during the life time of said Grantor." "This property is the sole property of said Margaret acquired before her marriage to her present Husband." Patrick's legal signature on this document was again his mark. This same property had been already deeded to the Fords by Margaret in Sept., 1863, but without the life occupancy agreement. Patrick now seems to be trying to recover some personal security from Margaret's forty acres, as he did from his own fifty-one acres in March, 1864. And even though Patrick had now deeded all of his and Margaret's property to William and Mary, he continued to pay the taxes which had risen to over $50/yr. in 1867.

On these tax receipts over the years, Patrick's name is spelled O'Hern, O'Heron, O'Herine, and O'Harron.[31]

In less than three years Margaret Ahern died. She was buried by William Ford in the Ford Cemetery, with a handsome obelisk marking her grave. The stone reads: Born 1786, Died Jan. 15,1870, Aged 84 yrs. Patrick is said to have revered Margaret, and to have kept her clothes neatly arranged in a closet for years after her death.[32]

William and Mary Ford now (1867) have all of the Ahern ninety-one acres, plus the eighty acres bought from Moir. In a short time these Fords are recognized as prosperous farmers. The 1876 Wayne County Atlas proudly depicts the "Farm Residence of William Ford, Esq., Springwell, Wayne Co., Mich." in its illustration section.

The year 1876, however, is the year that Mary (Litogot) Ford died on March 29, following childbirth. Son Henry was only thirteen. A cousin of Henry's (Jane Flaherty) came to keep house. His grandfather would mean even more to him now. Henry's father, William, was a good, quiet-speaking, hardworking man. He expected his eldest son to take an interest in the farm. However, Henry, a boy with vision, did not like farm work. This bothered his father, who is quoted as saying such things as, "Don't know what will become of him, just tinkers all night."[33]

Three years after his mother died, Henry, at sixteen, left home for the city. Grandfather Ahern stayed on the farm for another three years until his death in 1882. Patrick was buried in St. Alphonsus Church yard, Dearborn. The old church records[34] showed: "Patrick O'Hara died June 3, 1882, 83 years old. He was found improvidently dead in his bedchamber." The markings on the slab in the St. Alphonsus Cemetery were as follows: "Patrick O'Herin, Died June 1, 1882, Aged 84 yrs."

The fact that Patrick was a deserter from the British Army did not emerge until a few years before his death. It is said[35] that Patrick and William were in Detroit to buy fireworks for the Fourth of July, and William suggested going to the horse races in Windsor. Patrick didn't want to go, much to the consternation of William. William's insistence finally led to Patrick's explanation of why he was afraid of being apprehended by Canadian officials. So they came home to Dearborn without crossing the river.

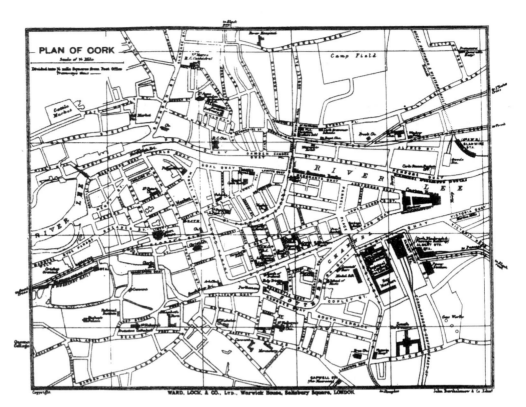

Map of the City of Cork, ca. 1910. Rev. O'Connor's St. Mary's Roman Catholic Cathedral and nearby Wolfe Tone Street, formerly known as Fair Lane, are located in the northwest section of Cork near the Cattle Market where Patrick's brother Cornelius is said to have worked.

Henry Ford later recalls his own youth in a short autobiographical sketch dated October 28, 1913:

I remember my father hauling wood and seeing the redhead woodpecker, swallows, bluebirds and robins. My grandfather told me the names of all these birds. My grandfather was my mother's foster father. He was born in Cork City, Ireland on the 17th of March, 1804. He came to this country about 1825. After my mother married here, my grandmother lived with my parents. She died in 1870 and he in 1881. I do not remember her very well, but I spent many happy days with him. When I was in Ireland in 1912, I went to the church in Cork and found the record of his birth. His name was Patrick Ahern.[36]

Henry Ford did indeed visit France, England, and Ireland during the summer of 1912, with Clara, Edsel, and Marvin Bryant in tow. This seems to have been a combined business and pleasure trip inasmuch as they were escorted much of the time by Mr. White of the Paris Branch, and Sir Percival Perry of the London Branch of Ford Motor Company. Clara Ford found the birthplace of her mother, Martha (Bench) Bryant on a street in Warwickshire, England.[37] In Ireland, Mr. Ford spent time in Bandon and Clonakilty as well as in Cork.[38] In Cork he conferred with Rev. C.C. O'Connor of St. Mary's Cathedral, Sunday's Well, and left a gift to the Sisters of the Assumption. Edsel's diary version of this same day is as follows:[39]

> August 10, 1912
> We arrived in Cork at 9.30 had breakfast at Metropole Hotel. Walked about town. Father walked off alone — waited for him until 11, then drove out to Blarney Castle saw some girls kiss the stone enough for me. Had lunch there, went to Bandon then to Clonakilty found Aunt Ann's house[40] took pictures saw church and school. Drove on through rain to Bantry Bay stayed at Vickery's Hotel — rather poor. Saw much bog, lots of peat.

This 1912 trip to Great Britain is thought to have been the impetus to a long and serious effort on the part of Mr. and Mrs. Ford to trace their ancestors.[41]

Correspondence from Rev. O'Connor began August 18, 1912, when the Reverend asked Mr. Ford for further information: "Can you let me know where your grandfather, Mr. Patrick Ahern was living in 1841? If he lived in Ireland, his name, as well as his age and parent's names will be found in the Census returns for that year. . ."

By October, 1912, Rev. O'Connor had located birth records of two Patrick Aherns: Patrick Ahern, son of Michael Ahern and Catherine Murphy, born March 13, 1804; and Patrick Ahern, son of Daniel Ahern and Catherine Neil, born March 17, 1804. It was some time before the Patrick of March 17 was established as the correct one. Rev. O'Connor stated that the Clerk would "be glad to get £1" for the search fee. The Reverend received £5 from Mr. Ford, "to use as your good judgement may direct." A newspaper clipping from O'Connor, with the heading "POOR CHIL-DREN'S EXCURSION" lists Henry Forde (per Rev. O'Connor) as donor of twenty shillings.

A letter from Henry Ford to Rev. O'Connor on November 23, 1912[42] includes the following paragraph which answers the Reverend's earlier inquiry:

> My grandfather, Patrick Ahern, lived here in Dearborn, Mich. in 1841, but sometime prior to that resided at Fair lane; and it would appear to me that if your clerk would institute a search among the Ahern families who resided there during earlier years, some trace of them might be found.

The Reverend replied on December 6, saying, "I shall certainly endeavor to do all I can to trace any members of the Ahern family that may still be living in or about Cork. Fair Lane is quite near this Cathedral, so there will be no difficulty in finding out if any of them are there or in the district around it."

In late December, 1912, advertisements appeared in the *News of the World,* the *Cork Examiner,* the *Irish Catholic,* and at least one London paper reading as follows:[43]

> INFORMATION WANTED
> Of the relatives of PATRICK AHERN, who resided at Fair Lane, Cork, about the years 1820-1840. He emigrated to America about the latter date, and lived at Dearborn, Michigan, in 1841.
> Any information which succeeds in locating them will be liberally rewarded. Apply to
> HENRY FORD, Ford Motor Co. Detroit, Michigan, U.S.A.

Letters responding to the advertisements were collected by Mr. E.G. Liebold, General Secretary to Mr. Ford, sorted and the most promising ones forwarded to Rev. O'Connor for further evaluation and follow-up. The majority of the letters, as might be expected, were from fortune hunters, thinking the name Ford meant that a very large reward, if not a legacy, was to be had. Lawyers insisted that their clients were relatives. Some respondents merely asked for a job, an automobile, or a little money, thinking they now knew how to reach Mr. Ford.

Rev. O'Connor was kept busy part time for two years on this project. One of his last letters seems to be in June, 1914. In it he says:

> I am sorry that we have not been able to locate Patrick Ahern; this, however, was perhaps only to be expected. It is a long cry from 1841 to 1912, and nothing having been committed to writing, it has proved

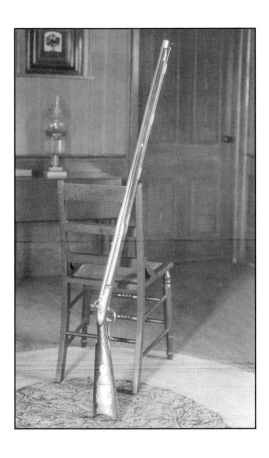

Patrick's muzzle-loading, double-barrel shotgun. Henry Ford remembered that the usual place for this gun was in Patrick's bedroom, leaning against the wall near the window. (188-7937)

practically impossible to say for certain who are now, in Cork, the living decendants of Patrick Ahern. But I agree with you in saying that "our efforts have been productive of some results.' To say the very least, it is probable — I am afraid I cannot say anything stronger — that Kate Ahern, Mrs. Barry, her sister, Mrs. McNamara and her sisters are true relations of Mr. Ford." (Letter addressed to Mr. Liebold).

It is quite obvious from this and earlier correspondence that Rev. O'Connor was never told that Patrick Ahern died in this country, and that Patrick Ahern was not Henry Ford's blood relative. Mrs. (Anne) Barry, who had answered the December 1912 advertisement, had indicated that she was the "oldest inhabitant living in Fair Lane." The information she had presented to Rev. O'Connor in an interview was considered by O'Connor as worthy of the reward offered by Mr. Ford. Rev. O'Connor suggested.[45]

Bits of information derived from the search initiated by Rev. O'Connor surfaced years later. The street called Fair Lane prior to Southern Ireland's independence is now named Wolfe Tone,

Patrick's bedroom in the William Ford home. Patrick lived with his adopted daughter and son-in-law from 1861 to 1882; from before Henry Ford's birth (1863) until Henry Ford left home (1879). (188-7920)

in honor of a leader of the Irish rebellion of 1798.[44] At an earlier time, Fair Lane was a nice residential section, later it became a poor neighborhood where the tinkers lived.[45] A certificate of marriage between a Timothy Ahern and an Eliza Ford, both of Cork, dated 1838, arrived at Ford's office in 1916. There is correspondence in 1926 with a Charles Ford of 2 Wolfe Tone Street, "late Fair Lane," Cork, who claimed relationship to both Fords and Aherns, and who sought work for his son in the new Cork Plant of Henry Ford & Son, Ltd.[46]

Mr. Ford personally acknowledged a Mrs. Katherine Gates of Maiden, Mass., as a niece of Patrick Ahern, and visited her in

March of 1924.[47] He also arranged to send her photographs of the old homestead in Michigan and the room occupied by Patrick. Quoting from a 1924 letter to Mrs. Gates, "One photograph shows his original gun and old clock. It was the custom in those days to carry the gun in and place it at the head of the bed each night. Another (photograph) gives a view of his dressing mirror, candlestick and old bible, all of which are original."

Mr. Ford's unusual fondness for his grandfather is evident in many ways. The meticulous attention given to Patrick's bedroom and his trusty shotgun in the restored homestead at Greenfield Village attests to a lingering love for his grandfather. And it is recorded that on the day of Henry Ford's death (April 7, 1947), "About 1:30 the chauffeur picked up Mr. Ford. They inspected the flood damage on the estate, at Greenfield Village, and in two cemeteries. Henry Ford wore his bedroom slippers — 'clodhoppers,' he called them — as he and Rankin (the chauffeur) plodded over the wet ground to inspect the Ahern tombstone at the Catholic Cemetery at Schaefer and Warren Roads, Then they returned to Fair Lane . . . ."[48] Henry Ford died at Fair Lane that evening.

Mr. and Mrs. Ford must have chosen the name for their stately new 1913–15 Dearborn home quite soon after the 1912 visit to Ireland and the section of Cork once known as Fair Lane. Mr. Ford, in particular, must have associated Fair Lane, Cork, with his cherished companion Patrick Ahern. It is not surprising, then, that Fair Lane became the name of the Dearborn estate which has now become a personal memorial to Henry and Clara Ford.

NOTES AND REFERENCES

1. Acc. 23, Henry Ford Office, Box 31, Ford Archives, Henry Ford Museum. Letters from Rev. C.C. O'Connor, St. Mary's Cathedral, Cork, Ireland (1912–1914).

2. *Ibid.*

3. Hood, Ann, "The Boy Henry Ford," unpublished manuscript dated April, 1940. Acc. 653, Ford Archives, Henry Ford Museum. Ann Hood was a pupil in the Edison Institute Schools, and one of Henry Ford's favorites. She managed to interview Henry Ford at length and thus obtain direct information of a personal nature which she recorded in this well written manuscript.

4. "Detroit Arsenal Funds" (7-31-1833) No. 24, Mechanics & Laborer's Wages. Reel 415, 17745, National Archives, Washington, D.C. (Copy located at Dearborn Historical Museum).

Patrick Ahern

5. Wayne County Land Tract Records, Liber 12, p. 86, Wayne County Register of Deeds, Detroit, Michigan. (S.W. $1/4$ of the SW. $1/4$, Section 7, Township 1 South, Range 11 East). On this deed to Margaret's property her name is spelled Stevenson. It is thought that John and Susan Stevenson may have been relatives of Margaret because the forty acres was sold without a profit and because a Susan Stevens was the only witness to Margaret's marriage which took place just a few days after the land transaction. Perhaps John was Margaret's brother. But henceforth Margaret's name appears as Stevens.

6. Acc. 940, Frank Hill Papers, Box 8, p. 70, Ford Archives, Henry Ford Museum. The marriage took place at St. Paul's in Detroit with Addison Searle, Rector.

7. Hood, Ann, op. cit. ref. 3.

8. Acc. 1, Fair Lane Papers, Box 1, Ford Archives, Henry Ford Museum. In a list of Scotch Settlement pupils, both "Fannie O'Heran" and "Mary O'Heran" are listed.

9. Ruddiman, Margaret (Ford), "Memories of My Brother Henry Ford," *Michigan History*, Michigan Historical Commission, Sept. 1953.

10. Litogot, Edward B., "Reminiscences," (Typescript) Acc. 65, No. 196. Ford Archives, Henry Ford Museum.

11. Mary (Litogot) Ford was an "acknowledged child" of the Aherns. There seem to be no records of legal adoption.

12. Acc. 1, Fair Lane Papers, Box 3, Ford Archives, Henry Ford Museum. These appear to be original documents warranting ownership of the Ahern-Ford homestead property.

13. Acc. 1, Fair Lane Papers, Box 4, Ford Archives, Henry Ford Museum.

14. *7th Census of the United States*, "1850 Census of Detroit and Wayne County Michigan, Vol. 1, (Dearborn Historical Museum).

15. Bryan, Ford R., "The Samuel Ford Family," *The Dearborn Historian*, Vol. 22, No. 4 (1982).

16. "Early Land Transfers, Detroit and Wayne County," Wayne County, Michigan Land Records, W.P.A. Vital Records Project, Michigan State Library & D.A.R. Louisa St. Clair Chapter (1940). "John Ford of Greenfield Twp. purchased from Henry Maybury of Detroit on Jan. 15, 1848 - W $1/2$ of SW. $1/4$ of Sec. 35, Twp. 1, S, Range 10 E" (County Records Vol. 32, p. 254).

17. Ruddiman, Margaret, op. cit. ref. 9.

18. Acc. 1, Fair Lane Papers, Box 1, Ford Archives, Henry Ford Museum. 1865 letter to William Ford from his brother, Henry, then prospecting in Idaho Territory.

19. Acc. 1, Box 3, op. cit. ref. 12.

20. Ruddiman, Margaret, op. cit. ref. 9.

21. Acc. 1, Box 3, op. ck. ref. 12.

22. *8th Census of the United States*, 1860 Census of Detroit and Wayne County Michigan, Vol. 19. (Dearborn Historical Museum).

23. Acc. 1, Fair Lane Papers, Box 12, Ford Archives, Henry Ford Museum. Letter of Certification signed by Edw. Dueroche, Missionary of the Congregation of St. Peter's Detroit.

24. Nevins, Allen, *Ford: The Times, The Man, The Company,* Charles Scribners Sons, New York, 1954. (Mr. Nevins differs with Margaret Ruddiman who said that the Fords were served their wedding supper in the new house.)

25. Litogot, Edward, op. cit. ref. 10.

26. Acc. 587, Ford Cemetery, Box 15, Ford Archives, Henry Ford Museum.

27. Acc. 1, Box 3, op. cit. ref. 12.

28. *Ibid.*

29. Acc. 1, Fair Lane Papers, Box 33, Ford Archives, Henry Ford Museum.

30. Acc. 1, Box 3, op. cit. ref. 12.

31. Acc. 1, Box 4, op. cit. ref. 13.

32. Ruddiman, Margaret, op. cit. ref. 9.

33. Author conversations with Miss Olive Ford, great granddaughter of John Ford, William Ford's father. (Dec. 29, 1980).

34. Acc. 23, Henry Ford Office, Box 30, Ford Archives, Henry Ford Museum. This information was collected in June, 1939, by R.H. Laird.

35. Hood, Ann, op. cit. ref. 3.

36. Acc. 1, Box 1, op. cit. ref. 8.

37. Acc. 889, Bryant Family History, Box 1, Ford Archives, Henry Ford Museum.

38. Henry Ford's grandfather, John Ford, had taken a life lease on twenty-three acres of land on the Madame Estate at Crohane near Clonakilty in 1819. Henry Ford's father, William (1826–1905) was quite likely born there. The family was forced to vacate the property in 1847.

39. Acc. 1, Fair Lane Papers, Box 31, Ford Archives, Henry Ford Museum.

40. Edsel Ford's Aunt Ann was most likely Anne (Nancy) Flaherty, younger sister of Henry Ford's father William. She was born near Clonakilty, Ireland, in 1834, and is identified in several photographs with Henry Ford at the Black Farm in 1911–12.

41. Ruddiman, Margaret, op. cit. ref. 9.

42. Acc. 23, Henry Ford Office, Box 31, op. cit. ref. 1.

43. *Ibid.*

44. O'Brien, Maire and Conor Cruise, *A Concise History of Ireland,* Beekman House, New York, ca. 1970.

45. Acc. 23, Henry Ford Office, Box 30, op. cit. ref. 34.

46. Acc. 23, Henry Ford Office, Box 31, op. cit. ref. 1.

47. *Ibid.*

48. Clancy, Louise and Davis, Florence, *The Believer,* Coward-McCann, Inc. New York, 1960. (Primary source: Rankin, Robert, "Reminiscences," Acc. 65, No. 4, Ford Archives, Henry Ford Museum.)

14
BEFORE FAIR LANE

Families, Farms, and Ford Activities at the
Fair Lane Site before the Mansion was Built

The Model-T automobile catapulted Henry Ford into a state of prosperity he had not known before. After having moved about Detroit from one rented flat to another for eighteen years, in 1908 he built a stately home for Clara, Edsel and himself at 66 Edison Avenue.[1] That same year, with his automobile business well on track, he was looking back to the farm and concentrating on the development of his gasoline tractor. He had by early 1909 already purchased more than a thousand acres in Dearborn Township near his boyhood home. Central to these purchases were the extensive Ten Eyck farmlands of over 800 acres, the adjoining Black Farm of 200 acres, and the 44-acre Degen Farm; the latter two properties bordering the north branch of the Rouge River.[2] This locality was well within sight of Henry and Clara's first home on the Moir Farm hardly a mile away, and within two miles of Henry's birth place.

The Ten Eyck home on Ann Arbor Trail just north of Chicago Road was at that time occupied by the Fred Gregory family. The Gregory-Ten Eyck connection provides a fascinating story. It seems that a Charles Gregory (1832–1870) came from England and operated the Saline Road (Michigan Avenue) tollgate near Trumbull Avenue in Detroit. He married Jane Whalen and in 1859 their first child, William, was born at the tollgate operated by his father.[3] The child was named William Ten Eyck Gregory because his mother and grandmother were good friends of Mrs. Conrad Ten Eyck of Dearborn. Later there were other children: Mary 1861, Fred 1865, and Edward 1869. The first earnings of William, at age five, were 50¢ obtained by driving a herd of cattle from the John Black farm out at Dearborn to a cattle yard in Detroit.

Eventually the Charles Gregory family moved to Dearborn, Charles becoming gardener and Jane housekeeper for the wealthy bachelor sons of Conrad (1782–1847) and Sarah (1794–1871) Ten Eyck. Jane also served as companion to Madame Ten Eyck who

The 1908 Edison Avenue home of the Henry Fords — first conspicuous evidence of Model-T profits. Close by on Glynn Court were built new homes for Clara's sister, Kate Richmond, and for Henry's sister, Margaret Ruddiman. These homes were all in the elegant Boston Boulevard-Second Avenue district, only about one mile south of the new Highland Park factory. (188-9282)

was widowed and becoming blind. It is said that often after supper, Charles and Jane would entertain themselves by walking down to the tollgate on Chicago Road and sitting on the porch with the people who ran it — Mr. and Mrs. James Cosbey, watching the people go through the tollgate and talking to the travelers.[5]

The sons, William and Charles Ten Eyck, had in 1858 built an elegant colonial home from which they managed about a thousand acres of Ten Eyck land. The older son, William Ten Eyck ("Uncle Billy," 1816–1899) never married, but his younger brother, Charles (1837–1894) in 1880 at age forty-three fell in love and married the exceptionally pretty Mary Gregory, their housekeeper's daughter who was nineteen. Charles and Mary had only one child, Jennie, who in turn became quite the darling of the premises. When Charles Ten Eyck died of typhoid in 1894, Mary's brother, Fred Gregory came back to Dearborn with his new family to look after Mary's estate. Thus the Gregorys figure prominently in Henry Ford's 1909 purchase of the Ten Eyck lands from Jennie (Ten Eyck) Ely and Mary (Ten Eyck) Boynton. Jennie had married Herbert Ely of Detroit, and her mother had been married again in 1904 to George H. Boynton. Both William and Fred Gregory would be later employed by Henry Ford as confidential land agents.

The Degen property purchased in 1909 from Anton (1841–1914) and Christina (Hollbach) Degen (1844–1919) bordered the Rouge River on the west side, providing about a half-mile of river frontage opposite the Black and Miller farms. (See 19th century map). The Degen children were married, and Anton

Pencil sketch (looking east) of Tollgate No. 3 located on Michigan Avenue at the intersection of Ann Arbor Trail which runs behind the house. After crossing Michigan, going west, Ann Arbor Trail leads to the Ten Eyck and Black farmhouses. The sketch was drawn by Orville H. Forster whose father was Superintendent of the Detroit & Saline Plank Road, and whose family at one time lived at the Tollgate. (188-8562)

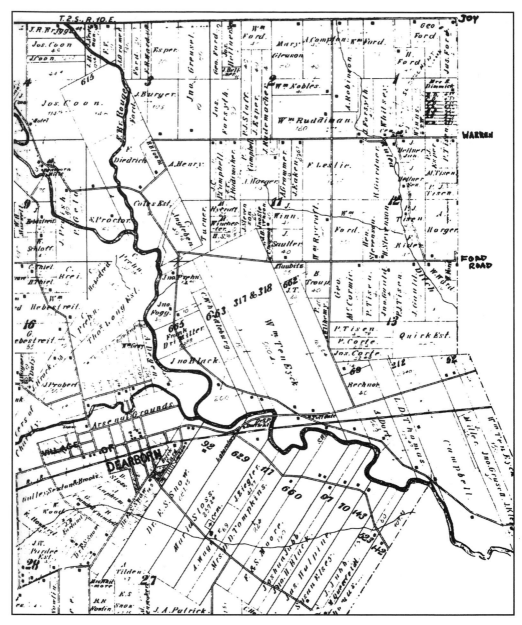

A map of the Dearborn area before the turn of the century, indicating only the Moir Farm (Ford and Southfield roads) belonging to Henry Ford's father, William. Ten Eyck, Black, and Degen properties were major among those acquired in 1909 for Ford Farms which later became Fair Lane Estate. (Map from files of Dearborn Historical Museum)

was no doubt ready to retire. Their home seems to have been located in Dearborn's present West Line district.

John and Alexina (McCallam) Black vacated their home when Mr. Ford bought their farm in July, 1909. John Black (1844–1914) was sixty-five years old and retiring from farming. He is described as having a "jolly face with red cheeks and a bushy beard, kind of curly." "He had a delightful Scotch accent, and so did Mrs. Black whose hair was in a 'cracker knot'."[6]

The Black farmhouse immediately became the "Ford Farms" operating headquarters occupied by Marvin Bryant (Manager) and Edgar LeRoy Bryant (Bookkeeper). They were Clara Ford's brothers. Edward L. Bryant, another brother of Clara, also worked there until his untimely death in 1913. Henry's cousin, Ester Flaherty, stayed at the house as housekeeper, and Alice Flaherty, another cousin, was a frequent helper. Although he tried, Henry Ford was unable to entice his father's widowed sister, "Aunt Nancy" Flaherty to make her home at the Black Farm.[7] Will Ford, Henry's youngest brother who then lived in Detroit and was in the farm implement business, became manager of the Farms about 1914, thus helping Henry with the testing and ultimately with the marketing of tractors. Will Ford's oldest son, Louis, also worked on the Farms testing tractors.

The lovely Ten Eyck home which became the residence of the Gregorys. Henry and Clara Ford occupied it while Fair Lane was being built, then had it torn down in 1917. (B-33855)

Fred Gregory and Jennie Ten Eyck in Jennie's pony cart near the Ten Eyck homestead about 1900. (B-33940)

The Fords, themselves, did not immediately occupy any of these newly purchased farmhouses.[8] Nor did they ever occupy the nearby William Ford homestead which Henry Ford had owned since 1902. Instead, a modest six-room California-style frame "Bungalow" or retreat was built in late 1909 on the west bank of the Rouge River opposite the Black Farm, on the property purchased from Anton Degen.[9] The Bungalow was located approximately where the Dearborn First Presbyterian Church stands today, and was there until after Mr. Ford's death in 1947. This isolated spot allowed the Fords to get away from the city on summer weekends, away from the prying public who were to greatly inhibit the Fords for the rest of their lives.

The heavily forested tract along the river offered not only a sheltered escape from the city but a prime animal and bird sanctuary as well. Mr. Ford loved birds and deer. One of his first acts upon owning this new property was to turn a number of deer loose into the "Deer Patch," a field of about ten acres surrounded by a ten-foot fence. A lane then led for some distance into another ten acres of woods called the "Deer Park." Mr. Ford treated some of the deer as pets, letting them run about as one might allow pet dogs. Billy, Fannie, and Bobby, for example would take sugar cubes from Henry's hand or from his coat pocket. Eventually, however,

Bobby became vicious and attacked Mr. Ford, knocking him to the ground and mauling him.[10] The deer herd was kept, nonetheless, for many years.

Mr. Ford's properties could easily be identified by his bird-houses. His grandfather, Patrick Ahern, had taught Henry the names of a great many birds so that he could cleverly imitate several bird calls. Henry would give bird identification books to the neighborhood children, hoping they too would take an interest in the birds. Mr. Ford at times had noticed broken eggs and little birds scattered on the ground. Suspecting it to be the mischief of red squirrels, he staged periodic red squirrel clean-ups on his properties. Other squirrels were apparently considered less destructive.[11] Davey Tree Surgeons were hired to care for the hundreds of acres of forest, and in many bare areas, additional trees were planted as shelter for the birds.

Mr. Ford sponsored a project with the Michigan Audubon Society, building 500 birdhouses and supplying special foods to induce flickers, bluebirds, goldfinches, cardinals and other species to remain all winter. Henry Ford was also active in promoting the Weekes-McLean Migratory Bird Bill which was passed by Congress in March of 1913. This bill gave the U.S. Department of Agriculture power to protect migratory and insectivorous birds from injury in their flights from one habitat to another.

Mr. Ford feeding deer in the "Deer Patch" at the Black Farm. (0-940)

One of the approximately one-hundred "capitol" birdhouses installed on Ford property in 1911. Each cost about $50, and were designed so that the house could be swung down for cleaning or repairs. (Photo from the Edward L. Bryant Collection) (B-40873)

Also in 1913, Mr. Ford made arrangements with the Shackleton Apiary in London, England, for the importation of 600 pair of English song-birds including chaffinches, larks, linnets, blackbirds, nuthatches, grosbeaks, warblers, thrushes, cardinals, jays, bluebirds and many, many more. Several hundred expensive birdhouses were placed over hundreds of acres of land. Feeding stations — suet cages with millet, sunflower seeds and cracked grain were hung in a multitude of places. Mr. Dye, a Shackleton ornithologist, accompanied the birds on the long trip across the ocean, attending the cages with food and water. Only three birds died on the trip. The birds were released on the grounds of the Black Farm before dawn of April 15, 1913. Henry Ford and Charlie Daniels, the local Dearborn game warden, witnessed the release. Newspapers described the Ford development as a "3,000-acre bird paradise." Mr. Dye stayed on the premises for several days to observe the adaptability of this homesick lot. It was quite disappointing that most of these birds soon vanished.

In the river near the Black farmhouse were the remnants of an old dam which had many, many years earlier supplied power for a grist mill. At this same location, contrary to professional advice,[12] Henry built a new dam and installed a generator to supply electricity to the farmhouse and the bungalow which was nearly a half-mile upstream. Along the way one could see robins in the winter at the electrically heated bird feeders. In only three years this dam and generator were torn out and replaced with the larger dam and twin turbine generators which are now there.

Henry Ford's prime objectives in owning extensive farmland during this period are thought to have been at least twofold. He first wanted to develop and test light-weight tractors to supplant horses on farms, and secondly he wanted to experiment with dairying and thus perhaps also rid farms of cows. Henry had an aversion to cattle — thought they were messy and stupid. He said he would never learn to milk a cow. "Don't ever learn to milk a cow and you'll never have to do it," he advised.[13]

Henry Ford was farming in 1906[14] when he was working the forty-acre Ford homestead which he had purchased in 1902, and the eighty-acre Moir Farm which his father had given him back in 1887. He is said to have been then experimenting with a large Avery steam tractor to pull a series of plows, although he owned a fine team of grays, "Dan" and "Ginny," and soon after another team, "Sadie" and "Stub."[15]

The "Square House" on the Moir Farm had been used somewhat as a summer house by the Fords prior to construction of the "Bungalow." Henry was then operating from that location what was called the "Butter Farm" where he had forty-four head of Jersey cattle and was producing 600 pounds of choice butter per week, which was delivered to Newman's store on Michigan Avenue. His dairy barn was a model of cleanliness. Men working in the barn wore white uniforms which were changed twice a day to be clean for each milking. One man in white was assigned to shoveling up droppings. It was asserted, however, that this immaculate dairy operation could not have been profitable.[16]

In late 1912, Henry Ford built a monster dairy barn, its attached twin silos located very near the Black Farm power house, the barn stretching eastward some 300 feet. Walls were constructed of glazed tile to the roofline. Designed to feed and house 156 head of Ayrshire cattle, provision had been made for waste con-

The Black farmhouse located on the east bank of the Rouge River where Fair Lane now stands. These farm buildings were torn down in 1914 to make way for Fair Lane construction. (B-37933)

veyors, milking machines, and refrigerated milk tanks. Mr. William Case, a graduate of Iowa State University, had been hired to manage the herd. The mammoth structure, largest of its kind in the State of Michigan, was dedicated on March 20, 1913. But on the very next day, a tornado lifted the entire roof of the barn and flattened it. No stock had yet been housed in the barn, so no casualties were inflicted; but passengers on the Michigan Avenue trolley line demanded the cars be slowed in order to view the spectacular wreckage.[17] The barn was not rebuilt. Mr. Ford had been planning to experiment with the production of powdered milk, the purification of milk using X-ray, and the possibility of synthesizing milk from plant products. These experiments were delayed but by no means abandoned.

The Ford gasoline tractor is said to have been under development as early as 1906. A still earlier but unsuccessful steam tractor purported to have been built by Henry Ford, cannot be substantiated. His first gasoline tractor, which he called his "automotive plow," utilized a 1905 Model-B automobile engine. The next, using a 1907 Ford Model-N engine, was probably also assembled at the Piquette Plant of Ford Motor Company and tested on the Ford homestead property. Later, several experimental Model-T tractors were built at Highland Park, somewhat to the annoyance of other Ford stockholders. It is said that as many as fifty different tractors were tested on the Black and Ten Eyck farms between 1909 and 1915.[18]

Henry Ford spent considerable time at the Black Farm and in the Village of Dearborn during this period of farm expansion. His accounts with Dearborn merchants show a number of farm-oriented purchases pertaining to wagons, harnesses, hand tools, feed, etc. Henry was known to pay his bills, but sometimes required considerable dunning. During this pre-Fair Lane period, Henry and Clara often drove from Detroit to the country to visit relatives and former neighbors. Mrs. Ford occasionally came to the farm with her "Detroit Electric" for eggs, butter, and dressed chicken. And she was sometimes stranded with a dead battery until Henry installed a charger at the Black Farm shops.

Before Fair Lane

Henry Ford with 1907 tractor powered by a Model-B engine. A Model-K Ford car is at right. (0-469)

When alone in a Model-T, Henry liked to drive fast. In going from the farm into Detroit, his dust could be seen a mile away as Henry raced up Reckner (Southfield), turning onto Bonaparte (Joy) heading east. At the Pere Marquette Railroad crossing, there was a sizeable rise in the road. Henry would hit this rise at full speed and fly through the air for a distance as much as fifteen feet before landing again on the road. This distance was witnessed and measured for Mr. Ford by his young cousin Earl Ford whose home was near the crossing and who was questioned each time by Henry as to how far the car had jumped that day. Earl was rewarded by being given an automobile ride down to the pasture lot to get his cows.[19]

Henry Ford with relatives in his Renault at the Black Farm in 1912. Left to right: Ester (Flaherty) McDonald, daughter of Nancy (Ford) Flaherty; Mrs. James Gardner, daughter of Nancy Flaherty; Nancy Flaherty, aunt of Henry Ford; Clara Ford; Henry Ford; Mr. James Gardner. Henry wanted his Aunt Nancy (his father's sister) to come and live at the Black Farm. Ester (standing), known as "Aunt Essie," lived at the Black Farm and worked as housekeeper. (0-6730)

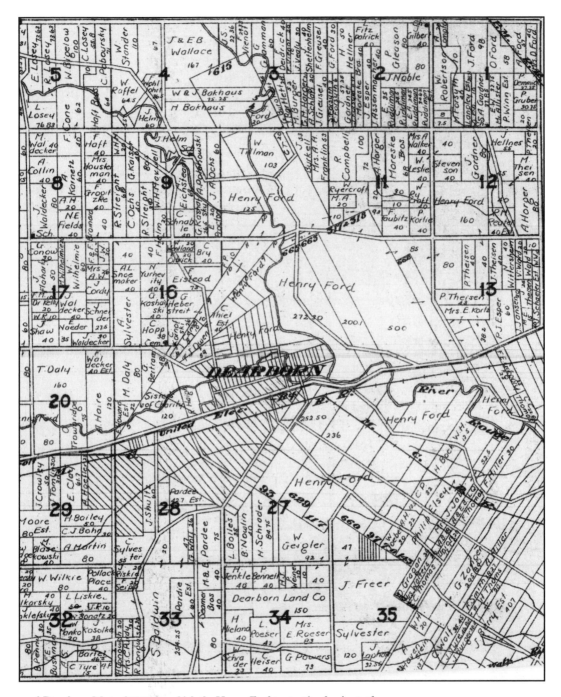

A Dearborn Map of 1915 in which the Henry Ford properties dominate the scene.
(D-1248)

Members of both Bryant and Ford families have indicated that Henry truly enjoyed taking them for rides in his early automobiles, and many photographs attest to this. He especially liked to take children for rides because they were not expecting big favors — even from Henry Ford. A ride in an automobile and perhaps a stop at Aggie Magoonaugh's Ice Cream Parlor in Dearborn were special treats to be remembered the rest of their lives.[20] And not infrequently, Henry would enjoy a walk out to the farms from Detroit, chatting with friends along the way. He often talked personally with neighboring farmers about selling their land to him. From some he couldn't buy, but many promised they would offer him first chance when they did sell, and remained loyal to that promise.[21]

Edsel Ford, a teen-ager, did not spend much time at the farms. He is said to have occasionally driven out from Detroit in a stylish, custom-built sports car. But Henry and Clara liked their Dearborn retreat well enough to decide to make Dearborn their primary home rather than Grosse Pointe where other wealthy Detroiters lived. By 1914, after only five years at their Edison Avenue home, the situation became intolerable due to people clamoring for five-dollar-a-day jobs. A move away from that location was imperative. The Gregorys were asked to vacate the Ten Eyck house to permit the Fords to move in. Correspondence at that time reveals some impatience on the part of the Fords regarding delays in getting possession of the house. With a minimum of remodeling the Fords moved into the Ten Eyck home as a temporary residence for the next two years. (The house had been equipped with furnace, bath and electric lights in 1912.) The buildings on the Black Farm were quickly leveled to provide a new homesite, and the spacious, 56-room Fair Lane residence immediately begun.[22] Two years after the completion of Fair Lane, the lovely old Ten Eyck homestead was demolished. Henry Ford had apparently not yet envisioned his Greenfield Village.

NOTES AND REFERENCES

1. Folsom, Richard, "Ford Residences," unpublished manuscript on file in Dearborn Historical Museum, 1983.

2. From Accession 62, Box 108, Edison Institute Archives. "549.68 acres, land located in P.C. 317, 318 & 662, purchased from Michigan Avenue Land Company, Jennie (Ten Eyck) Ely, and Mary (Ten Eyck) Boynton (part of Ten Eyck Farm), Jan.19, 1909 — cost $95,924."

"175 acres, the Easterly part of P.C. 663 lying between the River Rouge and rear claim in Dearborn T.2 S, R 10 E purchased from Jennie (Ten Eyck) Ely, Jan. 19, 1909 — cost $40,000."

"93.47 acres, P.C. 662, part of the Ten Eyck Farm between River Rouge and Michigan Avenue except MCRR right-of-way purchased from Strathern & Hendrie, April 5, 1909 — cost $23,367. 50."

"Lot 12 of the Subdivision of that part of the Military Reserve O'Flynn & McReynolds Subdivision, 43.85 acres known as the Degen Farm, purchased May 7, 1909 from Anton Degen and John Halvach in Village and Township of Dearborn — cost $6,577.50." (This is land upon which the "Bungalow" was built.)

"200 acres part of P.C. 663 & 665 purchased July 12, 1909 from John Black — cost $40,000." (This is land upon which Fair Lane Mansion is located.)

"Lot 145 of Detroit Arsenal Grounds, Village of Dearborn, 6.18 acres purchased July 12,1909 from John Black — cost $1,200." (This land is directly across the river from Fair Lane Mansion.)

"53.83 acres in P.C. 665 purchased March 13, 1909 from the heirs of Fritz Drey Miller — cost $6,000."

"60 acres in P.C. 663 known as the Moxon Farm, or the Weedleburg Farm, purchased from Emma Moxon April 2, 1909 — cost $6,000."

"45.33 acres, part of the Westerly part of the Northerly part of P.C. 665, between River Rouge and Plymouth Road, known as the John Fogg place, purchased April 15, 1909 from the heirs of Wm. W. Lovett — cost $6,680.97."

(Records for the period 1908–1915 show a total of approximately 125 land transactions involving about 5,000 acres in Dearborn Township.)

3. Arneson, Winfield, Dearborn Founders Series #47, Dec. 27, 1967.

4. Will of Conrad Ten Eyck, Liber 21, p.172, Wayne County Public Records, dated April 4, 1846.

5. Reminiscences of Mrs. Mary Louise Gregory Brand, daughter of Fred Gregory, Acc. 65, Edison Institute Archives.

6. *Ibid.*

7. Reminiscences of Mrs. Ester (Gardner) Davis, granddaughter of Nancy (Ford) Flaherty, Acc. 65, Edison Institute Archives.

8. The Ten Eyck home was occupied by the Fords during 1914–1915 while Fair Lane was being constructed, and 66 Edison was essentially under seige.

9. The "Bungalow" was a two-story, lap-sided building with brick foundation, wood shingle roofing, pine trim, pine finished interior with oak floors and natural fireplace. There were three rooms and lavatory on the first floor, and three rooms and bath on the second floor. The demise of the "Bungalow" seems not to be documented.

10. Reminiscences of Mr. A.G. Wolfe, son of Bert Wolfe, manager of the "Butter Farm," Acc. 65, Edison Institute Archives. (Mr. Ford disliked cats and was not especially fond of dogs.)

11. See Reference 5.

12. Henry Ford had in April, 1910, engaged Prof. Gardner S. Williams of the University of Michigan, Civil Engineering Department, to advise concerning the feasibility of water power at this location. Prof William's reply: "After an examination on the grounds, I became convinced from the smallness of the fall and the character of the location in general that the development of a water power plant would be an extremely expensive proposition for what the output would be."

13. See Reference 7.

14. "Henry Ford is threshing 70 acres of oats," *Dearborn Independent,* August 10, 1906.

15. See Reference 10.

16. *Ibid.*

17. *Dearborn Independent,* March 21, 1913.

18. Information from Edward L. Bryant notes.

19. Taped interview with Mr. Earl Ford, Archives, The Edison Institute Archives.

20. Reminiscences of Burnham Ford, Acc. 65, Box 27, Edison Institute Archives.

21. See Reference 7.

22. Reminiscences of Charles Voorhess, Electrical Engineer for Mr. Ford at Fair Lane, Acc. 65, Edison Institute Archives. (The Black farmhouse is said to have been approximately where the circular drive to Fair Lane is now located, and a hog pen was situated on the site of the present residence.)

15

A GLIMPSE OF FAIR LANE

A Short, Largely Pictorial Description of the Mansion, ca. 1920

Henry and Clara Ford had many homes during their lifetime, but none as permanent nor as elaborate as Fair Lane in Dearborn. Although they themselves had designed and built their honeymoon cottage, the small frame "Square House," in 1889 from lumber off the farm given to Henry by his father, Clara was soon

An aerial view of the mansion (left), and powerhouse (right) on the Rouge River in 1923. (0-2457)

coaxed to leave it for the city where Henry preferred to work. At the time they moved to the city (1891), Henry bought a residential lot in a Detroit subdivision, presumably with the intent of building a home. The lot was sold two years later. For nearly

twenty years, Clara kept moving from one rented dwelling to another — some ten in all[1] before they built their own home at 66 Edison Avenue in Detroit.

This spacious residence on Edison in 1909 was very appropriate to their station of newly acquired wealth, large enough for the family of three, and convenient to Henry's factories at Highland Park. But when Henry Ford began to offer the unheard of $5-per-day wage to his thousands of workers, he found he needed added protection from the mobs of employment seekers and from solicitors of every sort who were now fully aware that the Fords were ultra-generous multi-millionaires.

For seclusion, the Fords seriously considered following other wealthy Detroiters to Grosse Pointe, east of Detroit. But the little "Bungalow," the summer retreat they had built in 1909 on the Rouge River in Dearborn, appealed to both Henry and Clara to

Above: Clara's rose garden in the summer of 1927. (0-7168)

Opposite top: Front view of Fair Lane in March, 1916. (0-7170)

Opposite middle: River view of Fair Lane in March, 1916. (0-7169)

Opposite bottom: A lazy mid-summer afternoon at Fair Lane, about 1927. The cave-like entrance to Clara's boathouse is seen at the water's edge, far left. (0-130)

the extent that they decided to forsake Grosse Pointe and build their main house very close by the Bungalow on the same restful stream.[2]

In July, 1913,[3] word was out that Henry Ford was about to build a "Marble Mansion" on the Rouge. Henry denied that it would be a mansion, but conceded that he was moving to Dearborn and might spend about $100,000 on a new home. The Fords had engaged the firm of Van Holst & Fyfe, Chicago architects, who had inherited much of the business of Frank Lloyd Wright, so an element of "Prairie School" architecture was introduced.[4]

The Van Holst people were working on footings and foundations when Henry Ford noticed that they were extravagant in their use of materials, and that costs were likely to be excessive. He therefore dismissed the Van Holst concern and engaged the building contractor William H. Van Tine of Pittsburgh. Designs were modified somewhat and work was again underway in early 1914. Marblehead limestone from Ohio was unloaded at the Tractor

Plant[5] and hauled by steam traction engine to the riverside building site where stone cutters and masons went to work.

The house was to contain 31,770 square feet of floor space, bowling alley, field room, kitchen, service and storage rooms, divided into fifty-six rooms. Included were swimming pool, seven bedrooms and fifteen baths. The swimming pool and bowling alley were without a doubt amenities dear to the heart of their twenty-one-year-old son Edsel, as was the par-3 golf fairway outside. The building's gray outer walls eighteen to twenty-four inches thick and inner partitions averaging fourteen inches thick,[6] together with heavy carved oak interior trim and many massive fireplaces, presented a somewhat forbidding atmosphere — some might say oppressive. The Fords later had some of the dark interior paneling painted in light colors, and were inclined to favor use of rooms well lighted by outside windows.

Along with building the house, Henry was also constructing a new and larger dam and powerhouse. The powerhouse at the river's edge was a four-storied structure built of the same limestone block as the mansion at a cost of approximately $250,000. Thomas Edison, Ford's close friend, dedicated the powerhouse on August 26, 1914. Two water-driven turbines on vertical shafts turned electric generators to produce 110 kilowatts of electricity. From the powerhouse, private systems of electricity, telephone, steam, compressed air, hot, cold and refrigerated water were carried through a 300-foot tunnel to the mansion. These systems were completely independent of public utilities. Also housed in the powerhouse were a 12-car garage and a research laboratory. The powerhouse was Henry's domain while Clara managed the mansion.

All was essentially finished by November of 1915, after considerable landscaping of river banks, construction of gatehouse,

A Glimpse of Fair Lane

Front view of Fair Lane in 1951, after both Henry and Clara had died. (833-101694)

servants' cottages, pony barns, peacock and chicken houses, green house, boat house, etc. All is estimated to have cost in the neighborhood of $3 million. Mr. and Mrs. Ford, with Edsel, moved into their new home in January, 1916. Edsel did not stay long in Dearborn however, but married Eleanor Clay in November, 1916, and moved to the Grosse Pointe area close to his school chums. Henry and Clara occupied Fair Lane with their few servants for thirty-one years — Clara's living in the house three years after Henry's death in 1947.

Fair Lane promised to be an especially convenient homesite for Henry, then a man of fifty-two. It would be within five miles of his greatest creation — the mammoth Rouge Manufacturing Plant. And Fair Lane would be hardly a mile from his new Experimental Engineering Laboratory and Early American Museum and Village.

Clara's principal interest seemed to be her acres of gardens — the peony garden, iris garden, blue garden, rock garden, trail garden and nearly three acres of roses. She is said to have had 12,000 rose bushes of 300 varieties. When she invited groups to visit, it was usually to show the roses. Clara's friends and relatives were quite welcome at the mansion, but Henry usually met his elsewhere. The noted landscape architect, Jens Jensen, was employed to design portions of the 1,369-acre estate, although Clara is thought to have finalized most landscaping decisions. Henry's deer park, bird houses, maple sugar and private tree house were destined for oblivion, as eventually was Clara's rose garden. But we are still apprised of Jensen's Meadow."

The Fords were not adverse to leaving Fair Lane frequently and sometimes for prolonged periods. They occupied a winter home for years in Fort Myers, Florida, next door to their friends the Edisons. After the death of Thomas Edison in 1931, the Fords' winter home became the southern-style mansion at Ways, Georgia.[7] Summers often found them at Big Bay on cool Lake Superior or on their yacht *Sialia*. And the private railroad car *Fair Lane* served them on frequent vacation as well as business trips.

Fair Lane is now a sixty-acre property of the University of Michigan (Dearborn Campus). Although designated a "Conference Center," one gets the impression that it also serves as a "Faculty Club." The swimming pool is now converted to an attractive public dining room served by a student staff, and interesting tours of both powerhouse and mansion are conducted daily for a nominal fee by dedicated volunteer guides. Restoration of both buildings and furnishings to their 1920 condition is the object of an on-going program.

REFERENCES

1. Folsom, Richard, "Ford Residences," unpublished manuscript on file at Dearborn Historical Museum (1983).

2. Bryan, Ford R., "Before Fair Lane," Dearborn Historian, Vol. 26, No. 3, 1986.

3. *Detroit News Tribune,* July 13, 1913

4. Howcroft, Susan A., "Fair Lane, Henry Ford's Estate," unpublished paper, 14 pages, University of Michigan (no date).

5. Bryan, Ford R., "Henry Ford & Son—Tractors," *Dearborn Historian,* Vol. 42, No. 2, 2002.

6. "Fair Lane Fact Sheet," Ford News Department, Ford Motor Co., (1956).

7. Bryan, Ford R., "Henry Ford's Experiment at Richmond Hill," *Dearborn Historian,* Vol. 24, No. 4,1984,

16
CHILDREN AT FAIR LANE

Henry II and Benson Gardening, Henry Plays Santa Claus

When Henry and Clara Ford moved into their new Dearborn mansion, Fair Lane, in early 1916, their only child was Edsel, age twenty-one. Several features of this new home were designed especially for Edsel. These included a billiard room, an inside swimming pool, a bowling alley, and a three-hole golf course. None of these features was used by Henry and Clara by themselves. Edsel had attended the exclusive Detroit University School in downtown Detroit, and many of his best friends were from the Grosse Pointe area, a wealthy district on the opposite side of the city. Edsel did not spend much time in Dearborn, and it was less than a year before Edsel married the comely Eleanor Clay of Detroit and moved several miles across the city from Dearborn. So when we speak of the children at Fair Lane, we are speaking almost exclusively of Edsel and Eleanor's four children, Clara's nieces and nephews, and groups of children occasionally invited from Henry Ford's Greenfield Village Schools.

When Edsel's children, Henry II, Benson, Josephine, and William were small, Henry Ford enticed them to Fair Lane with all manner of attractions which might have been considered a bit old-fashioned for the times. For summer, there were swings and a playground slide, a playhouse with large sandbox, pony-carts and wagons, a treehouse, and a small farm lot with a vegetable garden of their own. For winter fun there were toboggans and a toboggan slide, a small horse-drawn cutter, a warm skating house on a large pond, a Santa's Workshop filled with toys, a Maple Sugar House; and no doubt more. Of what else could one think?

All sorts of pets inhabited the spacious premises — chickens, peahens, peacocks, rabbits, pigs, goats, deer, and ponies — a veritable menagerie. These animals had their proper permanent housing, but were available to amuse the children whenever called upon. But cats were scarce. Henry Ford did not appreciate cats.

Preparing a Fair Lane garden plot, Henry II at age four becomes a willing worker as his grandfather looks on. Benson, age two, does not seem to take the project seriously.
(0-889)

There was usually a dog, but Henry was not particularly fond of dogs either — especially the barking kind. Live cows were far too messy, and were kept at the Dairy Farm almost a mile away. The ponies, however, were kept at Fair Lane.

As Edsel's children grew older, the attractions became even more elaborate — scaled-down automobiles, a miniature farm yard with house, barn, and small-scale working steam engine, water wagon and grain harvesting equipment. Eleanor, their mother, was inclined to complain that the children were at Fair Lane too much. From about 1920 when grandson Henry was three, until perhaps ten years later when these children began to enter their teens, Fair Lane seems to have held their interest.

The children were always with an attendant. The safety of the Ford children was always a worry to the parents and grandparents. There was always the threat of kidnapping. Chauffeurs, often

Top: Henry II and Benson, with their pony, have dragged the ground and now begin seeding. Benson appears especially intent on the work at hand — perhaps more enthusiastic about farming than ever again. (0-1139)

Bottom: Pitching hay onto their small haywagon, Henry II learns to handle a 3-tine pitchfork, while Benson, on top of the load, watches the team. The ponies are obviously well behaved. This hay will be taken to their small barn nearby. (0-682)

Children at Fair Lane

armed, brought the Ford children from their Grosse Pointe home, and frequently acted as guards during the children's stay at Fair Lane. And from the number of still photographs and movies of the children that abound, there must often have been a photographer close at hand.

However, it appears that Edsel's children were seldom at Fair Lane as teenagers. They had outgrown the offerings of their grandparents, and had now been provided with new and lavish entertainment facilities at their new and more elegant home at Grosse Pointe Shores on Lake St. Clair. There is a feeling that the Grosse Pointe people may have looked down a bit at the Dearborn Fords because of their relatively simple and perhaps out-dated lifestyle. On the other hand, the Dearborn Fords abhorred the extravagant and seemingly frivolous activities prevalent on the other side of town.

On a warm early summer afternoon in 1923, Henry II and Benson pose with Henry and Clara in front of Clara's peony garden at Fair Lane. (0-5443)

This boy-sized steam engine is connected by belt to the grain separator in the barn. It is April 30, 1927. From left to right are Frances Bryant, Robert Bryant, Betty Bryant, Benson Ford, and Henry Ford II who is at the controls. (0-7601)

But Henry Ford now had his Greenfield Village children to please and to enjoy. The Village Schools had been started in 1929 with classes from first to eighth grade. These fortunate pupils, with the entire Ford Museum and Greenfield Village as their private playground, classroom and workshop, thus became recipients of Henry and Clara's love and generosity. Both Henry and Clara were very fond of children, although Henry was inclined to demonstrate his fondness more openly.

Nothing was too costly for the students at Greenfield Village which was less than a mile from Fair Lane. A chapel, a theatre, a ballroom and dance orchestra, laboratories, workshops, radio station, riding stables — this was a $10,000,000 investment — all for a very limited number of children. (Henry Ford Museum and Greenfield Village was not originally intended to be open to the public as it is now.) Several of Henry and Clara's nieces and nephews attended these Edison Institute Schools, along with other

Henry Ford II (in center) feeds loose grain into separator. Behind him in the dust stand Frances Bryant. At the far left is John Dahlinger holding a mouse — an object of scorn. Behind John is Betty Bryant. At the far right is Robert Bryant. (0-7602)

The younger grandchildren of the Fords, Josephine and William, here with Clara, are dressed as Tyrolese peasants on this February 1932 occasion in the gathering room at Fair Lane. (0-7603)

212

Outside Santa's Workshop, a group of Greenfield Village children gather in the snow beside the Christmas tree, holding their gifts presented to them by Henry Ford. Henry, in his Santa costume, stands in the background. This photograph, taken on December 19, 1946, was Henry's last appearance as Santa. He died the following April at age eighty-three. (188-74407)

Dearborn children from homes of average income. And it became commonplace for graduates of Edison Institute High School to receive a Ford car from Henry as a graduation present.

Henry and Clara visited the Village regularly to meet and be with the children, but on special occasions, such as Christmas time, the children of the Village were taken by horse and sleigh or haywagon to Fair Lane where they met Santa Claus in Santa's Workshop, and received presents from Mr. Ford dressed as Santa. As Santa, Henry would hand out toys — dolls, model trains, autos, toy animals, candy, and plenty of fancy fruit for everybody. He did

213

not condone toys of a military nature. There was always an ornately decorated tree, reindeer with sleigh, and Christmas music during the holiday season. In springtime, pupils from the schools were brought to the Fair Lane Sugar House where maple sap was cooked down to syrup and sugar.

Henry is said to have played Santa to children for over fifty years — from 1895 when his son Edsel was two, until the Christmas of 1946, just four months before he died. His guests had included children of neighbors, his nieces and nephews, his grandchildren, and lastly the children of the Greenfield Village Schools.

So from one lone son (Edsel) at Fair Lane in 1915, Henry and Clara Ford enlarged the number of their young guests to a dozen or so in the 1920s, and finally to literally hundreds more with their informal adoption and entertainment of the Village school children beginning in 1929. Thus children certainly played a major role in the life of the Fords at Fair Lane.

17
OLD-FASHIONED HARVESTING

Henry Ford's Collection and Demonstration of Antique Farming Equipment on Neighborhood Farms

Once sufficient land had been cleared for farms in lower Michigan, the typical farmer devoted the bulk of his acreage to such crops as wheat, oats, barley, rye, corn, and timothy hay. These crops were all marketable, but some were retained for the livestock — these included oats and hay for the horses and corn fodder for the cattle. The market price of the grains largely determined the farmer's cash income for the year; while a variety of other home products from the sugar bush, the orchard, the vegetable garden as well as an abundance of beef, pork, mutton, butter and eggs, all bolstered the family standard of living. On a farm of this sort, there was food for all and work for all. As to the work, a farmer of that period once lamented, "It seems I've been milking and spreading manure from the day I was born."

Farmers in Dearborn were no different. They too were largely general farmers. Dairy farms, which later became so commonplace, did not exist as such before refrigeration and rapid transportation made it possible to truck fresh milk into the cities. The early farmer had to make butter from his souring milk, and people kept cows in the city. To the general farmer, the harvesting of grain was the principal event of the year. There were no monthly milk checks.

We'll start this story back in 1881 when James (Jack) Gleason, a farmer on Bonaparte (Joy Road) between Evergreen and Recknor (Southfield), bought a 10 h.p., 225 rpm horse-drawn, Westinghouse, portable steam engine to power his grain separator. As most farmers would, he had some trouble operating the thing and called upon the neighborhood mechanic, "Lyin' Hank"[1] to make the thing run properly. This Hank Ford learned to love this little steam engine, as well as Gleason's pretty daughter, Christine[2],

215

and almost begged to operate the engine all summer for far less than a pittance. He operated it so well all around the neighborhood,[3] that the Westinghouse people hired him to service their machines in all southern Michigan for upwards of a full pittance.

Years later, after Henry had married Clara, gone to the city and made his fortune, he came back to the old neighborhood in 1908 to revolutionize farming with a gasoline tractor. To do this he was collecting and researching old as well as new farm machinery. And Henry had not forgotten Mr. Gleason and the little Westinghouse No. 345 he had once so admired. But lo, he found from the now elder Mr. Gleason that the little engine had been sold twenty years earlier and its whereabouts were completely unknown.

But Mr. Ford was now well acquainted with Mr. Westinghouse, himself, and there was little trouble initiating a joint effort to find what, if anything, was left of the old engine. "I will trace it to the melting pot if necessary" said Mr. Ford. This search went on during much of the year 1913. On Westinghouse records the engine had changed hands several times and had been rebuilt twice

Edward Hendry standing on a ten (count 'em) horsepower sweep. A driveshaft ran from the center of the sweep to the grain separator in the barn. This machine was the property of Henry Ford who in the mid 1920's demonstrated old-fashioned threshing methods on his own farms and those of his neighbors. (B-35528)

Top: An early grain separator used by Henry Ford on Dearborn farms to demonstrate how threshing was done during his boyhood. (188-6469)

Bottom: The 1881 Westinghouse Portable Steam Engine located in Pennsylvania and rebuilt by Westinghouse in 1913 for Henry Ford. Henry liked this engine because it was about half the weight of other engines of like horsepower, and required much less fuel due to its efficient boiler configuration. (188-6470)

While others — Jim Kennedy and Milton Bryant — stand and talk to James Gleason (with white beard), Henry has put his coat and hat on the water wagon and is stoking the engine. This little engine which Henry operated for Gleason in 1882 is now in the Ford Museum. (B-35303)

at their factory. Finally, an engine with "No. 345" fastened to its boiler was located on a farm near Edinboro, Pennsylvania. The farmer, Mr. C.R. Hayes, was paid $200 for it, and Westinghouse again rebuilt it to Mr. Ford's specifications for an additional $445.[4]

A concurrent episode is described quite adequately by Earl Ford,[5] a Dearborn farmer in his own right. During the summer of 1913 or shortly after, as Henry Ford drove by the farm of his cousin John N. Ford on Joy Road in Dearborn; Henry spotted an old Ypsilanti Steam Works "Monitor" portable engine of 1890 vintage, which had sat in the farmyard until a good-sized sapling had grown up between the spokes of one of its wheels. Henry asked John if he could have the engine since it was old and rusty — and jokingly said he would give a new hat for it. Henry was given the engine and, sure enough, a few days later John received a large hat box with an expensive high hat in it. But when John's son, Earl, asked his father what he was going to do with the hat, John's response was, "I wouldn't wear that damn thing milking cows." Some days later, Henry, again driving by, asked Earl how his father liked his new hat; and Earl answered quite honestly, "Dad says he wouldn't wear that damn hat to milk the cows." To that, Henry drove off down the road with great guffaws of laughter.

To Henry, the hat was merely a joke. Soon, John was to receive in exchange for his old engine, the use of a like-new Westinghouse steam engine in bright nickel trim. This was the rebuilt engine Henry had operated in his youth for Jack Gleason. Henry loved to operate this engine, and arranged to have it at John's farm to be used for neighborhood threshing bees. Eventually this same Westinghouse No. 345 was placed in the Henry Ford Museum.[6]

Henry has the draft wide open on his little Westinghouse as he fills the firebox with wood. There'll be plenty of steam for blowing the whistle as well as threshing grain. (0-1658)

The threshing bees mentioned by Earl Ford must have begun as early as 1913, when photographs show Henry Ford employees such as Ray Dahlinger eating at the John N. Ford threshing table. Later photographs, 1922–1923, show Henry, himself, much involved in the harvesting activities. Emma Ford, John's daughter,[7] relates that one evening when the Westinghouse was being moved into their farmyard, the door on the firepot had been broken and Ray Dahlinger had hastily scheduled overnight repairs so that Henry would not know of the accident. That night, lights of a car were seen in the back lane, and there was fear that Henry had found out. The next morning Henry arrived very early, inspected the engine, felt the firepot and said, "Hmm, fresh paint!"

Harvestors eat at the dining table of John N. Ford in October, 1913. John and his wife, Mary, are standing at the far corner of the room. Myrtle, their daughter, stands at the door. Seated from left, 1) Earl Ford, 3) Edgar Johnson (Henry Ford's cook at the Black Farm), 5) Dick Wright, 6) Will Ford, 7) Ed Vokers, 8) Pete Theisen, 9) Henry Ford, brother of Will, 10 & 11) Laird boys, 12) Clyde Ford, 13) Ralph Ford, leaning forward; extreme right Ray Dahlinger. (B-35297)

Neighborhood crew with their wives are served a noon meal from the "chuck truck" during corn harvesting at Dilly Ford's place about 1923. The Lincoln sedan which brought the women is just visible between the corncrib and barn. Dilly had been the widow of James Ford since 1902. Henry helped her with farming, and soon after this picture was taken bought her farm which was located on the southwest corner of Joy and Greenfield Roads. (Photo from the Orla H. Ford Collection)

Aside from the pictures presented, herewith, the most adequate and concise description of these harvesting bees is that given by Orla Ford[8] whose father, James, participated with the threshing crews.

During the 1920s, Henry Ford worked thousands of acres of farm land, raising wheat, corn, soybeans, and vegetables. In the Dearborn vicinity, his farm manager, Mr. Ray Dahlinger, scheduled harvesting crews on the Ford properties, and also at additional farms designated by Mr. Ford. These additional farms were those of old-time friends, neighbors, and relatives. On the day scheduled, the Ford farm crew would move in its harvesting equip-

Some of Henry's old friends shed their coats and put on a demonstration of threshing grain by means of "flails," at the Michigan State Fair (1922). (833-33321)

ment — steam traction engine, separator, wagons, and tractors or teams as necessary to get the job done. He also sent a cook with chuck-truck to prepare the noon meal for the crew and neighboring farmers. Just before the meal, a limousine was sent to the various nearby farms to pick up wives of the working crew, and they too were treated to the same hearty meal. Henry would often be there at that time to meet his friends. Henry Ford was especially fond of observing the operation of his steam traction engines used to harvest grain.

Orla's collection of pictures, given to him by his father, verifies his description of the proceedings. Henry Ford was basically a farmer and felt most at ease with rural people. He liked to volunteer help to people who were trying their best. The old-fashioned harvesting bees provided enjoyment to him and offered a means of helping his friends. These friends and relatives knew better than to ask Henry for money. John N. Ford ("Big John," there were five John Fords in the community) was paying off a mortgage most of

222

his farming days, but he would never accept money from Henry. As a result, according to his son, Earl, John and Henry were always on the best of terms.

William Ford, Jr., youngest brother of Henry and also very mechanically inclined, provided steam-powered threshing service to Dearborn farmers, including his brother, Henry, during 1911–1913. William then went to work full time for Henry on the Ford Farms — Henry's buying Will's equipment.[9] John Ford, Henry's other brother, also operated a steam-driven threshing rig when he was farming his Chase Road property. But the brothers could not afford to indulge in all that antique equipment. It was Henry who left us a most astonishing accumulation of solid, tangible evidence of farming's nostalgic past — prominently displayed in the northwest corner of his marvelous museum. Right here in Dearborn is quite likely the most complete historical collection of farm harvesting equipment in the world.

Henry Ford celebrates his 60th birthday with neighborhood cronies at his Dearborn homestead, Ford and Greenfield roads, July 30, 1923. Standing: William Streeter, Jr., John Ford (Henry's brother), Fred Gleason, Charles Ward, Jim Ford, H. F. Brand, Alex Ford, Emil Morrell, Harvey Ford, John Bryant. Sitting: Charles Reynolds, Henry Ford, George Troop, Jim Gleason, George Ford, Sam Ford, Jim Kennedy, William McFarlane, William Streeter, Sr. (0-1459)

THE STORY OF DAVID YOUNG

The following letter is from Henry Ford's correspondence files

McGregor, Ia.
1-21-1917

Mr. Henry Ford
Detroit, Mich.

Dear Friend.

You will no doubt be surprised when you read this and know who it is from. I have been keeping tab on you for the last ten or twelve years and have planned a good many times to come and see you. There is not a man living that I would rather see.

You will remember me when I say that you and I ran Mr. Jack Gleason's threshing outfit. You as his engineer and me as his feeder, if you will remember back to 1880 or 1881 or 82. You will remember that Gleason bought a Westinghouse threshing outfit. We hauled the engine around with horses. He hired you for his engineer and me for one of his feeders, and as near as I can remember we were good ones. And my heart grows sad when I think of those good old days. I often speak of you, telling how I knew you. A good many say yes, you know Henry Ford from what you read of him in the papers. My wife often says why don't you go and see your friend Ford? She knows why I don't. I know why and you can guess.

When winter sets in here in McGregor (on the Mississippi River) work stops. There are no factories of any kind and when navigation opens up then we get busy, no time to visit. We dig in and save our earnings for the next coming winter.

Well Mr. Ford, I guess I have made all plain to you and probably more than you will care to read, but I will ask one little favor of you which is this, if you will write me if only two or three lines with your name signed to them, believe me it will ever be esteemed a particular favor and be acknowledged with the sincerest respects of

Respectfully,
David W. Young
McGregor, Iowa.

The following is an excerpt from the reminiscences of Fred Gleason, son of Jack Gleason:

A supposed murder story that Mr. Ford cleared up, has been on my mind for many years, a murder story in which the accused was a very well-known man by the name of Jeremiah Sheahan, who was the first county auditor that Wayne County had. My only object in writing this story is to vindicate Mr. Sheahan.

Mr. Dave Young and Mr. Jeremiah Sheahan and two other men were playing cards many years ago in a log house at the corner of what is now known as Southfield Road and Plymouth. Mr. Young and Mr.

Sheahan got into an argument over the game. Both went outside to settle it. Mr. Young was never heard of after that night. There were many conflicting stories told as to just what became of Mr. Young. One version of the story had it that he was buried under a certain pear tree at the northeast corner of Plymouth Road and Southfield.

This is how Mr. Ford cleared up the mystery. He was out to our farm talking to my father who was complimenting Mr. Ford regarding his kindness of instructing Mr. Campsell (Ford's secretary) to make out checks to several of his old acquaintances as the essence of Father-Time had knocked at their door. Mr. Dave Young was one of the names he mentioned. I interrupted the conversation to ask Mr. Ford if Mr. Dave Young were still alive. His answer was "yes." He said Mr. Campsell mailed him a check just a few days previously.

NOTES AND REFERENCES

1. Henry Ford was so far ahead of his neighborhood contemporaries in his thinking and in his predictions that his statements were quite often unbelievable — sometimes absolutely preposterous. Thus he was given the nickname "Lyin' Hank." As late as 1910, when Henry Ford announced he was going to increase production of Model-Ts at Highland Park from 1,000 to 5,000 per day, Addison Ford remarked, "Henry's lyin' as much as ever."

2. During this period, Henry Ford was kicking up his heels on the dance floor of Joe Coon's Tavern with the Phelps & Brace Orchestra and caller William Cox. Henry's dancing flair roused the girls to a state of ecstasy. Christine Gleason was particularly smitten and singled out Henry for marriage. Henry, it seems, was more than agreeable but Henry's parents objected because the Gleasons were Catholic. Both families had come from southern Ireland. Christine then decided to drop Henry in favor of the equally promising young blacksmith, Joseph Shefferly. (See the unpublished reminiscences of Fred Gleason, Acc. 65, Edison Institute Archives.)

3. In early days, the neighborhood extended for miles in nearly every direction. Now with the automobile, the neighborhood can be less than a city block. Do you know all your neighbors living within 500 feet?

4. Correspondence between E.G. Liebold, Carrolton R. Hayes, and G. Westinghouse Co., April–Sept. 1913. Acc. 13.1, Office of Registrar, The Edison Institute.

5. Earl Ford, lived in Ann Arbor with his son, Keith. (Both are now deceased) Earl worked the John N. Ford farm for several years after his father died in 1916, and was Trustee of the Ford Cemetery for most of his life.

6. Indeed both the old Ypsilanti steam engine with the young tree still clinging to its wheel, and the little Westinghouse, No. 345, are as yet on display in the Ford Museum, both having survived the latest auction.

7. Emma was the daughter of John N. Ford and became the wife of Raymond H. Laird. See, "I Worked for Henry Ford," by Raymond H. Laird, *Dearborn Historian*, Vol. 10 No. 1, 1970.

8. Orla H. Ford was well known in Dearborn during the 1920s. He was head of the Service Department at the Clyde M. Ford, Ford Lincoln-Fordson dealership in Dearborn.

9. Burnham Ford, Reminiscences, Acc. 65, Box 27, Edison Institute Archives. Burnham was son of William Ford, Jr., thus nephew of Henry Ford.

18
EARLY FORD DEALERS

Addison and Clyde Ford,
First Ford Dealers in Dearborn

This chapter relates to descendants of one of the six sons of Samuel Ford, the first of the Fords to settle in Dearborn. This son, George, inherited a portion of the original 1832 homestead and deeded some of his property to a family board of trustees in 1893 for the Ford Cemetery. Descendants of this George Ford included Addison and Clyde Ford who both became Ford automobile dealers, the latter was also elected first Mayor of the City of Dearborn.

It was in the extreme northeast corner of Dearborn Township that Samuel Ford settled in 1832. After Samuel had died (1842), his wife, Nancy, operated the eighty-acre farm until her death in 1873. One of her ten children, George Ford (1835–1901), who already owned neighboring land, inherited that portion of Nancy's farm which adjoined his own and included the Ford Cemetery where Samuel and Nancy were buried. This George Ford and his wife, Mary (Jones) Ford had two children, Ida and Addison. This story features Addison Charles Ford (1864–1920) and his son Clyde McKinloch Ford (1887–1948), both early Ford dealers.

Addison C. Ford grew up on the George Ford farm, the farmhouse facing Joy Road just west of the cemetery. Addison was very close in age to Henry Ford, a neighbor boy and a second cousin. In 1887 Addison married Mary Althia Ward (1866–1940) a neighbor girl who with Addison had attended the Scotch Settlement School and later taught in the same school. Mary's father was Francis R. Ward a graduate of Michigan State Normal School at Ypsilanti, and a teacher for forty years in the Dearborn locality.

Addison took over his father's farm in 1901, and was at first primarily a farmer, but unlike many of Henry Ford's relatives, was inclined to endorse Henry's mechanical bent. On his own farm, Addison set up a grist mill operated by a large single-cylinder Otto gasoline engine, and it is said that Mary, doing her chores in her sunbonnet, was often seen with an oil can filling the oil cups on the bearings of the engine. (Refined women wore sunbonnets in those days because sun-tan was considered unbecoming.) The flywheel of this engine was about five feet in diameter, and a man would jump onto one of the spokes of the wheel to push the piston into firing position before turning on the spark. When the engine backfired, the noise was so loud that it was heard on the farm of James Ford, nearly two miles west. The mill was primarily a grain mill, but one of the machines in the mill would separate seeds from the ripe tomatoes, which Addison raised on the farm for the D.M. Ferry Seed Company.

Addison had a reputation as a prankster. Typical is a story of how "Molly," his wife, had waited hours for him at suppertime. It became dark and she was worried. She took a lantern and headed for the barn to search for Addison. As she left the house, she glimpsed a ladder against the house and to a second-story window. She went back into the house to investigate, and found Addison chuckling to himself in the bedroom — the caper being a big joke to Addison.

Henry Ford, another prankster, was a frequent visitor at the Addison Ford farm with his early cars, the Model-R, the Model-S, and occasionally the big Model-K. After the Model-T was introduced, Addison sensed an opportunity. From the vantage point of his grist mill office, he would sell these popular cars.

The Model-T was a big improvement over previous automobiles. First of all, to quote a 1908 brochure, "The control (steering) is on the left side, the logical place for the following reasons: The driver is then nearest the vehicle he is passing, running in the opposite direction. When the driver is seated on the right side, he is at a great disadvantage in learning if a vehicle is overtaking him on his left — as required by traffic regulations, and, "With the control on his left, the driver and his front seat passenger step out directly on the clean curb. With the old way they walked around in the mud."

Crankshaft, drive-train, springs, front axle, and many other vital parts of the Model-T were fabricated from the new ultra-strong Vanadium Steel. And this new vehicle did not require the battery which, on the older models, needed to be recharged every two or three weeks in order to supply the ignition. Now, instead of a battery, the Model-T had a magneto requiring essentially no attention.

Left: Addison Ford, from a re-touched photograph taken about 1915. Right: Mary (Ward) Ford, wife of Addison Ford and mother of Clyde M. Ford, ca. 1920. (Photos courtesy Rylma [Ford] LaChance)

Drivers of previous Fords had to be constantly warned not to test the power of the battery by laying a file across the positive and negative poles. Henry Ford, with the Model-T, was building a car for the multitude, and the multitude at that time was on the farm. The Ford car was designed with the farmer in mind. It was light, would go through deep sand and mud, and was easy to extricate if it became stuck. On firm ground, one stout man could lift any one wheel or the entire rear end.

In the year 1910, the Ford factory was being moved from the Piquette Avenue Plant to Highland Park where Model-T production would eventually reach its peak. There is some evidence that Addison Ford sold Model-Ts for Henry Ford without a license as early as 1908. However, Addison petitioned the Detroit Branch of the Ford Motor Company on Feb. 10, 1910, for a Dealer's License.

From the beginning, Ford dealers were chosen with care. Only men financially reliable, of good standing in the community, and occupying presentable homes were accepted. The license was granted to "A.C. Ford" on March 16, 1910, the assigned territory being "Dearborn and Vicinity."

Dealers at that time were likely to handle more than one make of car, and sell wherever they wanted. The popularity of the Model-T, however, allowed Ford Motor Company to begin to demand the "one-make" franchise, and restrict the dealer to a given territory as well. Year by year, as sales increased, it was the policy of the Company to reduce the area alloted one dealer and increase the number of dealers. Addison's address was Dearborn, and he was the only Ford dealer in the area. The Dearborn Village population was 800. The 1910 Model-T price for the Roadster was $900, and for the closed "inside driven" Town Car, $1,200. Regular equipment included three oil lamps, tube horn, and gas lamp brackets. Commission to the dealer was 25% of the price. Addison

The Addison C. Ford homestead on the south side of Bonaparte (Joy) Road just west of Division (Greenfield) Road. The Ford Cemetery and St. Martha's Episcopal Church are on this property which was purchased from the U. S. Government by Samuel Ford, Addison's grandfather, in 1832. The house was built about 1860 by Addison's father, George Ford, and was only recently demolished. (B-35402)

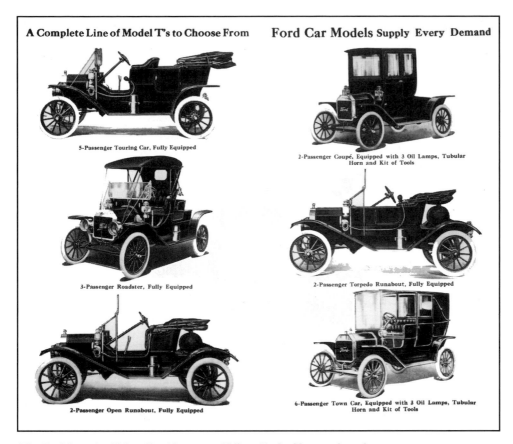

The Ford line of vehicles offered in 1911. Addison Ford sold approximately ten cars that year, and had to teach pratically every one of his customers how to drive. (0-3452)

is credited with having sold seven vehicles that year, and having "contracted" with Ford Motor Company for $5,600 worth of cars.

Dealers are said to have seldom read the details of their contracts; they had that much confidence in Mr. Ford. But to quote one early dealer verbatim et literatim, "What in the hell is the use of reading it? After it tells who the first party is and who the second party is, the whole damn thing is for the first party."

A Ford Motor Company statement in 1912 indicates Addison Ford had purchased ten vehicles and had estimated his annual number of sales to be thirteen. And part of the selling job was teaching new owners to drive. Being able to drive a horse and buggy gave

231

buyers some initial confidence. A newly cut hay field was an ideal place to practice — no ditches, no horses in the way. So both Addison and Mary became Model-T driving instructors. A few customers gave up trying to learn and wanted their money back.

Performance of cars needed to be demonstrated. In this vicinity vehicles were taken to farms where the car would be driven in a plowed field to show that the farmer could get anywhere on his farm with it. In mountainous country, hill-climbing duels were popular. In California, one dealer carried dynamite in his Model-T to demonstrate its soft ride. A 1909 cross-country race (New York-Seattle) won by a Model-T, had been well publicized. The car was shown fording streams, climbing over rocks, and plowing through mud.

Many farmers were afraid that an automobile would set fire to the barn where they would want to keep the car. Some farmers hand-pushed their Model-T in and out of the barn. One dealer said he paid farmers to store his surplus cars in their barns during the winter months in order to prove that the barns would not catch fire. "It didn't burn their barn down during the winter and it certainly won't burn it down in the summer," he said. Addison built himself a "Tin Shed" next to his grist mill, and in it he is said to have been able to store as many as thirty Model-Ts, in order to be ready for the summer selling season.

The dealer would ordinarily order a car from the factory for a customer with a deposit of $25, and the dealer paid the factory 10% of the wholesale price when he ordered the car. Delivery required full cash payment of the balance. Often, however, dealers accepted a personal note from the purchaser, carrying some of the paper themselves, and discounting some. A small percentage of the notes always turned out to be "slow notes," no matter who carried them.

The Model-T had left-hand drive which helped sales, but for years, dealers begged for front doors which Mr. Ford was reluctant to furnish. Another weakness was in the ignition system which employed four problematic vibrators, one for each cylinder. Henry Ford would never okay a master vibrator which both owners and dealers preferred. Hand-cranking the engine was no easy task either, although Henry Ford insisted it was. A variety of foot starters operated from the car seat could be purchased for $25, but Ford Motor Company did not market one. In 1910, one could also buy a "Sunbeam" battery-operated lighting system for $45, "Mott"

Clyde Ford home ar 22149 Long Boulevard in Dearborn, about 1930 when it was new. (Photo courtesy Dearborn Historical Museum)

wire wheels for $20, "Comfort" shock absorbers for $7, and a "Gemco" front bumper for $8. But early Model-T dealers were not encouraged to sell such accessories.

Trade-ins were common from the beginning. It was not unusual for early car salesmen to take a horse in trade for a Model-T. Some car dealers made considerable money on the resale of horses. One dealer admitted taking a horse appraiser with him when he called on farm prospects. City dealers were more likely to accept a piano in trade, and one Model-T dealer in Minnesota accepted 500 gallons of maple syrup. The salesmen themselves were responsible for getting rid of these extraneous assets. One slight obstacle in selling the 1910 Model-T was the Selden Suit which was then in progress. Henry Ford did not think it right that his customers should have to pay Mr. Selden a 5% royalty fee on each car purchased. Other automobile manufacturers were charging their customers the extra money. Mr. Ford was fighting Mr. Selden's patent in a New York court. Meanwhile, Model-T purchasers, who might be liable for the fee if Mr. Ford lost the case, needed some protection. Most Ford dealers posted a bond for people who bought the Model-T. A certificate was given with each car, guaranteeing that if Mr. Ford lost the suit, the buyer would be reimbursed. Mr. Ford won the lawsuit in January, 1911.

Model-Ts were not always black. They were obtainable in a variety of bright colors from 1908 until 1914, at which time even the brass radiator and lamps were black "Japaned." Again in 1925, muted body colors were introduced and were available until the demise of the model in 1927.

The new Model-T owner was given a price list of parts by Ford Motor Company; front fender $4, rear fender $3, et cetera. Dealers were not required to have a service department per se. Some small dealers operated with little but pliers, screwdriver, and monkey wrench — the choice of "English" or "Metric" not being paramount. However, a few large city dealers had sufficient stock and mechanics to build from parts a complete Model-T within 24 hours.

But Ford owners did get good service. Henry Ford would stop the assembly line at times to furnish repair parts to dealers for service. He would say, "If that one is giving trouble out there, why send two out there to give trouble." One dealer said that after he sold a car to a doctor, the doctor expected him to come over and start it as a daily service. This he did for a while. In starting the Ford car, it often helped to put the vehicle in "high" and jack up one of the rear wheels before cranking.

Addison's only son, Clyde, twenty-three years old in 1910, immediately became a salesman. He did not like to operate the dusty grist mill because of troublesome asthma. But he did like going from farm to farm with a demonstrator flivver to take orders. On one of these selling excursions, in 1915, he visited the James F. Glass homestead near Plymouth. Young Camilla Glass, a very pretty but innocent farm girl, was overawed by this highly polished salesman and his shiny new automobile. Her father bought a car, and the salesman and the farmer's daughter were married in October, 1916. As a wedding present, Addison and Mary built them a large new house next to their own on Joy Road.

The year that Clyde and Camilla were married finds Addison's business in exceptionally healthy condition. A "Commercial Statement" of August 15, 1916, reveals Addison's having had auto sales of $60,280 during the previous year, with operating expenses of only $1,000. The statement indicates there were no new or used

*Clyde McKinloch Ford, son of Addison
and Mary Ford, ca. 1920.*

*Camilla (Glass) Ford, wife of Clyde M. Ford,
ca. 1920. (Photos courtesy Rylma [Ford] LaChance)*

cars on hand on the date the statement was submitted. He had
$16,000 in the bank and $2,500 in notes and accounts due him. He
had no debts, and was able to borrow $10,000 from the Dime
Savings Bank of Detroit if necessary. Garage, machinery, tools, fix-
tures, and other equipment used in the automobile business were
valued at $800. Some of his major service work he was referring to
John Tyre, who ran a garage in an old blacksmith shop on Michigan
Avenue in Dearborn Village. Addison's "other real estate" was valued at $30,000. He estimated his own "net worth" at $50,000.

The dealership quite soon outgrew the old grist mill location.
It next became Addison Ford & Son, and a large garage was built

in Dearborn Village at 86 East Michigan Avenue (now 21925 Michigan Avenue), between Porter and Centre Streets (Oakwood and Monroe). The "Tin Shed" was moved from the farm to Dearborn, and erected between Mechanic Street and the Railroad, directly behind the garage. This dealership was opened for business in August of 1917.

When Addison entered Dearborn Village with his Ford Agency, he by no means found a business vacuum. The *Dearborn Independent* was advertising the Saxon Roadster for $395; John W. Theison was running large advertisements for his Paige automobiles; and the thirty h.p. Chevrolet with electric starter and lights, and providing twenty-five miles per gallon of gasoline, was being sold by John D. Hull for $560. To help Addison, however, the Ford Branch at 1550 Woodward, Detroit, occasionally issued a large announcement in the Dearborn newspaper, emphasizing a new lower price for each Ford model with the statement, "New prices guaranteed against price decreases for one year." It is also interesting that in 1917 one could obtain from Citizens Mutual Auto Insurance Co., a $5,000 Fire, Theft & Liability Insurance Policy for $1 per policy, plus 25¢ per horsepower. Insurance for the twenty-two h.p. Ford was $6.50 per year.

The year Addison and Clyde moved their business to Dearborn Village, reveals their having scheduled 180 vehicles for the coming year, up slightly from the 175 contracted the previous year. Of these, 118 were touring cars, 23 roadsters, 9 sedans, 9 coupelets, 14 chassis, and 7 trucks. It is interesting that, although 15 vehicles were scheduled for each month, the "mix" shows chassis and truck models were to be delivered largely in cold weather, while open cars were being handled throughout the year. Closed cars accounted for only 10% of the total, with the Town Car apparently not at all popular in this area.

Within a year, Addison Ford & Son received the Wayne County franchise for the new Fordson Tractor being manufactured less than a mile away, and for which Henry Ford's brother, William, was a major distributor. Henry Ford had been showing his new Fordson tractors to dealers in May of 1916. He offered alcohol and kerosene carburetors as well as gasoline. Gasoline was more scarce than kerosene, and the quality was not uniform. The cracking process to control gasoline quality had not yet been introduced, and much of the gasoline sold was adulterated with 10–15%

The Clyde M. Ford dealership at 21825 Michigan Avenue in May of 1930. Model-A Fords are in the showroom. Note the Ford Benzol in the curbside pump, and in the window to the left the Ford Ammonium Sulfate Fertilizer, both of these products from the Rouge Coke Ovens; also the Ford Hardwood Charcoal from the forests of the Upper Peninsula. (Photo courtesy Dearborn Historical Museum)

kerosene or diesel oil. And as for alcohol — according to one midwestern dealer, "You know the farmer can take the corn that he feeds his hogs, take the alcohol out of it, increase the feeding value and have his own power. That was corn liquor. Then the country began to go dry (1917) and that carburetor never did run." Thus kerosene became a standard fuel for the Fordson.

But on July 1, 1920, Addison Ford died quite unexpectedly at age fifty-six. Addison's funeral was on July 3rd, and it is said that the slow procession from Joy and Greenfield Roads to Grand

Lawn Cemetery, including a few horse-drawn carriages, was harassed by boys throwing firecrackers at the horses.

Clyde M. Ford thus became sole owner of the Ford agency. Addison's wife, Mary, stayed at the old homestead until 1922, when Henry Ford bought the farm as part of his large collection of Dearborn farms. Mary then moved to Detroit, living on Greenway Street for several years, but was again living at the farm at the time of her death in 1940. Clyde and Camilla, with their young daughter, Rylma, moved into Dearborn in 1922 where they bought the Kalmbach house at 318 West Garrison Street.

The old farmhouse, built about 1860, was vacant for several years with Henry Ford's "service men" checking it frequently. Occasionally a Girl Scout group would have permission to camp there overnight. The big engine from the mill is said to be in the Henry Ford Museum. The large Addison Ford barn, where Rylma played with her cats as a girl, was carefully dismantled and moved to Greenfield Village. And Henry Ford had the relatively new Clyde-Camilla wedding-present house moved away because it was not part of the landscape as he remembered it as a boy. After Henry Ford died (1947), Clara Ford arranged a life lease of the original farmhouse to Raymond and Mabel Ford, cousins, who lived in it until 1974. The house, then adjacent to St. Martha's Episcopal Church, was owned by the Episcopal Diocese of Detroit, and served as the St. Peter's Home for Boys. The boys lived together and maintained the property under the direction of the Church. Quite recently the old farmhouse was torn down.

In 1923, Clyde, now living in Dearborn, was selling Fords, Lincolns, and Tractors. Dearborn was booming, business was some thirty-five employees working at the dealership. About this time, Clyde hired his cousin, Orla H. Ford, as Service Manager, and Orla worked at the dealership for the next twenty years. In neighboring Springwells, Henry Ford's nephew, Robert Ford, opened a Ford agency in 1923. There was plenty of business for both, as Model-T prices were down to $269 for the Roadster and $595 for the Sedan. Model-Ts accounted for the majority of vehicles sold in the United States. And in 1927, with the blessing of Henry Ford, Clyde's agency expanded, establishing the "Westwood Ford" dealership at 26927 Michigan Avenue, just east of Inkster Road.

Soon after Clyde Ford moved into the Village of Dearborn, he became involved in politics, and found public service to be more

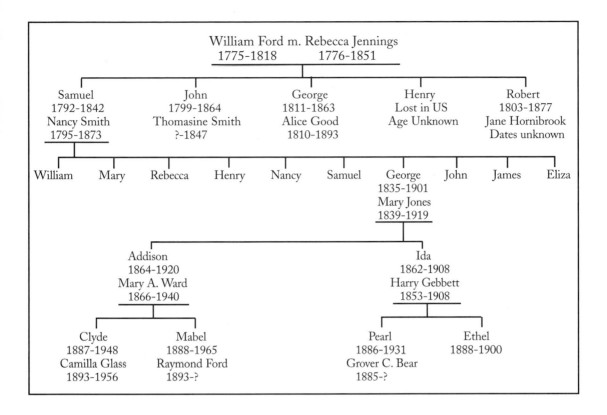

challenging than the auto business. He was also extremely interested in local history. In 1926 he wrote a fairly lengthy account of early Dearborn, with emphasis on the role of Henry Ford. (This manuscript is now in the Dearborn Historical Museum.) By 1928, Clyde Ford was Mayor of the new City of Dearborn and also Chairman of the Consolidated Cities Association, an organization sponsored by Henry Ford to promote the merger of Fordson (East Dearborn) with Dearborn (West Dearborn). In November of 1928, Clyde M. Ford, James P. Casey, and Floyd Yinger (Mayor of Fordson) ran for Mayor of the new Consolidated Dearborn. Clyde Ford carried Dearborn and Floyd Yinger carried Fordson in a close primary race. But during the campaigning for the run-off election, Mr. Casey gave his support to Clyde Ford, and the following letter was distributed widely prior to the final date.

> To whom it may concern:
>   We the undersigned, do hereby whole-heartedly endorse the candidacy of Clyde M. Ford for the office of Mayor of the new City of Dearborn. In so doing we are thoroughly convinced that Mr. Ford is

WELL qualified for the office through his extensive and diligent service in public office, and the confidence placed in him by the citizens of
the consolidated cities, by placing their stamp of approval on consolidation as organized and propagated by Mr. Ford.

Further in endorsing Mr. Ford, we do so because we do heartily
believe that this new City should be placed in the hands of its friends
for administration this next three years so that consolidation will not
have been in vain.

Edsel Ford
Chas. E. Sorenson
B.J. Craig
Harry Bennett

This particular time was perhaps the high point of Clyde
Ford's career. He had won the election by a large majority. He was
now Mayor, the auto business was flourishing, he had a beautiful
new home at 22149 Long Boulevard, a new Lincoln to drive, and
a happy family with his wife, daughter, and small son. But trouble
was in the offing. The 1929 stock market crash and Great
Depression were to affect both his political career and his business.
Although he again won mayoral votes against Floyd Yinger in
1931, and against David Jones in 1933, the Democratic landslide
of the depression years, together with alleged corruption in his
Police Department, prevented further major political victories for
this staunch Republican. Clyde Ford withdrew from the Dearborn
mayoral race in September, 1935, after three terms as Mayor, and
became Councilman. That year he gave his support to Clarence
Ford, brother of Robert Ford, the East Dearborn Ford dealer. But
it was a dark horse candidate, John L. Carey, who received the
backing of the Ford Motor Company and Harry Bennett's political action groups such as the Knights of Dearborn. Carey won
with ease. Attempts on the part of Clyde Ford to obtain a seat in
Congress in 1932 and 1934, running against John Lesinski, Sr., a
Democrat, had also failed. Nonetheless, Clyde Ford was to hold
various positions in Dearborn city government for nearly thirty
years. A large percentage of the profits from the Ford agencies had
gone toward Clyde's campaign expenses. Although auto sales were
very depressed during the thirties, Clyde Ford did have the advantage, if any, of handling Henry Ford's personal "gifts" to local people. Henry Ford, it is said, did not like to pull cars directly from the
assembly line. He asked Clyde to order and deliver them.
However, there may not have been much profit to Clyde in these
particular cars. In the summer of 1942, when car rationing had

gone into effect, Clyde Ford sold his dealerships to Stuart Wilson. Shortly after he had sold his business, Clyde Ford told the writer that one of his difficulties in the car business at that time, in addition to the unavailability of new cars, was the large inventory of boats, trailers, and other non-automotive items previously taken in trade. These were difficult to sell, and they tied up capital.

Stuart Wilson stayed at the Michigan-Oakwood location until 1945 when materials became available to build a new sales-and-service dealership at 23535 Michigan Avenue, west of Outer Drive. This dealership became the property of Village Ford in 1982. So although Addison and Clyde Ford were the first in Dearborn, their combined thirty-two years as Ford dealers (1910–1942) do not come close to matching the Robert Ford family's fifty-nine years (1923–1982).

Clyde M. Ford subsequently held the office of City Controller and was City Assessor when he died in 1948, at age sixty-one. His wife, Camilla, died in 1956. Both are buried with Clyde's parents and grandparents in Grand Lawn Cemetery. Clyde and Camilla's offspring include several grandchildren — none of whom lives in Dearborn.

The author acknowledges with great appreciation the material provided for this article by Clyde M. Ford's daughter, Rylma (Ford) LaChance, and Orla H. Ford, cousin of Clyde Ford.

19
MODEL-T TRAVEL IN THE EARLY 1920S

A Trip from Detroit to Richmond, Virginia, to Visit "Aunt Becky" Ford

One cannot usually recall his obvious first mode of travel — in his mother's and father's arms. However, I can vaguely remember, in 1915 at age three, having experienced horse and buggy, auto, and train — in what sequence I am not certain. The horse and buggy belonged to my uncle who lived on a farm near Mt. Morris, Michigan; the auto belonged to a doctor at Byron, Michigan, where my father was superintendent of schools; and the train was at the station in Durand, Michigan, where the railroad connections allowed us to travel from Byron to Mt. Morris, my parents' hometown.

The auto I remember was most likely a Model-T Ford. I recall the mahogany dash, the leather straps holding the top forward, the brass radiator, and the bumps on the all-brass acetylene headlights as I sat on my father's lap in the front seat. My father was devoted to horses, my mother enjoyed the luxury of travel by train, and I was to become an auto advocate at an early age.

We did not own an automobile until 1922. My father was then school superintendent at Columbiaville, Michigan, on the Michigan Central Railroad which provided frequent trains directly to Detroit, or also to Flint via connections at Lapeer. We had been traveling by train to Lapeer where we did most of our shopping. In almost no time, it seemed that our neighbors were offering us rides to Lapeer, our relatives were coming to see us in their touring cars, and my father reluctantly admitted that maybe we should consider having an auto. It was when my father's older brother came from Royal Oak for Christmas, 1921, in his new Ford sedan that I believe my father succumbed.

At age nine (early 1922) I began to study the classified auto advertisements in the Detroit News. My mother and sister wanted a closed car. My dad insisted on its having a self-starter and demountable rims. In these particulars, my father was much more knowledgeable about a car than the rest of us.

Most Model-Ts had had only a magneto (generator) to furnish electricity — first for ignition and later for electric headlights. The magneto generated electricity only when the engine was running. When the engine raced, the headlights were bright as necessary. However, when the engine idled the headlights became very dim. Therefore, with only a magneto as a source of electricity, auxiliary kerosene front lamps and a kerosene tail lamp were necessary for safety on the road. As one slowed down to meet another car on a narrow road, one's electric lights were lost at the worst possible time. Sometimes two Model-T drivers would pass each other in almost total darkness. Some drivers put their cars in "neutral" and raced their engines while they coasted past the oncoming car. When the engine was not running there was, of course, no electricity available to start the engine; therefore it had to be manually cranked. Many a driver's arm was broken when the engine misfired and momentarily reversed its direction of rotation. Also, if the hand-brake was not drawn back, the car would leap forward when the engine started, sometimes knocking the man down, or pinning him to a barn wall.

Adding a battery and starter allowed an all-electric lighting system, but did not completely free the driver from occasional need to hand-crank the engine. At low engine speed, the magneto generated too little electricity to provide, in addition to ignition and electric lights, a fully charged battery. Thus the battery was often insufficiently charged to be totally dependable for starting the car. Therefore, the crank remained a permanent fixture on the Model-T, with or without a starter.

The "demountable rims" allowed one to replace flat tires by simply loosening four lug-nuts and exchanging a tire-rim combination without having to separate tire from rim. This could be accomplished in just a few minutes. The damaged tire, together with rim, could then be left at a garage for repair, or repaired at home instead of on the road. A second flat on a single trip, however, required getting out the tire irons, separating tire from rim, and patching the inner tube — a lengthy, difficult task.

We did not consider any other than Ford automobiles because my mother belonged to the Ford family of Dearborn. Other pop-

ular small cars at that time were the Star, Gray, Dort, Chevrolet, and Overland. In early 1922 the price of a new Ford runabout was $319, and the touring car $328. However, a new sedan with starter and demountable rims was $645. I read many, many advertisements in the *Detroit News* describing used Fords for sale. Typical was: "Ford Touring, excellent condition, four new tires, side curtains, starter, demountable rims, $150." Very few sedans were for sale. Essentially all sales of both new and used cars were cash sales. Most used cars were sold privately.

I would have preferred an "open" car, but my father learned that a relative of ours had a 1920 Ford sedan in his barn right there in town, where it had been standing for a year or so because it was not a "gear shift" car — the type our cousin had been accustomed to driving. In 1920, this car had cost over $900, and was available for $300. This was our first car.

Many people who owned touring cars said they would be afraid to ride in sedans because of the danger of being cut by broken glass if the car turned over. The large difference in price, however, was more likely to have been the reason for the greater popularity of touring cars. A few owners of touring cars bought "winter tops," allowing them to replace the open top with a glass enclosed top for winter weather. Sedans and "winter tops" offered better protection from wind and rain, but most had no heaters, and it was therefore necessary to bundle up in the winter. We all had feet and fingers numb with cold on long winter trips. Rather than contend with the added problems of winter driving, some owners "blocked up" their car in the barn, drained the radiator, removed the battery and skipped the winter season entirely.

My father quickly learned to drive as well as most drivers. He was first inclined to turn wide on corners, occasionally forcing another driver into the ditch. Going into the ditch was not an uncommon occurrence on the narrow dirt roads. On a twenty-mile trip one might help push more than one car out of the ditch, and also see several cars beside the road with tires being patched. One day we had three flat tires on our way from Columbiaville to Lapeer, a distance of ten miles.

Whereas some autos carried two or three spare tires, we only carried one, inflated and mounted on a rim. Under the rear seat were jack, socket wrench, tire irons, inner-tubes, tire boots, spare valves, a tube patch kit good for at least a dozen patches, a hand pump, and a tire pressure gauge. Along with the tire maintenance gear would be a screwdriver, pliers, monkey wrench, some soiled rags, a spare "timer" (timers tended to become oily and cause misfiring), a fan belt, a few new and used spark plugs, and maybe some radiator hose. With all these things under the seat, some fancy packing was required to permit the seat, itself, to fit into place.

Pumping up a tire was strenuous work, and if there were two men in the party, they would alternate at the job. Women and children would sit at some distance from the roadside to avoid dust from passing cars (and profanity emanating from the worksite). Water in a roadside ditch was helpful if one needed to locate an otherwise undetectable inner-tube leak before patching.

There were many brands of tires. Among the more popular were: "United States," "Goodyear Diamond Tread," "Firestone Non-Skid," "Kelly-Springfield," "Sears," "Fisk," and "Vacuum

Cup." Cord tires were taking the place of fabric, and were more expensive. Tires for the Model-T (30x3½) cost from about $5 to $15, and were usually advertised to last from 1,000 to 3,000 miles. Our sedan had been equipped with five Firestone "Non-Skid" tires which looked like new, but which hardly lasted out the year. Tires blew out long before they wore out. The natural rubber oxidized readily, the weak carcasses, often overloaded, together with bumpy, stony roads, forced drivers to expect blowouts at any moment. A blowout could very well mean the ditch on one side of the road or other for a Model-T driver, because maintaining steering control was very difficult with a flat.

There was much argument in those days whether a front or rear blowout was more hazardous. On the Model-T, with its low-ratio steering and small diameter steering wheel, it was generally conceded, at least by amateurs, that a blown front tire was the more dangerous. The driver needed to hold the steering wheel firmly even for normal driving, inasmuch as a large stone, rut, or pocket of sand in the road could otherwise swing the front wheels abruptly either right or left.

Air pressure in tires was high (60–70 lbs./sq. in.), and many a tire blew up while just parked in the sun. Burlap bags were commonly seen draped over tires on cars standing in the sun. I knew of no one at that time who owned a car without having a garage or barn in which to protect it.

A good many Model-T owners did considerable maintenance work on their own cars. My father, who loved horses more than cars, and who was not very mechanically inclined, learned to replace light bulbs, clean and replace spark plugs and commutator (timer), polish coil contact points, adjust and change transmission bands, and grease front hubs. It was almost a necessity to be able to do these things inasmuch as the car could sputter and stall anywhere on the road. There were few garages, no tow trucks, and miles of almost deserted roads in the rural districts where the Model-T was especially popular.

The Model-T engine developed about twenty horsepower and would propel a touring car to about forty miles-per-hour on a level road with amazing acceleration. (If this ratio had been maintained, our present 200 h.p. engines should produce a top speed of 400 mph.) Gasoline was about twenty cents per gallon, and one might expect to travel twenty-five to thirty miles on one gallon. We had

George Gilson and wife Rebecca (Ford) Gilson, circa 1900. Rebecca (Aunt Becky) was the eldest daughter of Mr. and Mrs. William S. Ford of Dearborn Township. (Photo from author's collection)

no speedometer, nor a gasoline gauge, other than a stick to dip into the tank. They were not standard equipment on the Model-T at that time.

Our sedan had two pieces of optional equipment of which I was especially proud. On the driver's side was a large spotlight which was designed to illuminate the right edge of the road, including pedestrians and bicyclists. It worked beautifully, but has now become all but abandoned as an accessory. The other was a more rare item for a Model-T, a "foot feed" which has now become the standard accelerator pedal. This was a touchy thing, difficult to control steadily, and tiresome to use. Being a novelty, we often demonstrated the "foot feed" to passengers, but much preferred to use the more convenient and less tiring steering column lever.

My first driving was backing the Model-T out of the garage and between two trees, allowing about six inches of space on either side. If I had backed slowly into a tree, the fender would have merely sprung inward a few inches and sprung back out, no harm done. One could have run forward into a solid barrier at five mph, and merely bounced back — possible damage, a blown front tire. There were no bumpers as such. I was not aware of the local Ford dealer's having a "body shop." A badly damaged fender or running board was replaced for a few dollars. Somewhat bent fenders were commonplace on Model-Ts, usually the result of the owner's personal skill in manipulation of the shape following an accident.

I anticipated that it would be fun to drive on the road if one did not have to make that one shift from "low" into "high" and experience that forward lurch; that jerking, chattering, and perhaps stalling sensation as one leaped ahead at maybe double his previous speed. Owners of cars with "gear shifts" were constantly and proudly demonstrating the very low (4–5 mph) speed at which they could travel in "high" without the engine stalling. I was to find that delicate coordination of hand and foot motions were required to shift the two-speed Model-T smoothly, and that trying to idle the engine in "high" usually resulted in several sharp jerks followed by a complete stall.

For two years my father frequently drove us to Mt. Morris weekends (fifty miles round trip), and to Troy, Michigan, for vacations (sixty miles each way). By the summer of 1924 we were ready for a more extended trip. My mother had relatives in Richmond, Virginia, whose letters indicated they were anxious to see us again. (We had previously gone by train.) So we planned to visit my mother's Aunt "Becky" (Rebecca Ford Gilson) who was born in Dearborn Township (1845) and who lived and taught school in Delray before marrying George Gilson and moving to Richmond. Aunt "Becky" was the eldest daughter of William S. Ford, a Dearborn pioneer (1819–1893).

My mother also planned to visit her Uncle William Newsome and his son Howard, who were associated with the Ford dealership in Richmond. Uncle "Willie" and Howard were husband and son respectively of Josephine Ford, the youngest daughter of the same William S. Ford of Dearborn. "Aunt Josie" (1864–1918) had died subsequent to our previous visit. She had been an attractive girl, the same age as Henry Ford of Model-T fame. She was rumored to have been Henry's favorite cousin, and was said to have been offered transportation from Richmond back to

Dearborn in Henry's private railroad car if she would come. She never returned.

Our trip started from Troy, Michigan, where we were living during the summer of 1924. I had just turned twelve, had joined the Boy Scouts, had bought a Scout uniform and looked forward to wearing it with my Tenderfoot badge on the trip. My father joined the Automobile Club of Michigan (AAA) for $10.00, received maps and other travel information, but did not purchase insurance. Auto insurance was not the business it is today. My impression is that few automobiles, especially Model-Ts, were insured. The Auto Club was well known, however, and sponsored progressive automotive legislation, and road safety innovations including route markers and reflective and electric warning signals at intersections and sharp curves. These improvements were initiated as early as 1917, much in advance of governmental agencies. The Auto Club also had pioneered in providing "Safety Patrol" and teaching supplies for traffic education in the schools in 1919.

We studied the maps, picked the route, and prepared for sleeping, as was the current mode of auto travel. Some carried tents. The 1923 Overland "Champion" had an interior designed to convert for sleeping. Model-T owners had to improvise. We had a sectional mattress, the larger section fitting the car almost perfectly. The front bucket-seat backs folded forward and down to support the front end of the mattress, the back end of the mattress resting on the back seat. With our heads to the back three could sleep on the mattress. My little sister, Bonnalyn, then six years old, was to sleep crosswise of the car on the blanketed flat floor between the foot pedals and the front seats. She remembers it as having been a bit tight-fitting. During the day, the mattress would be rolled up and carried outside the car with one end between the left front fender and hood, the other end in the running board luggage rack. A canvas cover would keep it from getting wet. Running board luggage racks were very common — more common than windshield wipers. Only one rack could be used inasmuch as it interfered with the opening of the car door. A large suitcase was tied to the right headlight, and allowed to rest on the fender. A covered picnic basket would carry sandwiches, milk in Thermos bottles, paper plates, cups, etc.

Two new "Vacuum Cup" tires had been installed on the rear wheels, a new "Sears" tire as spare, and my dad and I were anxious to get started. My mother and sister were admittedly not very enthusiastic about this mode of transportation. The trip would be more primitive than to their liking. It was late July (after raspberry season) that we started, and the weather would be hot and dry during the whole trip.

Paved roads were not too plentiful. The main road (Livernois) in front of our house was being graded for paving that summer. As we left Troy, we zigzagged between mule-team dump wagons on our way to Royal Oak and to a gas station for a full tank. Our sedan had a square-shaped gas tank under the driver's seat. The gas hose was put through the driver's window and, with considerable spilling of gas, the tank often was filled to slightly overflowing. The car always smelled of gasoline. Engine oil was replenished, tires were checked for air, the radiator for water, and the wooden-cased battery for water at nearly each gasoline stop, especially during this hot weather. A really prepared motorist carried a three-compartment tank on his running board, containing emergency gas, water, and motor oil.

Our route was to be south to Columbus, Ohio; thence east on the Lincoln Highway (U.S. 40) to Hagerstown; down the Shenandoah Valley (there was no Skyline Drive) to Staunton; then east again to Richmond — a total of about 600 miles. With the best of luck, we estimated it would require three days. We had heard that Aunt Josie's son, Howard, had driven the distance with a Model-T touring car in twenty-four hours — average speed over 25 mph. However, we planned a more leisurely trip. The sedan was not as speedy as a touring car, and was also a bit top-heavy.

We left Royal Oak at 10:00 A.M., drove over to Telegraph Road, south through Dearborn, and to Toledo. When we reached Ohio there was a conspicuous difference in the paving. Instead of concrete there was a preponderance of brick, both in towns and on U.S. 23 south. In the country these were rather narrow red brick roads with no center line markings, thus behooving a driver to run off the edge if an oncoming driver was a bit piggish. Thankfully, there were very few trucks on the roads outside of cities, excepting a few local farmers taking milk or grain to the nearest town. More often, horse-drawn vehicles were encountered.

As near as Ohio we were introduced to the then current custom of blowing horns and waving arms and flags when meeting other cars with Michigan license plates. It should be explained

*Josephine Ford at age
twenty-one (1885).
Josephine was the youngest
child of Mr. and Mrs. William
S. Ford and an acknowledged
favorite of young Henry Ford.
(188-28828)*

that, especially during the month of July, cars were decorated with small American flags. Almost universal was a neat array in the shape of a fan attached to the radiator cap. Other flags were attached to windshields and lights, while children held flags in their hands, waving them outside in the breeze. As we proceeded farther from Michigan, these highway greetings became more vociferous, and if a Michigan driver noticed an apparently disabled Michigan car, he was expected to stop and offer assistance.

It was about sundown when we came to Delaware, Ohio, some fifty miles short of our intended mileage for the day. We stopped at the south edge of town, at a new, clean gas station where other cars were parked for overnight. The owner would usually charge about a dollar per car, keep the rest rooms open for washing, shaving and such, keep the premises lighted, and sometimes sell groceries and hot coffee. As alternatives, there would have been the downtown city hotels or an occasional house bearing a sign, "Tourists." There were no motels, although in the next few years the tourist "cabins" would appear.

The sedan had roll-down curtains around the rear seat. Newspapers were pinned up to cover the front windows. Anyone who has ridden the upper berth of a Pullman car can visualize the contortions involved in getting into and out of bed. Needless to say, we were up at sunrise and preparing to leave. Again following U.S. 23 to Columbus, we reached U.S. 40, the famous Lincoln Highway across the U.S.

A few miles east out of Columbus, however, we found miles of road where the brick pavement was built only in one driving lane. Sometimes it was the right lane, sometimes the left. In meeting a car, one or the other vehicle had to go onto the bumpy, dusty, gravel half of the road. Brick along these roads were sometimes red, sometimes yellow, but there was no concrete.

That day was bright and cheerful, and we rolled merrily along over flat country and through Zanesville, until mid-afternoon when we came to a down-grade. The down-grade lasted and lasted, and my father held his foot steadily on the brake pedal to control the speed of the car. The hill seemed endless. At last we came to the bottom; there was a smelly, scorched odor, and my father announced that he had no foot brakes at all. We found the nearest garage. They said the brake band had worn out coming down the hill. They were fully prepared for such repairs and would have it fixed that day. No doubt the hill produced a steady source of such customers.

We learned we were in Bridgeport, Ohio, just across the Ohio River from Wheeling, West Virginia. We found a place to eat and a place to stay in our car overnight. The mechanics gave my father some pointers about driving in the "hills," knowing that many longer, steeper ones were yet to come. Their advice was to use all three transmission bands when going down a hill. Push on the "brake" a bit, then the "reverse" pedal, then the "low" pedal, back to "brake," and soon down the hill. Especially the "reverse" band should be involved in descending hills because it gets very little use otherwise, they explained. They also reminded us that if the "low" band gives out while going up a hill, one was to turn the car around and "back" the car the rest of the way up. As a result of their advice, we didn't burn out any more transmission bands on the trip.*

Early the next morning we crossed the bridge into Wheeling and headed toward the mountains with scant knowledge of what was to come. Otherwise we might have returned home at that point. We turned to our maps which provided topographical profiles of road elevations. The horizontal axis was compressed in relation to the vertical axis, greatly exaggerating the steepness of the mountains and increasing our apprehensions. Washington and Uniontown, Pennsylvania were taken in stride, but then the trouble started. The road was macadamized, but narrow and crooked. One of the first mountain climbs — probably to an elevation of about 2,600-2,800 feet — wound upgrade endlessly. The Model-T crept along in "low" speed. Occasionally a "gear shift" car would creep by us in "second." Part way up the mountain we began to see boys with water pails. A little later we saw cars stalled beside the road with radiators steaming. The boys were selling their water for 25¢ a pail. There were very few "turn outs where one could drive off the road to cool the engine. The few there were were clogged with cars of all makes, but nearly all were other tourists not accustomed to negotiating the mounatins. With a container, one could usually find a roadside spring (where the boys obviously obtained their water) and replenish the radiator.

It was along this stretch of road that we first experienced the "magnetic hill" effect. After ascending a steep grade, we would come to a section of road less steep, giving us the illusion that we

---

*This flexibility of the planetary transmission on the Model-T reminds one of the popularity of the Model-T chassis equipped with big front bumper and roll-hoops for the game of auto polo. The cars could lurch forward then backward without waiting for the gears to mesh; turn sharply, collide with one another, roll over and be turned back upright by the driver in almost no time. The object of the game was for one of two opposing teams of cars to push a giant white ball to its designated end of the field. These bright colored skeleton cars with their red-hot exhaust manifolds, no mufflers, and red flame shooting out, produced a spectacular display, especially at night. The game was a popular attraction at the Michigan State Fair in the early twenties.

were going slightly down hill. However, the engine labored and my father pulled over to investigate the trouble, only to find that the car tended to coast backward. On scrambling out, we could see that we were still on a fairly steep upward grade.

We were several hours ascending that one mountain. The roads did not slice through the mountains; they went from the very bottom to the very top, via a succession of loops with sharp turns, ascending essentially perpendicularly to the direction of the range. On the peak of one mountain was an observation tower and restaurant. From the tower we could see three states — Pennsylvania, Maryland, and West Virginia. My mother enjoyed a cup of coffee anytime, any place. The coffee was 15¢ — an outrageous price compared to the standard 5¢ cup. She had her coffee, but we certainly felt that we had been exploited. The year 1924 was an inflationary year, and the time of the popular quip, "With a Harvard diploma and 10¢ one can get a cup of coffee almost anywhere."

The ups and downs over the mountains became almost routine for us and other tourists. We learned to check our radiator frequently, preferably at mountain tops. We learned to drive more like the natives who raced down the mountains, swung around the usual sharp curve at the bottom using the entire width of the road, across the inevitable bridge, and up the next mountain at full throttle as far as possible, shifting at the last possible moment

255

before stalling, and grinding the rest of the way to the top, ready to descend again at break-neck speed. Traffic was light and almost the only deterrent to speed was the frequent sighting of a wrecked car, caught in the trees, down the mountainside. In this fashion we reached Cumberland, Maryland by nightfall.

On the outskirts of the city of Cumberland we found a gas station and a lot beside it with perhaps a dozen tourist cars camping for the night. The location was in a valley with towering mountains on either side. The sun had set very early in the valley and there was a long period of dusk. I remember thinking that the people who worked from sunrise to sunset would have a short work day. The mountainsides were steep, and houses on the hillsides seemed to be directly above us, ready to topple down.

The next day we went on to Hagerstown where we left the Lincoln Highway to go south, down the Shenandoah Valley. The road was narrow but paved, and my father wanted to see the famous apple orchards around Winchester, Virginia, and the beautiful valley farms leading to Staunton. Through the orchards the limbs were already drooping with the green fruit. The orchards seemed to extend miles on end. These, of course, were commercial orchards, much different than the typical Michigan farmer's family orchard.

In late afternoon we realized that this might be our last night on the road before reaching Richmond. It was time to spruce-up for our arrival the next day. On the road just outside the town of New Market, a very reputable farmhouse displayed a "tourists" sign. We drove in and were greeted at the door by the housewife. We apparently met the requirements and were to experience our first-ever exposure to true southern hospitality. We were shown to our rooms, brought tub and water for bathing, and were invited for "supper." (Farm families, both in the north and in the south, served "dinner" at noon and "supper" at approximately 6 p.m. "Lunch" was associated with children at school and with workers in the factories.) Supper was with the family of four, who had apparently lived there all of their lives. They were very curious about us, our trip, and life up north. We were impressed with their southern terms and accent, genuine charm, and strange foods. After eating, we were invited into the parlor where there was more conversation and singing of songs to organ music. A daughter, in her twenties, had considerable talent and sang a few solos. We certainly had never expected to be received in this fashion at a tourist home —

never had been before, nor have been since. Next morning breakfast was served — a typical hearty, southern farm breakfast. Again to the parlor and some songs before we could leave. My father had to force upon them payment for the meals, and with much too much ado we finally returned to the road.

From New Market we drove past Harrisonburg, where I remember the railroad yards extending along the auto road and river, on the west side of the city. When we reached Staunton, to me in my Scout uniform the famous Staunton Military Academy was prominent in my mind, and I did get a glimpse of its entry portals and impressive buildings. I remember Charlottesville as a very pretty city, and was informed by my father that much of the elegance was that of the University of Virginia campus. Before reaching Richmond, however, we had a flat tire requiring us to put on the Sears spare. It was midday and my father removed his coat and became quite disheveled in the tire-changing process.

We reached Richmond in mid-afternoon at a time of intense heat and humidity as we slowed down in the city traffic. My father stopped the car at the curb and, in shirt sleeves, got out to inquire regarding directions to Seven Pines, our destination. As he crossed the street, he was very conspicuous, as he was the only man in sight without a coat, despite the heat. The South had retained a gentlemanly formality that had been more or less discarded in the North.

Continuing through the city and to the east, six miles out the Williamsburg Stage Road, brought us to the home of our Aunt Becky and Uncle George Gilson. Their home was in a modest suburb of Richmond, adjacent to a woods where the Civil War Battle of Seven Pines had taken place. The battle earthworks were still there after sixty-two years. Trees had grown on the ridges and in the trenches, but I was able to find, in the few days we were there, three corroded lead bullets from the battle. (Although the battle was classified as a draw, from 6,000 to 8,000 men were lost to each side. Confederate wounded, including their commanding general, were taken directly into Richmond, the Confederate Capitol. From a morale standpoint, some believe the battle to have been the turning point of the war.)

My mother was busy visiting with her Aunt Becky, and my father and I played carom with Uncle George. In relating her experiences in moving to Richmond from Detroit, (this might have been about 1910), Aunt Becky divulged to my mother that when she first arrived in Virginia, her neighbors found her doing her own housework, and there were many snide remarks about her being very low-class for not having "colored help." She apparently capitulated to their feelings and hired a black lady to help with the housework. Next, the neighbors learned that Aunt Becky was eating meals with her help, which practice was also taboo in the Richmond area. By the time we had arrived in 1924, Aunt Becky, although now nearly eighty, was again largely doing her own housework, but in the less conspicuous, easy, southern way. The war between the states had not been forgotten in Richmond, however, and we were cautioned to make no reference to it in conversation with the natives.

We did some sight-seeing in Richmond, including a visit to St. John's Church where Patrick Henry delivered his "Liberty or Death" speech for independence in 1775. The James River through Richmond was wide but not navigable because of the rapids. One day we were taken on a picnic to Jamestown, about thirty miles down the river from Richmond. We drove in Ford and Maxwell touring cars on mostly gravel roads. On approaching the small island, we crossed a swampy marsh on a long, narrow, wooden bridge. The island was essentially deserted. An old church, said to have been built in 1639, was in ruins, with a large tree growing inside the crumbly walls. A small, newer but seemingly neglected church, and statues of Capt. John Smith and Pocahontas were nearby. There appeared to be no attempt to maintain the area, let alone restore it. It was my father's interest in American history that had inspired the outing.

We had brought swimming suits, and waded into the river. The water was somewhat salty, and jellyfish were quite abundant. Howard Newsome, a born prankster, feigned losing his dentures in the water, and we spent some time looking for the alleged missing teeth on the river bottom. There were no picnic facilities other than the grassy ground and our car running boards which served admirably on such occasions. There was no mention of nearby Williamsburg. (Historic Jamestown became a part of Colonial National Monument in 1930. The Williamsburg restoration was to begin in 1926.)

Another outing was an early evening drive to the residence of Uncle William "Willie" Newsome, who lived in a large white plantation mansion some miles out of Richmond. Uncle Willie was upstairs in bed as a result of an auto accident. A distant cousin of about my own age was with us, and we spent time before dark exploring the house and grounds. His mother had asked him to bring his violin so that he could play for us that evening. His rendition of "The Wreck of the 97" was acclaimed most popular, and was played several times with gusto. He was fairly accomplished as I could appreciate, having had a few violin lessons myself. My mother saw to it that I was to continue with my lessons that fall — all ultimately to no avail.

The heat had been almost unbearable. There seemed to be little breeze except when riding, and nights did not cool off appreciably. I do not remember any rain on the trip at all. It was somewhat a relief from a comfort standpoint to be thinking of heading home. Having been there about a week, we again loaded our gear and said our goodbyes. We never saw most of these relatives again. (Our Aunt Becky passed away in 1926.)

Washington, D.C. was to be the highlight of our trip back to Michigan. We drove slowly through Fredericksburg and on to Mt. Vernon. We were in Washington that afternoon and drove from the Washington Monument to the Capitol and White House, all without traffic mishap, albeit not without making a few improper turns, undoubtedly. The Washington police must have had instructions to pamper tourists.

We stayed on the northern edge of Washington that night, and proceeded to Frederick, Maryland, the next morning, where, from a second story window on the main street, there waved a flag reminding us of the legendary "flag-waving patriot" Barbara Fritchie. Gettysburg Battlefield, as I recall, was quite inconspicuous from the road, with scattered monuments over the distant hillsides; but with no accumulation of cars, tourists, souvenir stands, nor high observation towers. It was peaceful countryside, as a military cemetery should be.

The rest of the trip must have been anti-climax, inasmuch as I remember few details. U.S. Highway 30 would take us homeward most directly. I don't remember where we stayed the next two nights. To avoid driving through Pittsburgh, however, we left U.S. 30 and headed toward Butler, Pennsylvania. Somewhere in this area we became lost, encountering roads alternating between deep sand and rocky cattle lanes. We spent a few apprehensive hours hoping we would find a farmer who could direct us before we completely ran out of gas. However, we eventually went through New Castle, skirted Youngstown and Cleveland, and arrived home in three days from Washington. Before we arrived home, the Sears tire had split down the middle of the tread and had to be discarded. It was the only tire we lost, but was not the only one we had patched in the 1,200 miles of travel.

On the trip I had learned to read road maps, keep my sense of direction (when the sun was shining), and act somewhat as navigator by watching the highway route signs. It would still be two years before I would obtain a driver's license.

We kept this Model-T until it was ten years old, finally using it somewhat as a truck before selling it for ten dollars while it was still in running condition — depreciation $29/yr., insurance nothing — typical of Model-T ownership. Although considerable maintenance was required, the bulk of this was likely to be for tires and batteries. The black finish on the ten-year-old sedan was worn and dull, but not rusty. Serious rust was no problem with Model-Ts. The metal was heavy gauge, and sand rather than salt was used on roads to increase traction when icy. The high clearance and narrow wheels helped in mud and snow. Rocking the car forward and backward was easily done with the unique planetary transmission. It was a sad sight to see the old car driven away. Luckily, we already had a younger Model-T sedan to take its place.

After 1924, auto travel changed rapidly — many more paved roads, tourist cabins, more gas stations, fruit and vegetable stands, restaurants, billboards — all the trappings to induce more such travel. Auto travel in the early twenties may seem very primitive to the one who only reads about it, but please don't feel sorry for those of us who experienced it.

20

FORD FAMILY TREE

Created by Raymond H. Laird,
a Ford Motor Engineer,
Principally during the Years 1924-1925

The Ford family tree, in whatever form it is found, is based on the work of Raymond H. Laird, a Ford Motor Company engine engineer and husband of Emma Ford, a cousin of Henry Ford. The tree is depicted in botanical form in a drawing by Laird, in four looseleaf genealogical books assembled by Laird, and in charts prepared by this author. Impetus and support for the years of work done by Laird were provided by Henry Ford.

When Henry, Clara, and Edsel Ford traveled to England and Ireland in the summer of 1912, Clara found the home of her mother in Warwick, England; Henry inquired in Cork, Ireland, regarding his foster grandfather, Patrick Ahern; and Edsel reported in his diary that they found the house in Clonakilty, Ireland, where his great-aunt Nancy had lived. Serious work on Ford genealogy did not start, however, until twelve years later. Laird tells of this beginning in a letter dated November 8, 1965, to some friends:

> As I recall, your main question was regarding the origin of the Ford family tree of which you have a print. Here's how it started. In 1924 Mr. Ford called me into his office and showed me a sketch of the Ford family tree that Mabel Ford had drawn from what data she had been able to gather. This had kindled Mr. Ford's interest and he designated me to obtain all information that I could, and draw as complete a tree as possible.
>
> During the next few years I drove tens of thousands of miles to interview people; gather data from family Bibles, photographs, letters, gravestones and cemetery records; arrange these data in order to draw the family tree of which you have a copy. We also checked all available records in Ireland. This investigation was suggested by Mr. Grace as he managed the Ford Plant there, and he was aided greatly by Charles A. Webster, D.D., rector of Blackrock, Cork. Only fragmented data was available, however. During World War I, all records of the area from which Mr. Ford's ancestors came were sent to the Four Courts Building in Dublin for safekeeping. This building was bombed and most of the records were destroyed.

The Ford family tree as drawn by Raymond Laird between 1924 and 1927, with a few later additions to the William Ford branches. The original drawing, 31 by 20 inches, allows individual names to be read.

From the time I completed the data until I retired from the Ford Motor Co. in 1949, all correspondence claiming relationship to Mr. Ford was referred to me for my comments before being answered.

In a letter to Henry Ford's secretaries E. G. Liebold and Frank Campsall, Laird had occasion in 1939 to summarize the results of the 1925 Irish research:

In 1585 Queen Elizabeth selected a number of English gentlemen who were to people Munster (one of four Irish provinces) with settlers from England. Among those gentlemen was Sir John Starvell who was to bring to Ireland and settle on the estate granted to him "such of the gentlemen of the country of Somerset as he found able and willing to come." It is also an historical fact that about the year 1601 a large number of the gentry of Somerset and Devon, mostly younger sons, went over to Ireland. From time to time in the succeeding years others came over to settle the nearly 600,000 acres granted in Munster. Queen Elizabeth was bound on her part to maintain certain forces for security of the settlers.

Early in the seventeenth century an Anthony Starvell had property in the neighborhood of Clonakilty, as had also a member of the Honner family. These two families were united by marriage in 1694

WILLIAM FORD

REBECCA JENNINGS

Please fill the blanks below, and add on the other side of this sheet any information you can, not embraced in the blanks. Kindly give your ancestry as far back as possible, the history of each person, their residence, occupation, what they have accomplished of note, when and where graduated, whether in the army and what company and regiment or in the navy, what boat, what church if any, what offices, either church, military or civil, public or private. Write full name and middle name, if any, and underline the name by which usually called. Be careful to give correct dates, name and facts, and write **PLAIN**.

Yours respectfully,

FAMILY RECORD

Of..... Henry Ford .....of. Bath,Placer Co. Cal.

Occupation..... Miner .....Church, if any, Cathlic,Forest Hill
Last place of residence

Society, if any,.....

Military Record .....

Offices held .....

Born..... 1830 *When* Ireland *Where* .....Died. May 4, 1901 *When* Forest Hill, Cal. *Where buried*

Married. Aug. 25, *When* 1857 San Francisco, Cal. *Where* .....Katherine O'Leary *Whom*

Born..... Nov. 1829 *When* Ireland *Where* .....Died. August 15, 1912 *When* Forest Hill, Cal. *Where buried*

Church and Society.....

Offices held .....

REMARKS: .....

CHILDREN

	NAME	BORN When and Where		DIED WHEN	Where Buried
1	Mary Jane Ford (Bayles)	July 24, 1858	Bath	July 14,1910	Forest Hill
2	Rebecca Ford (Henning)	Sept. 4, 1859	Bath	July 1, 1914	Forest Hill
3	Henrietta Ford(DeBons)	June 19, 1861	Bath	Sept 20,1910	Forest Hill
4	William Henry Ford	Feb. 5, 1864	Bath	Dec.13,1931	Forest Hill
5	Anna Agusta Ford	Dec. 1, 1965	Bath	1870	Forest Hill
6	George Samuel Ford	Oct. 19, 1867	Bath		
7	Francis Albert Ford	Nov. 29, 1869	Bath	Feb.11,1928	
8	Alice Ford (Bequette)	Sept.27, 1871	Bath		
9					
10					
11					
12					

FATHER OF FIRST PERSON NAMED IN THIS RECORD

Full Name..... John Ford .....Residence. Dearborn, Mich.

Born. 1799 *When* Ireland *Where* .....Died. Mar. 22, 1864 *When* Ford Cemetery *Where*

Married. Feb. 14, 1824 *When* Ireland (Parish of Desertserges) *Where* Thomasine Smith

Born..... Klonekilty, Ireland *When* Died. 1847-On ship enroute to America *Where buried*

GRANDFATHER ON FATHER'S SIDE

Name..... William Ford .....Residence..... Klonekilty, Ireland

Born. 1775 *When* Ireland *Where* .....Died. 1818 *When* Ireland *Where buried*

Married..... *When* Ireland *Where* .....Rebecca Jennings *Whom*

Born. 1776 *When* Ireland *Where* .....Died. May 1,1851 *When* Grand Lawn, Detroit *Where buried*

GRANDFATHER ON MOTHER'S SIDE

Name..... .....Residence.....

Born..... *When* *Where* .....Died. *When* *Where buried*

Married..... *When* *Where* .....*Whom*

Born..... *When* *Where* .....Died.

REMARKS: .....

NAME..... Alice Ford Bequette
Person making out the above

ADDRESS.....Auburn, Placer Co. Cal.

A one-page sample of the genealogical sheets collected by Laird.

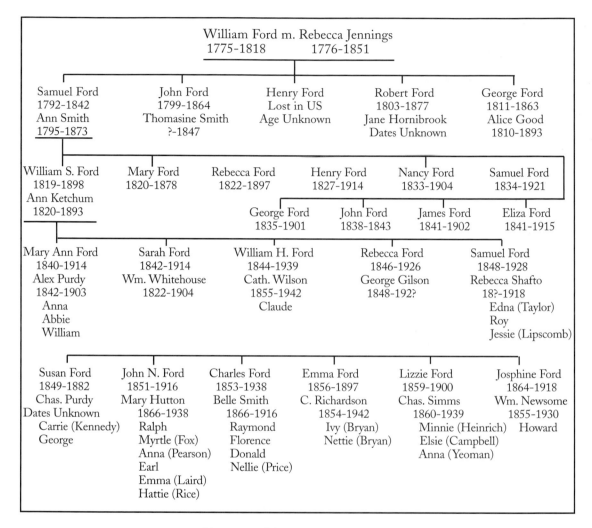

William Ford m. Rebecca Jennings
1775-1818   1776-1851

Samuel Ford	John Ford	Henry Ford	Robert Ford	George Ford
1792-1842	1799-1864	Lost in US	1803-1877	1811-1863
Ann Smith	Thomasine Smith	Age Unknown	Jane Hornibrook	Alice Good
1795-1873	?-1847		Dates Unknown	1810-1893

William S. Ford	Mary Ford	Rebecca Ford	Henry Ford	Nancy Ford	Samuel Ford
1819-1898	1820-1878	1822-1897	1827-1914	1833-1904	1834-1921
Ann Ketchum					
1820-1893					

	George Ford	John Ford	James Ford	Eliza Ford
	1835-1901	1838-1843	1841-1902	1841-1915

Mary Ann Ford	Sarah Ford	William H. Ford	Rebecca Ford	Samuel Ford
1840-1914	1842-1914	1844-1939	1846-1926	1848-1928
Alex Purdy	Wm. Whitehouse	Cath. Wilson	George Gilson	Rebecca Shafto
1842-1903	1822-1904	1855-1942	1848-192?	18?-1918
Anna		Claude		Edna (Taylor)
Abbie				Roy
William				Jessie (Lipscomb)

Susan Ford	John N. Ford	Charles Ford	Emma Ford	Lizzie Ford	Josphine Ford
1849-1882	1851-1916	1853-1938	1856-1897	1859-1900	1864-1918
Chas. Purdy	Mary Hutton	Belle Smith	C. Richardson	Chas. Simms	Wm. Newsome
Dates Unknown	1866-1938	1866-1916	1854-1942	1860-1939	1855-1930
Carrie (Kennedy)	Ralph	Raymond	Ivy (Bryan)	Minnie (Heinrich)	Howard
George	Myrtle (Fox)	Florence	Nettie (Bryan)	Elsie (Campbell)	
	Anna (Pearson)	Donald		Anna (Yeoman)	
	Earl	Nellie (Price)			
	Emma (Laird)				
	Hattie (Rice)				

and by terms of the marriage settlement the Madame estate came into the possession of the Starvell family. Early records show that the Fords were tenants of Starvell at Madame and of Honner at Croghane, and indicate that these Fords were descendants of the Fords of Somerset and Devon who came to Ireland to help people the confiscated lands. It is also an interesting fact that the connection between the Ford and Starvell families existed in Somersetshire as early as the first part of the thirteenth century before either family came to Ireland.

I have a fairly complete record of the descendants of Mr. Ford's grandparents, William Ford and Rebecca Jennings, who were born in 1775 and 1776. William Ford died in Ireland, but his wife Rebecca, and their sons Samuel (1792), John (1799) and George (1811) came to America and all settled in the vicinity of Dearborn. John was Mr. Ford's grandfather. They came to America in 1847. This was the year of the great potato famine when times in Ireland were exceedingly hard.

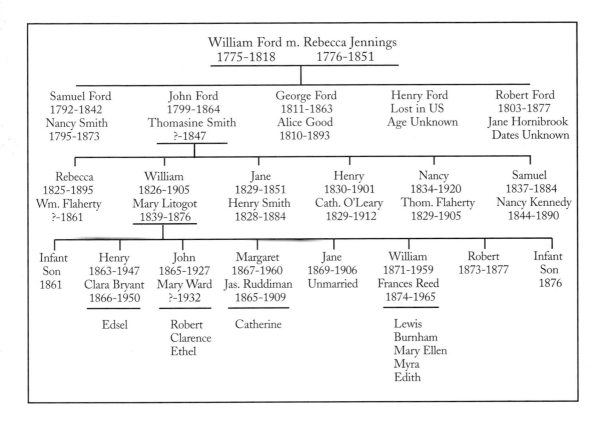

In the early records the name Ford is variously spelled; Ford, Forde, Foord, De Ford and De La Ford, two or more spellings sometimes being used in the same article. The two latter spellings indicate Norman origin.

So the Ford family tree is well established following the names of William Ford and Rebecca Jennings. Laird assembled genealogical material quite steadily until he was needed by Henry Ford to work full-time on the Model-A engine in 1927. Only a few items were added after that. Copies of the Laird genealogy papers were kept by Ford in his office files at the Engineering Laboratory in Dearborn. A story that Ford ignored the tree because he learned of a horse thief among his forebears has no credence.

The family tree drawn by Laird as a botanical tree twenty by thirty-one inches in size was incomplete as of 1927 because he had not yet had time to include the limb representing the Robert Ford family. The tree thus gives the impression of having been struck by lightning. Names of individuals are legible on the tree only when reproduced at full size. Laird's most complete data, by far, are in

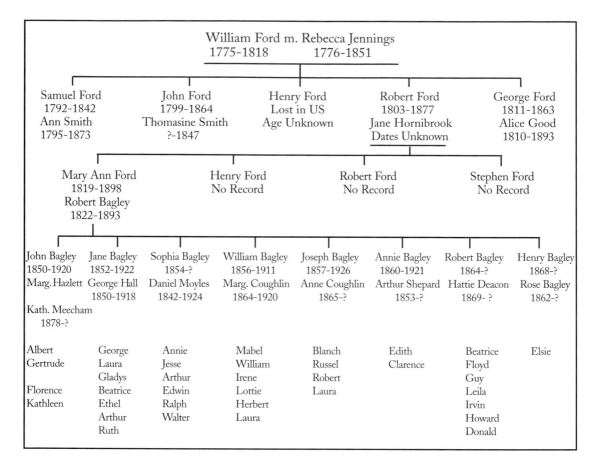

the form of hundreds of genealogical sheets sent to heads of families who supplied needed information. These sheets are in separate books representing the four main branches of the Ford family. From data in those books, four individual tables representing the four family branches have been prepared.

The illustrations in this chapter include a much-reduced copy of the Ford family tree drawn by Laird, a one-page sample of the large number of genealogical sheets collected by Laird, and four charts prepared from genealogy sheet data and each representing one branch of the family.

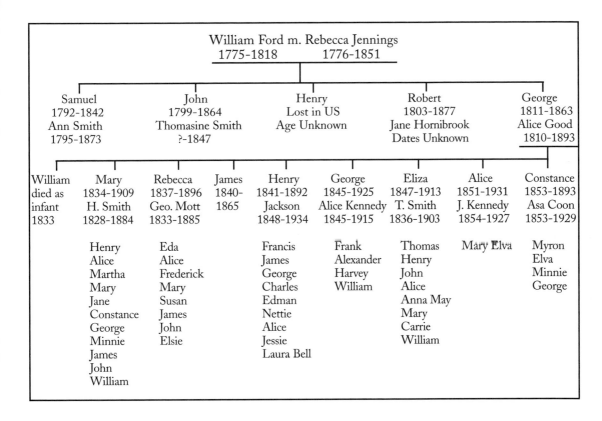

| William Ford m. Rebecca Jennings |
| 1775-1818   1776-1851 |

Samuel	John	Henry	Robert	George
1792-1842	1799-1864	Lost in US	1803-1877	1811-1863
Ann Smith	Thomasine Smith	Age Unknown	Jane Hornibrook	Alice Good
1795-1873	?-1847		Dates Unknown	1810-1893

William	Mary	Rebecca	James	Henry	George	Eliza	Alice	Constance
died as	1834-1909	1837-1896	1840-	1841-1892	1845-1925	1847-1913	1851-1931	1853-1893
infant	H. Smith	Geo. Mott	1865	Jackson	Alice Kennedy	T. Smith	J. Kennedy	Asa Coon
1833	1828-1884	1833-1885		1848-1934	1845-1915	1836-1903	1854-1927	1853-1929

	Henry	Eda		Francis	Frank	Thomas	Mary Elva	Myron
	Alice	Alice		James	Alexander	Henry		Elva
	Martha	Frederick		George	Harvey	John		Minnie
	Mary	Mary		Charles	William	Alice		George
	Jane	Susan		Edman		Anna May		
	Constance	James		Nettie		Mary		
	George	John		Alice		Carrie		
	Minnie	Elsie		Jessie		William		
	James			Laura Bell				
	John							
	William							

References

Accession 28, Box 27, Henry Ford Office. Benson Ford Research Center, HFM & GV.

Accession 1635, Box 1, Ralph Laird Papers. Benson Ford Research Center, HFM & GV.

Laird, Raymond H. "I Worked for Henry Ford." Dearborn Historian, Vol. 10, No. 1, 1970.

21
THE FORD CEMETERY

The Burial Site of Samuel on His Farm, Which Became a Cemetery for the Descendants of Samuel, George, and John Ford

In 1832, Samuel Ford and Ann (Nancy) Smith Ford, both of Ireland, settled on eighty acres at what is now the southwest corner of Joy and Greenfield roads in Detroit. There were no roads at that time, and the property was in the northeast corner of what was to be Dearborn Township, on the town line between Dearborn and Redford Townships. After only ten years in this country, Samuel Ford died in 1842 and was buried on his own property. This was the first burial in what became the Ford Cemetery. George Ford, a brother of Samuel, also had purchased eighty acres east of Samuel in 1832, and another brother, John, arrived from Ireland and settled on the same town line a mile west of Samuel in 1847. Members of these other Ford families also began to be buried in the same lot with Samuel.

Following the death of Samuel's wife, Nancy Ford, in 1870, his eighty acres were left to her sons, James and George, each receiving forty acres. George received the forty that contained the Ford Cemetery. In 1893, a deed of trust was formulated. George Ford and Mary Jones Ford, his wife, conveyed the cemetery property to a board of trustees to be operated "as a place of burial for the heirs and descendants and the families of heirs and descendants" of Samuel Ford, George Ford, and John Ford — the three brothers from Ireland. Each of the three trustees was to represent his or her respective branch of the family.

When George Ford, the owner of the farm surrounding the cemetery, died in 1901, his wife, Mary, deeded the farm to Addison Ford, their only son. In 1919, Mary died, and Addison died in 1920. Addison's son, Clyde M. Ford, inherited the farm. By then, Henry Ford was buying up Dearborn land and acquired from Clyde Ford the forty acres in which the Ford Cemetery was locat-

ed. Henry neglected to inquire about the cemetery trust deed, assumed he had bought the cemetery, and took over its maintenance, about which none of the relatives complained.

About this time, Raymond Laird was assigned by Henry Ford to compile a record of all persons buried in Ford Cemetery and to draw a plat showing the location of all graves therein. Arrangements for additional burials were made at first through M. H. Sipple of Henry Ford's staff. Following Sipple's death, permission for burials was obtained through Henry's secretary, Frank Campsall, who granted permission for people to make their own arrangements for burial. No death certificates or reports were filed.

When Henry Ford died on April 7, 1947, he had that very same day commented to his chauffeur, Robert Rankin, that he was

St. Martha's Episcopal Church and the Ford Cemetery on Joy Road near
Greenfield Road, where Henry and Clara Ford are buried. The tall 1876 obelisk
to the left in the cemetery marks the grave of Henry's mother, Mary. The long
flat stones near the obelisk mark the graves of Henry and Clara. The photograph
was taken in May 1954, only a few months after the dedication of the church.
Henry's sister Margaret and brother William are buried in this cemetery, but his
brother John is not. Clara is the only Bryant in the cemetery. (Photograph courtesy of Dearborn Historical Museum.)

to be buried in the Ford Cemetery. He was buried there, but it
immediately became a problem for his wife, Clara. The grave had
to be guarded day and night. Whether the little cemetery was the
proper place for such a prominent figure was much debated. There
were suggestions that Ford's grave should be moved to Greenfield
Village, and it was suggested that perhaps the whole cemetery
should be moved there. It was rumored that Ford's body already
had been moved to St. Paul's Episcopal Church in Detroit, and

Edison Institute people attending a ceremony at the gravesite of Henry and Clara Ford in the Ford Cemetery. The date is April 11, 1966, the hundredth anniversary of Clara Ford's birth. (B.61683-2)

there are people to this day who question whether Henry Ford is really buried in the Ford Cemetery.

It was not until Clara Ford suggested that an Episcopal church be built next to the cemetery on adjoining land that Ford Motor Company lawyers discovered the existence of the 1893 trust deed of ownership of the cemetery. The assumption had been that Henry Ford had owned the cemetery since 1920. This posed a very serious problem. There were two options: contest the trust deed, or activate the board of trustees and gain its permission for control of the cemetery. The latter choice was adopted. It was found that two of the original trustees of the cemetery had died and that Earl Ford, representing Samuel's branch of the family, was the only one living. Earl Ford had been a trustee since 1921, having replaced his father, John N. Ford, who died in 1916.

Then living in Ypsilanti, Michigan, Earl Ford was asked to call a meeting of all living descendants of the original three brothers

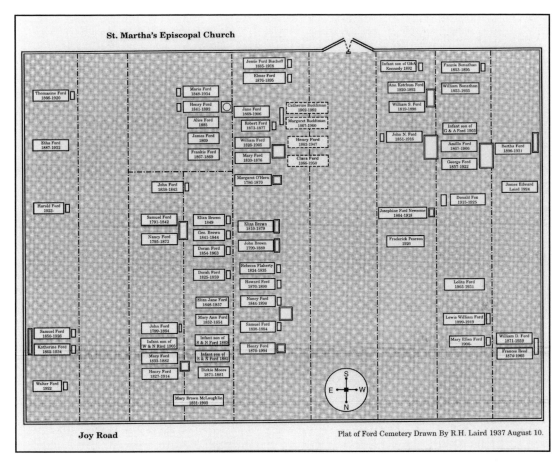

St. Martha's Episcopal Church

Joy Road

Plat of Ford Cemetery Drawn By R.H. Laird 1937 August 10.

Plat of Ford Cemetery, drawn by R. H. Laird, August 10, 1937.

for whose families the cemetery was established in 1893. To prepare this list of descendants, the genealogical data previously collected by Laird were of tremendous value. The meeting was held at the Edison Institute on November 23, 1948. A relatively small number of people — perhaps seventy-five — attended. Notice of the meeting had briefly explained the history of the cemetery, referring primarily to the need to elect two new trustees. The following statements were included in the meeting notice:

> This letter is meant to notify you as an heir that we will meet on the day mentioned at which time you will be asked to name, vote on, and elect two successor trustees to act with me in the carrying out of the purposes and uses for which the Ford Cemetery was created.
>
> At the meeting you will also be requested to pass on the matter of certain improvements in the Ford Cemetery and the care thereof, and such other business as appropriately may come before the meeting.

273

Earl Ford chaired the meeting with the object of voting for two additional trustees. Elected were Mabel Nancy Ford and Laurence Ford. Clara Ford was there, and her attorney, Clifford B. Longley, used drawings to explain her generous offer to fence and care for the cemetery. The meeting, as this writer remembers, was similar to a Ford family reunion, with relatives who hadn't seen one another for months, or even years, anxious to chat.

Clara Ford devoted the next year and a half to planning how to protect the little Ford Cemetery for posterity. Her final decision was to purchase enough land adjacent to the cemetery to build an Episcopal church, including a parish hall, a rectory, and a sexton's house, to be called St. Martha's in honor of her mother. In June 1950, Clara Ford offered to the Episcopal Diocese of Michigan a gift of eight acres of land surrounding the cemetery, sufficient property in trust to raise $700,000 to be used in building a church and its future maintenance, and a perpetual trust valued at $300,000 derived from Ford Motor Company stock for maintenance of the cemetery and St. Martha's Church.

During 1949 and 1950, Clara Ford had given her architect, Arthur Hyde, and her personal secretary, H. Rex Waddell, detailed descriptions of the type of church she wanted. But she died on September 29, 1950, and did not live to witness the construction of St. Martha's Church. Groundbreaking ceremonies were held on June 22, 1952, and the church was dedicated in 1954. The Ford Cemetery, together with St. Martha's Church, is now under the jurisdiction of the Episcopal Diocese of Michigan. The cemetery is open to the public, and both church and cemetery can be seen readily on the south side of Joy Road, a short distance west of Greenfield Road in Detroit.

References

Accession 1, Box 27, Fair Lane Papers. Benson Ford Research Center, HFM & GV.

Accession 23, Box 28, Henry Ford Office. Benson Ford Research Center, HFM & GV.

Accession 587, Box 15, Office of Henry and Clara Ford Estate. Benson Ford Research Center, HFM & GV.

Accession 1635, Ralph Laird Papers. Benson Ford Research Center, HFM & GV.

Index

Note: To distinguish among individuals with identical names, birth (or death) years are given if included in the text; otherwise, names (and years, as needed) of parents or spouses are given. When a female's married name is known, she is listed under that name; when it is not known, or if she did not marry, she is listed under her birth surname. (For example, Jane Ford and Jane Elisha Hornibrook Ford are two different individuals and have separate index entries.)

Ford Bryan has written six other books about Henry Ford:

ROUGE: PICTURED IN ITS PRIME
Covering the Years 1917–1940

HENRY'S LIEUTENANTS

BEYOND THE MODEL T
The Other Ventures of Henry Ford

HENRY'S ATTIC
Some Fascinating Gifts to Henry Ford and His Museum

CLARA
Mrs. Henry Ford

FRIENDS, FAMILIES AND FORAYS
Scenes from the Life and Times of Henry Ford

For more information, please see this web site:
http://wsupress.wayne.edu

To order books, call Wayne State University Press
1-800-978-7323